The American South and the Atlantic World

UNIVERSITY PRESS OF FLORIDA

Florida A&M University, Tallahassee
Florida Atlantic University, Boca Raton
Florida Gulf Coast University, Ft. Myers
Florida International University, Miami
Florida State University, Tallahassee
New College of Florida, Sarasota
University of Central Florida, Orlando
University of Florida, Gainesville
University of North Florida, Jacksonville
University of South Florida, Tampa
University of West Florida, Pensacola

First cloth printing, 2013
First paperback printing, 2015

LIBRARY OF CONGRESS CATALOGING-IN-PUBLICATION DATA
The American South and the Atlantic world / edited by Brian Ward, Martyn Bone, and
William A. Link.
p. cm.
Includes bibliographical references and index.
ISBN 978-0-8130-4437-8 (cloth: alk. paper)
ISBN 978-0-8130-6138-2 (pbk.)
1. African Americans—Southern States—Social conditions. 2. Southern States—History.
3. Southern States—Social conditions. 4. Southern States—Race relations. I. Ward, Brian,
1961– II. Bone, Martyn, 1974– III. Link, William A.
E185.A477 2013
305.800975—dc234   2012046699

The University Press of Florida is the scholarly publishing agency for the State University
System of Florida, comprising Florida A&M University, Florida Atlantic University,
Florida Gulf Coast University, Florida International University, Florida State University,
New College of Florida, University of Central Florida, University of Florida, University
of North Florida, University of South Florida, and University of West Florida.

University Press of Florida
15 Northwest 15th Street
Gainesville, FL 32611-2079
http://www.upf.com

THE AMERICAN SOUTH AND THE ATLANTIC WORLD

Edited by Brian Ward, Martyn Bone,
and William A. Link

University Press of Florida
Gainesville · Tallahassee · Tampa · Boca Raton
Pensacola · Orlando · Miami · Jacksonville · Ft. Myers · Sarasota

Contents

Preface

Understanding the South

In 2008, the Arts and Humanities Research Council in the United Kingdom agreed to fund an international research network dedicated to the theme "Understanding the South, Understanding America: The American South in Regional, National and Global Perspectives." The network was based at the University of Manchester, with the Universities of Copenhagen, Cambridge, and Florida as partners. Between May 2008 and August 2010 each of these institutions hosted a network conference. These meetings brought together scholars from a range of disciplines and allowed them to explore together the current state and future prospects for the study of that section of the North American continent that eventually became known, with all due disclaimers about the definitional slipperiness of the term, as the American South.

This series of books from the University Press of Florida extends the work of the network, initially in three volumes grouped around the themes of creating citizenship in the nineteenth-century South, the South and the Atlantic World, and creating and consuming the South. While each volume stands alone as a valuable contribution to a particular aspect of southern studies, collectively they allow us to take stock of a rich and diverse field, to ponder the substantive disagreements and methodological tensions—as well as the common ground—among scholars of the South, and to think about new areas and techniques for future research. Each volume and many of the individual essays are marked by an interest in interdisciplinary and multidisciplinary approaches to the region. Indeed, one aim of the series is to juxtapose the work of historians with that of scholars associated with the New Southern Studies in the belief that historians and those working out of literary and cultural studies traditions have much to learn from each other in their quest to understand the American South in a variety of overlapping temporal, geographic, symbolic, cultural, and material contexts.

The coeditors of the series wish to thank all those colleagues who participated in the four conferences. Special thanks are due to Tony Badger at the University of Cambridge for his generous financial support and for hosting the Cambridge conference; to James Broomall, Heather Bryson, Angela Diaz, and Angie Zombek at the University of Florida for their logistical help; and, at the University of Manchester, to David Brown for coediting the *Citizenship* volume, Michael Bibler for his consistently constructive engagement with all aspects of the network, and Tom Strange and Jennie Chapman for their invaluable administrative assistance. We would also like to express our gratitude to the Arts and Humanities Research Council for its sponsorship of the network, to the British Academy and the United States Embassy's Cultural Affairs Office in London for important additional funding, and to Meredith Morris-Babb at the University Press of Florida for her enthusiastic support of the Understanding the South series of books.

Brian Ward, Northumbria University
Martyn Bone, University of Copenhagen
William A. Link, University of Florida

Introduction

BRIAN WARD

....

> They could hear a stream running down to the ravine where it met the
> other stream and then the river. . . . From there it met the Ohio and the
> Ohio met the Mississippi and then down to the Gulf of Mexico and the
> Atlantic, it was all connected.
>
> Philip Meyer, *American Rust*

Individually and collectively, the essays in this volume showcase, but also
interrogate, the value of Atlantic World frameworks for understanding
the histories and cultures of the American South. Although the majority
of the chapters are broadly historical in nature, several are from literary
or cultural studies perspectives and others are avowedly interdisciplinary.
They range temporally from colonial times to the modern era. Thematically, they embrace economics, migration, religion, revolution, law, slavery, race relations, emancipation, gender, literature, performance, visual
culture, memoir, ethnography, empires, nations, and historiography. Geographically, they focus mainly on the southern region of the North American continent and the lands in and around the Atlantic Ocean—although
the physical location of a putative "Atlantic World" and, for that matter, of
something we can call an "American South" are among the many definitional issues with which the volume wrestles.

This is an opportune moment to think about the utility of Atlantic
World models for scholars of the American South. The fields of Atlantic
history and its interdisciplinary cousin Atlantic studies are now well established. Within southern historical, literary, and cultural studies there
has been an enormous complementary interest in hemispheric or New

World approaches to the region alongside work dealing more specifically with the Black Atlantic.

These Atlantic-oriented analytical moves have intersected with, and sometimes come into conflict with, broader "transnational" and "post-national" turns in southern and American studies and a growing commitment to globalizing the study of region and nation. According to their advocates, both moves promise to rescue southern and American studies from the tyranny of nationally circumscribed narratives that bear the ordure of a discredited southern regional and U.S. national exceptionalism. This quest, in the words of Kathryn McKee and Annette Trefzer, to "unmoor the South from its national harbor" and embed it "in a larger transnational framework" has become commonplace among the loose conglomeration of southern literary and cultural studies scholars broadly associated, some more willingly and appropriately than others, with the New Southern Studies.[1]

Meanwhile, books like *Grounded Globalism*, anthropologist James Peacock's sprawling examination of how southern regional identity might be recast in an age of heightened global economic, military, and cultural interconnectedness, the collection of essays on *Globalization and the American South* edited by historians James Cobb and William Stueck, diplomatic historian Joseph A. Fry's survey of the "vast and often decisive impact" of the American South on U.S. foreign policy in *Dixie Looks Abroad*, sociologist Wanda Rushing's investigation of globalization in Memphis, and the birth of proudly interdisciplinary journals such as *Global South* suggest that similar concerns are animating many southernists working in a variety of disciplines.[2] It is in the context of these ever-expanding comparative, transnational, and global perspectives on the American South that this volume revisits the merits of narrower Atlantic World perspectives for those seeking to understand the region. At the same time, of course, many of the essays also remind us of the importance of the American South in shaping a series of overlapping and unstable Atlantic worlds. Indeed, the South's status as simultaneously co-creator and product, beneficiary and benefactor of various Atlantic systems forms a powerful theme throughout the volume.

The collection opens with my own essay, which samples an eclectic range of literature, scholarly and creative, to examine the main conceptual and practical issues raised by Atlantic approaches to the American South. Using the memoirs of author-critic Caryl Phillips and the theoretical modeling of historian David Armitage to frame the discussion, it considers the strengths, weaknesses, and potential of various Atlantic perspectives for southern studies and offers an intellectual context for the volume as a whole. While embracing the possibilities opened up by closer dialogue across traditional disciplinary divides, the essay also reaffirms the value of uni- and multi-, as well as inter-disciplinary work on the South's Atlantic connections.

Given the enormous technical challenges posed by situating the American South within a comprehensive Atlantic World framework, I note that "granular" approaches to the mutually constitutive relationships between the South and the Atlantic World have been especially productive. This granularity is evident in studies that focus primarily on particular places, individuals, groups, moments, or themes in order to trace and evaluate the impact of much broader Atlantic forces as they flow into and out of the South. Many of the essays in the volume also adopt granular approaches of one sort or another, revealing the significance of the South's Atlantic World connections by examining the lives of certain individuals, or the collective histories of particular groups and locales, or else by tracking Atlantic-South interactions at certain historical moments, or along distinct thematic lines.

Jon Sensbach, for example, focuses on the remarkably diverse, globally inflected religious life of the South in the colonial and the early republic periods to complicate our understandings of the region's Atlantic heritage. Sensbach points out that transatlantic imports, not least African traditions and Anglo-Protestant evangelicalism, were important features of the southern religious landscape but hardly the only, nor necessarily always the most important ones. However, with the end of the transatlantic slave trade and the growing defensiveness and cultural isolation of the South in the antebellum period, the dynamic religious cosmopolitanism of the colonial era dwindled. According to Sensbach, it was only in the early to mid-nineteenth century that European-derived evangelical Christianity increasingly dominated the region, if never absolutely and never in anything resembling a "pure" form given the importance of African influences and adaptations. The belated triumph of a relatively narrowly Atlantic, and then of a still more narrowly construed "southern" style of evangelical Christianity, he charges, has generated a literature that largely ignores more than two centuries of dynamic religious experimentation and diversity.

In another mode of granular study, the essays by Natalie Zacek, Jennifer K. Snyder, Martha S. Jones, Leigh Anne Duck, Kathleen M. Gough, and Natanya Keisha Duncan all focus primarily on individuals or distinctive groups to illuminate the South's complex relationships to various Atlantic worlds. Zacek considers the political and personal career of the murdered Virginia-born, British-sponsored Leeward Islands governor Daniel Parke to show how fatally difficult it could be to juggle the contradictory demands of yoked yet differentiated Atlantic worlds in the eighteenth century. Jennifer K. Snyder's essay focuses on the story of James Moncrief, the Loyalist chief engineer for Georgia and South Carolina, and his slaves as they fled the South into the Caribbean in the wake of British defeat in the American Revolution. Highlighting the personal dilemmas faced by southern Loyalists and their slaves amid a transatlantic power struggle, Snyder demonstrates how mobility and settlement, in many ways the key tropes of Atlantic studies, were experienced differently in different locales by different peoples in the Atlantic World.

Martha S. Jones uses the story of Saint-Domingue slave Jean Baptiste to illustrate how competing legal regimes in the New World and even within the North American mainland profoundly affected the lives of those who lived there, free and unfree. Indeed, Jones's deft analysis of Baptiste's travails in Port-au-Prince, New York, Baltimore, and New Orleans in the aftermath of the Haitian Revolution affirms the importance of rival legal codes, themselves connected to competing imperial and national jurisdictions, in defining the Atlantic World, particularly in matters pertaining to race and slavery.

In chronological terms, the essays by Sensbach, Zacek, Snyder, and Jones fall squarely within the period, roughly from 1500 to 1830, on which Atlantic historians have focused most intently. In his historiographical overview, Trevor Burnard argues that, for all its many achievements, Atlantic history's early modern fixation has exacerbated an unhelpful division between American colonial historians, who have been increasingly committed to Atlantic perspectives, and colleagues working in the later nineteenth century and beyond, who use such paradigms relatively rarely. As Burnard suggests—and as Natanya Duncan's essay with its twentieth-century focus illustrates—there is great potential in a more elastic temporal approach to the Atlantic World among southern, and other, historians. Certainly, colleagues in southern literary and cultural studies have been much bolder in exploring the region's Atlantic coordinates and relationships into the modern era, as the essays in this volume by Duck, Gough, and Keith Cartwright demonstrate.

Like fellow historian Trevor Burnard, Jeffrey R. Kerr-Ritchie adopts a transnational perspective to challenge some of the most powerful paradigms operating within the historiography on the nineteenth-century American South. In critically reappraising the enormous literature on U.S. emancipation and Reconstruction, much of it comparative in orientation, Kerr-Ritchie exposes a surprisingly strong residual commitment to ideas of southern exceptionalism. In a productively provocative account, Kerr-Ritchie looks to the Atlantic and other worlds to reevaluate what, if anything, was really distinctive about the southern experiences of civil war, emancipation, and reconstruction.

Like many of the essays in this book, Leigh Anne Duck's study of the Baltimore-born African Methodist Episcopal bishop Levi Jenkins Coppin is concerned with how ideas of race and racial, as well as regional, identity were generated and circulated in a transoceanic context. Under Duck's scrutiny, the turn-of-the-twentieth-century writings and photographs of Coppin, a proud, self-declared "Southerner by birth" who became the first AME bishop of Cape Town in South Africa, demonstrate how conceptions of the Atlantic World and its constituent parts and peoples were at some level created by acts of imagination. Duck reveals the Atlantic World, like the American South, as in part a symbolic construct enacted through textual and visual representations and misrepresentations, as well as through the kinds of commercial, demographic, military, and legal encounters and exchanges that historians tend to privilege. Coppin's fraught, sometimes contradictory and patronizing attempts to work through notions of diasporic black identities, while also critiquing different regimes of racial oppression on both sides of the Atlantic, complicates how we think about the Black Atlantic and its manifestations in Africa and the United States.

Kathleen M. Gough's essay juxtaposes the careers of two remarkable female writers and ethnographers of the early twentieth century—Florida's Zora Neale Hurston and Ireland's Lady Augusta Gregory—to illuminate the creation of both Black and Green Atlantics. By exploring these women's creative and folkloric work and their subsequent public reputations, Gough reveals how powerful notions of Irish and black—especially southern black—identity and related ideas of cultural authenticity were generated, disseminated, and redeployed around the Atlantic World, often with recourse to strikingly similar invocations of agrarianism, religiosity, and resistance (cultural and political) to oppression. In the process, Gough also critiques a tendency to ignore or marginalize women in Atlantic studies—a tendency that Natanya Keisha Duncan's essay on the Accraborn Princess Laura Kofey and her Garveyite political, economic, and cultural activities in the interwar South also reverses. Duncan emphasizes the special place that the American South occupied in Kofey's plans for greater commercial and educational exchange between Africans and African Americans and, ultimately, for repatriation. By noting the regional, gender, class, and racial dimensions of Kofey's transatlantic experiences, Duncan joins Snyder, Jones, Kerr-Ritchie, Duck, and Gough in adding nuance to our appreciation of how the Black Atlantic functioned.

In the final essay in the volume, Keith Cartwright reminds us that subjective judgments and personal knowledge of the Atlantic World, whether recorded in memoir, expressed in the creative arts, or, as with Cartwright's own Peace Corps experiences in Senegal, channeled into a particular brand of scholarship, have been important elements in generating understandings of the South's relationship to places around the Atlantic. In a bold, multi-layered, and temporally expansive interdisciplinary essay that circumnavigates the Atlantic World several times, Cartwright demonstrates how experiences, real and imagined, of the American South, of the Atlantic World, and of the connections between them have always varied according to precisely whose perspective is being examined, privileged, or obscured.

This volume reminds us that comparative and transnational approaches to the American South can illuminate both the similarities and the differences between various sites in the Atlantic World. Indeed, one strength of Atlantic perspectives on the South is that they can simultaneously, if somewhat paradoxically, challenge exceptionalist narratives about the region without gratuitously ignoring the truism that each locale within the Atlantic World, including the South and its subdivisions, is in some way distinctive, though never isolated from or immune to transnational currents. Attempts to unravel the complex relationships among, and the competing explanatory power of, various regional, national, hemispheric, Atlantic, and global contexts for understanding the American South animate many of the essays in the collection.

Ultimately, the value of any grand conceptual paradigm, such as Atlantic history, or Atlantic studies, or the Black Atlantic, rests on its capacity to explain past or present social realities; it is valuable insofar as it helps to reveal the workings of the material, emotional, and symbolic worlds in which real people and social groups, in real places, have lived. By those criteria, this volume's mix of case studies and state-of-the-field essays and its blend of notionally historical and literary as well as interdisciplinary contributions indicates that much remains to be learned about both the Atlantic World and the American South by considering them together.

Notes

1. Kathryn McKee and Annette Trefzer, "Preface: Global Contexts, Local Literatures: The New Southern Studies," *American Literature* 78, no. 4 (2006): 678.

2. James Peacock, *Grounded Globalism: How the U.S. Embraces the World* (Athens: University of Georgia Press, 2007); James C. Cobb and William Stueck, eds., *Globalization and the American South* (Athens: University of Georgia Press, 2005); Joseph A. Fry, *Dixie Looks Abroad: The South and U.S. Foreign Relations, 1789–1973* (Baton Rouge: Louisiana State University Press, 2003), 4; Wanda Rushing, *Memphis and the Paradox of Place: Globalization in the American South* (Chapel Hill: University of North Carolina Press, 2009).

1

Caryl Phillips, David Armitage, and the Place of the American South in Atlantic and Other Worlds

BRIAN WARD

In 2000, the St. Kitts–born, British-raised, American-based writer Caryl Phillips published *The Atlantic Sound*, an account of his travels around the Atlantic World. Against the ineluctable backdrop of the transoceanic slave trade which had brought his ancestors from Africa to labor in the Caribbean, Phillips chronicled the complex circum-Atlantic mix of connection and rupture, belonging and estrangement from which his own sense of self, of his place in the world, and his hopes and fears for the future had emerged.[1]

In *The Atlantic Sound*, and in some of the essays collected in *A New World Order*, Phillips contemplated the interpenetrating histories and cultures of Europe, Africa, and the American South. Visiting Liverpool in England, the Elmina slave castle in contemporary Ghana, and Charleston in South Carolina, he explored an Atlantic heritage that for "countless millions" who "have traversed this water" accounts for a sense of permanent displacement.[2] And yet if, in the words of another modern Atlantic sojourner, British-Guyanese author Fred D'Aguiar, this means that "home is always elsewhere," the same mix of roots and routes also accounts for Phillips's identification with multiple Atlantic homes.[3] Those identifications are rarely unproblematic, and Gregory Smithers is probably right to suggest that for Phillips "existential questions of home and identity"—the central preoccupation of his writing—"are constantly in flux."[4] Nevertheless, it is through his encounters with an Atlantic World conceived as a fractured whole that Phillips can process and reconnect the "remembered fragments of a former life. Shards of memory."[5] For Phillips the Atlantic functions, much as the Caribbean did for Martinique poet, philosopher, and Faulkner scholar Édouard Glissant, as "a synthesizing space in which opposites can live comfortably together."⁶

Phillips's experiences in Liverpool, Elmina, and Charleston reveal a plethora of concrete historical connections between and symbolic echoes among each of these Atlantic sites enshrined in buildings, monuments, festivals, dances, music, foodways, religion, literature, academia, commerce, and tourism and embedded in shared social memories and individual consciousnesses. As he navigates this mix of the foreign and familiar, Phillips soaks up the commercial, cultural, symbolic, and human relationships that have bound together Africa, Europe, and the Americas since at least the fifteenth century, and exposes an Atlantic past that pours into the personal and collective present. Thus *The Atlantic Sound* offers a personal insight into the kinds of historical intersections and enduring cultural reverberations that more academic Atlantic studies often promise to explicate. Indeed, one justification for starting this essay with a nod to Phillips's work is that it shares some of the major preoccupations of Atlantic studies in general, and scholarly efforts to use that framework to investigate the American South in particular.

Phillips's memoirs form part of a long tradition of travel narratives that plot the material, symbolic, and emotional coordinates of the Atlantic World. Alongside the theoretical work of Atlantic historian David Armitage, they also serve as a useful structuring mechanism and interpretive foil for this essay, which examines, in four thematic sections, how scholars from many disciplines have addressed the American South's relationship to the Atlantic World. The first section deals with struggles to define an Atlantic World geographically, temporally, and substantively and the implications of those struggles for how the concept has been used to examine the histories and cultures of the American South. The second section considers the virtues and limitations of Atlantic perspectives in relation to other transnational moves in southern studies, notably the growing emphasis on a global South. The third section examines how scholars have dealt with the relationships between the South and the United States, indeed with nations and empires more generally, in the context of the growing commitment to transnationalism.

The final section commends various particularist or "granular" approaches to the South's links to the Atlantic World. It is worth acknowledging at the outset that it may seem counterintuitive, even heretical, to argue for studies of the local, the regional, and the national, or of the experiences of individuals and distinct social groups, or of particular themes in order to maximize the interpretive potential of Atlantic perspectives on the American South. Committed Atlanticists see the Atlantic Ocean not as a vast physical entity that has separated the lands and peoples around it into discreet entities, but rather as the principal mechanism by which histories and cultures have become entwined in a transoceanic system that is best understood holistically. For its partisans, the Atlantic World constitutes what Trevor Burnard has described as "a particular zone of exchange and interchange, circulation, and transmission" created by a series of migrations, encounters, networks, negotiations, and fusions that transcend national borders and imperial projects.[7]

Nevertheless, some of the most impressive Atlantic scholarship for those interested in the American South has been decidedly granular in nature: it has concentrated on how the Atlantic World has affected and been affected by particular groups and individuals in particular places at particular times; or else it has taken explicitly thematic approaches to the Atlantic World, focusing on issues such as race, slavery, emancipation, religion, law, disease, gender, sexuality, economics, diplomacy, literature, performing arts, and other cultural practices in ways that seldom entirely slip the yoke, if yoke it be, of the imperial and national histories that Atlantic studies sometimes claims to have transcended.

Where, When, and What? Defining the Atlantic World

Caryl Phillips has a very clear sense of the territorial scope of his Atlantic World: "I know my Atlantic 'home' to be triangular in shape with Britain at one apex, the west coast of Africa at another, and the new world of North America (including the Caribbean) forming the third point of the triangle."[8] By contrast, scholars interested in the Atlantic World, whether coming to praise or bury the concept, have often agonized about its geographical location as part of wider anxieties about its analytical value. Writing in 2002 about the proliferation of scholarship on the Atlantic during the previous quarter century, David Armitage mischievously declared "we are all Atlanticists now." However, Armitage appreciated that Atlantic World history, like the more interdisciplinary field of Atlantic studies with which it overlaps, still "has no agreed canon of problems, events, or processes. It follows no common method or practice. Like the Atlantic itself, the field is fluid, in motion, and potentially boundless, depending on how it is defined; that is part of its appeal, but also one of its drawbacks."[9]

This lack of definitional precision stems partly from recognition that there have always been multiple concurrent, successive, and interconnected Atlantic worlds. Sir John Elliott, a pioneer of Atlantic history, has observed that "there was not one Atlantic—at least during the sixteenth and seventeenth centuries—but a minimum of three, defined by different climatic and environmental conditions and different movements of winds and currents." According to Elliott, it was only in the late seventeenth century that a North European Atlantic, a Spanish Atlantic, and a Luso-Atlantic began "to merge, in a process of mutual interaction in which the slave was an involuntary and all too prominent participant."[10] Even then, several distinct yet entwined Atlantic worlds persisted, prompting Peter Linebaugh and Marcus Rediker to use the idea of a "many-headed hydra" to frame their book on the unruly Atlantic of the Revolutionary era.[11]

This conceptual fuzziness—part blessing, part curse—is compounded for anyone hoping to use the Atlantic World as an instrument for studying the American South, since that region is a similarly unstable geopolitical and symbolic terrain whose precise location, and even existence, has sometimes been quite contentious. Indeed, despite the region's growing reliance on plantation-based staple crop production and slavery, for much of the colonial period and even into the early nineteenth century there was only a limited concept of "the South" as a distinct cultural or political entity occupying the lands that later constituted the Confederacy, itself a rough-and-ready guide to the geographic location of "the South."[12] Because the South has never been geographically fixed or racially, politically, socially, culturally, and economically monolithic, any attempt to study it in an Atlantic context necessarily involves utilizing not one but two notoriously imprecise and shifting units of analysis.

Fixing an Atlantic World in time has proved as problematic as fixing it in space. For Atlantic historians, the paradigm has proved most useful for the period from roughly the mid-fifteenth century to the early nineteenth century. These early modern and early *modern* Atlantic worlds have thus been defined principally by reference to European imperial and colonial expansion, to the rise of the transatlantic slave trade and the systems of New World slavery it enabled, to shipborne and shipboard exchanges of peoples, cultures, capital, and goods, and to the encounters between those peoples and their cultures in the lands around the Atlantic Ocean.

More recently, however, there have been efforts to extend the temporal scope of Atlantic history by the likes of Donna Gabaccia and Toyin Falola and Kevin D. Roberts, whose edited collection on *The Atlantic World, 1450–2000* pushes the paradigm to the start of a new millennium.[13] Significantly, the essays in that volume are mainly concerned with aspects of the Black Atlantic, a concept that, since the 1993 publication of Paul Gilroy's *Black Atlantic*, has been widely, if inconsistently, used to explore the flows of peoples and cultures derived from Africa around the Atlantic Ocean.[14]

The Black Atlantic, the African diaspora, the transatlantic slave trade, New World slavery, emancipation, legal and extralegal regimes of racial discipline, and race relations more generally are interconnected themes that occupy a central place in attempts to put the American South in an Atlantic context.[15] Broadly defined, Black Atlantic concerns have also prompted some of the more chronologically adventurous approaches to the entwined histories of the Atlantic and the modern U.S. South, easing the field away from its traditional temporal moorings in the early modern era.[16]

This shift toward the contemporary period mirrors Gilroy's preoccupation with how the slave trade and the dispersal around the Atlantic of forcibly displaced Africans helped to fashion an emerging transoceanic modernity. Gilroy was hardly indifferent to the circulation of black bodies and cultures around the early modern Atlantic, or to the racialized violence that accompanied forced migrations and New World slavery. Still, like Phillips, he was even more interested in how these phenomena produced the fluid, hybrid identities and syncretic modern cultures that have subsequently been engaged in an endless process of making and remaking, remembering and forgetting, that Atlantic past.

While relatively few Atlantic historians have ventured much beyond the mid-nineteenth century, when the end of the slave trade and New World emancipations have conventionally been taken to mark the end of a particular incarnation of the Atlantic World, scholars working from literary, cultural, and sociological perspectives, along with creative artists, have been more comfortable pursuing their interests in the symbolic, creative, and affective relationships between the American South and the Atlantic World into the twentieth and twenty-first centuries. Helen Taylor's *Circling Dixie*, for example, focuses on the transatlantic production and reception of modern southern culture (*Gone with the Wind*; *Roots*;

Tennessee Williams's plays; the music and literature of New Orleans; and Maya Angelou's life and writings—"the very spirit of circum-Atlanticism," according to Taylor).[17] Recent novels by Patrick Neate (*Twelve Bar Blues*), Dave Eggers (*What Is the What: The Autobiography of Valentino Achak Deng*), and Cynthia Shearer (*The Celestial Jukebox*) all deal with contemporary passages from Africa to the American South. As Martyn Bone notes in reviewing these novels, Texas and Virginia and cities such as Atlanta are among the most favored destinations for "voluntary migrants from the African continent," who are, "like their predecessors, thrown and drawn together by the shared experience of crossing the Atlantic; moreover, many confront the legacy of slavery and racism that has so profoundly shaped U.S. history in general and U.S. Southern history in particular."[18]

For good reason, slavery and racism remain central to much of the work, scholarly and creative, on the modern South and the Atlantic World. As Joseph Roach argues in *Cities of the Dead*, his study of circum-Atlantic performances and rituals from the eighteenth century to the late twentieth century, it is impossible to underestimate the "centrality of the diasporic and genocidal histories of Africa and the Americas, North and South, in the creation of the culture of modernity."[19] But, unlike for most Atlantic historians, it is the psychological, material, social, and cultural legacies of the Atlantic slave trade and the racial, class, and gender inequalities that they helped to create that are at the heart of many contemporary literary and cultural studies. "The burden of slavery is not the past itself but the legacy of narratives that still provide room for the kinds of social, racial, and gender divisions from which the slave owner, during another time, profited," explains George Handley.[20]

Of course, the operational mechanics of the modern Atlantic World are very different from those in the early modern period. Ship-bound oceanic links have been superseded by air travel; the slave trade is no longer at the center of transatlantic commerce; developments in mass media and electronic communications have brought together people and facilitated financial transactions and cultural exchanges among Atlantic dwellers who have never met, as well as embroiling the Atlantic World ever more fully in global flows of capital, cultures, commerce, and peoples.

Yet, historians readily concede that the early modern Atlantic World was never homogeneous or static, but rather multivalent, fluid, held together in different configurations by a messy and constantly shifting blend of commerce, transportation links, migrations, military power, laws, cultures, and acts of creativity and imagination. Modern Atlantic worlds are equally, if differently, diverse, complex, and unstable when compared to earlier Atlantic worlds. Consequently, there remains interpretative mileage in focusing on the connections among peoples inhabiting a variety of modern Atlantics: connections born of continued personal, commercial, and cultural interactions but also born of shared Atlantic histories that are very much alive in the present.

Navigating the Transnational Turn: The American South in Atlantic and Global Perspectives

In a valiant attempt to pick through the definitional uncertainties regarding the geographical location and temporal scope of the Atlantic World, David Armitage has identified three main approaches: *circum*-Atlantic histories focus on transnational aspects of the Atlantic World; *trans*-Atlantic studies are comparative and deal with the international history of the Atlantic World; and *cis*-Atlantic approaches examine particular nations or regions, their peoples and cultures, within an Atlantic context.[21] As we will see, each model provides a useful way to conceptualize how the American South has been slotted into an Atlantic framework.

Although Phillips's *Atlantic Sound* has elements that in Armitage's terms might be considered trans-Atlantic and, even more so, cis-Atlantic, his book comes closest to Armitage's idea of a circum-Atlantic approach. Phillips focuses primarily on the port cities of Liverpool, Elmina, and Charleston, which are physically in contact with the Atlantic Ocean, and his main concern is with how the Atlantic facilitated the circulation and transformation of bodies, goods, capital, cultures, symbols, identities, and memories around those coastal locations.

Citing Roach's *Cities of the Dead* as an exemplary model, Armitage suggests that circum-Atlantic studies are usually more attentive to cultural matters than the other two approaches, which tend to focus on economic links and expressions of imperial/state power, at least in the hands of historians. However, as Armitage appreciates, strictly defined circum-Atlantic studies, restricted to only those lands lapped by the Atlantic Ocean, have serious limitations. The contacts and exchanges made possible by the Atlantic were shaped by and had serious ramifications for peoples and places located far beyond the coasts of Africa, Europe, and the Americas, as well as in Asia and other regions of the globe.

In a similar vein, François Furstenburg has argued for the penetration of Atlantic World influences deep into the American interior, and vice versa, urging more attention to the significance of the "Trans-Appalachian frontier" in Atlantic history. Furstenburg wants to see what happens when we look at colonial America and the early republic, "not from the perspective of the East Coast looking out toward the Atlantic, but rather from the multiple perspectives of the Atlantic world looking in toward the trans-Appalachian West and vice versa."[22] At one level, this capacious approach to the Atlantic World risks diluting the value of the paradigm until everything in continental North America is reduced to a mere extension of Atlantic history, thereby underestimating the significance of more local, internal dynamics as the United States emerged from its colonial past and expanded westward. Still, Furstenburg's perspective promises to recalibrate our understanding of what was going on among the diverse peoples occupying the southern section of North America during the late eighteenth and early nineteenth centuries by extending the reach of Atlantic studies across the Appalachians, into the Mississippi Valley, and beyond to the Southwest.

From the other side of the ocean, African historians have also been concerned to explore how far the Atlantic World penetrated into that continent and with the related issue of how far into the African heartlands we can still discover people who helped to create an Atlantic World. John Thornton, Linda Heywood, Toyin Falola, Matt Childs, and Sheila Walker have all highlighted the importance of various West Central African, as opposed to coastal West African, societies in the Atlantic World, describing their involvement in transatlantic commerce, including the slave trade, as partners as well as victims, and tracing their distinctive contributions to the emergence of African American and African Caribbean cultures in the New World.[23]

Asking how deep into the interior of lands in and around the Atlantic we can legitimately trace the influence of a discernible Atlantic World before it expires, or morphs into something qualitatively and quantitatively different, raises fundamental questions about the relative merits of Atlantic, or more circumscribed hemispheric, or more expansive global approaches to the study of the American South. For some, the Atlantic is simply too small, too pinched, and too parochial as a frame of reference. It is also held that by privileging the Atlantic basin, Atlantic studies risk undervaluing the significance of other zones of economic, demographic, and cultural interaction affecting the American South, while also effacing other important encounters that occurred in continental North America, such as those on the west coast. Moreover, despite its best intentions, Atlantic studies can perpetuate a Eurocentrism that marginalizes Native Americans and Africans.

Summarizing some of these concerns, economic historian and committed global southernist Peter Coclanis has argued that "the obsession with the Atlantic world *qua* unit continues to impede our understanding of the degree to which this unit drew its lifeblood from and hemorrhaged into others."[24] From the standpoint of European history, Coclanis claims that "by fixing our historical gaze so firmly toward the West the approach may, anachronistically, give too much weight to the Atlantic rim, separate North West Europe too sharply both from the other parts of Europe and from Eurasia as a whole, accord too much primacy to America in explaining transoceanic trade patterns, and, economically speaking, misrepresent through over statement the place of America in the order of things."[25]

Coclanis has a point. For most of the early modern period, Europeans devoted far more time and resources to developing intra-European and Asian trade connections than in opening up the Atlantic World. Even European discovery of the Americas was a consequence of trying to find a navigable water route to the much-coveted Indies. With regard to the American South, Coclanis concludes that "the South was born of global forces, and, if we think hard enough and look deep enough, we come to understand that the region, economically speaking, has remained in and of the world ever since."[26] By way of example, he notes how Indian pigments found their way to colonial North America via the European, especially Italian textile trade, even "displacing indigenous Native American pigments of major ceremonial importance in the Southeast United States."[27]

Other historians of early America have similarly noted that European adventurers, merchants, and colonists were always part of a world much larger than the Atlantic. For example, global connections clearly informed European encounters with the indigenous peoples of the American South: the responses of Captain John Smith to the Native Americans he met in Virginia were shaped by his earlier experiences with Ottoman Turks in the eastern Mediterranean; John White's paintings of Native Americans around Roanoke—important in creating understandings and misunderstandings of the South and its inhabitants for Europeans—reflected assumptions derived from his prior knowledge of other "exotic" peoples such as Picts, Uzbeks, and Turks.[28]

Fast-forward from the colonial period to the modern South and there is even more evidence of the region's place within global networks of culture, commerce, and diplomacy. Caryl Phillips certainly appreciated that global forces flowed through the modern Atlantic World in general and the American South in particular. One hero of his South Carolina trip is J. Waties Waring, a federal judge ostracized by white Charlestonians after World War II, partly for divorcing his local blueblood wife to marry a liberal Yankee, but mainly because of his steady opposition to Jim Crow. Equally significant for Phillips, Waring was an internationalist whose cosmopolitanism helped to explain his relative racial progressivism. Phillips quotes at length from a 1951 speech Waring made during an immigrant naturalization ceremony in Charleston:

> What is good has come to us from other lands. We have acquired from the Northern European countries systems of law and order, forms of government. We have acquired from the Southern countries of Europe literature, and architecture, and beauty. We have acquired from the people of Africa the Egyptian culture, music, rhythm, softness and beauty. We have acquired from the Asiatic countries most of our systems of philosophy, and all of our leading religious ideas.[29]

Just about all of the particulars here, as well as many of the underlying assumptions about regional and racial characteristics, are deeply suspect. But what appeals to Phillips is that Waring offered an unusually forthright recognition of the South's global situatedness and diverse heritages at a time when most white southerners were proclaiming the virtues of a fictionally pure white Anglo-Saxon Protestant culture and fighting to protect its all-too-real privileges.[30]

Economic, demographic, and political accounts of the contemporary South have become increasingly attentive to these kinds of global connections. Marko Maunula's *Guten Tag, Y'all* examines the impact of foreign capital and corporate interventions in the South Carolina Piedmont since World War II; James Peacock's *Grounded Globalism* argues that distinctive southern regional identities have been transformed, though not erased, by the region's deep immersion in a global economic and cultural nexus; a similar argument appears in Wanda Rushing's *Memphis and the Paradox of Place*, which concludes that "new forms of local identity, cultural expression, and economic development, integrated with old ones and mediated by the processes of globalization, will sustain the *genius loci*, or spirit of place, that makes Memphis distinctive"; and James Cobb and William Steuck's *Globalization and the American South* is dedicated to the proposition that the region has always been understood best in the context of "criss-crossing currents of global interaction."[31]

This global turn in southern studies, itself related to transnational and post-national turns in American studies more generally, has increasingly shaped literary and cultural studies of the region.[32] Selecting contributions for a special issue of *American Literature* dedicated to the New Southern Studies, guest editors Kathryn McKee and Annette Trefzer sought essays that "point to *shared* cultural and historical legacies within the global South in interpretations that effectively counter old narratives of regional and national exceptionalism."[33] Melanie Benson's *Disturbing Calculations*, an innovative study of how the fixation on mathematics in late-nineteenth- and twentieth-century southern literature reflected efforts to calculate, literally to account for and thereby legitimize, social hierarchies based on class, gender, and race, takes as axiomatic that "the South [is] inherently and historically transnational, born of early global forces."[34]

A parsimonious sampling of the many other works that explore how global currents flow through the literatures of the American South in ways not easily contained by an Atlantic World framework might include *Global Faulkner*, edited by Trefzer and Ann J. Abadie; Frank Cha's work on literary depictions of Korean immigrant experiences in the modern South; and Scott Hicks's analysis of how the mid-twentieth-century writings of Zora Neale Hurston and George W. Lee linked the experiences of African Americans in the rural, segregated, cotton-dependent black belt to global histories of migration, financial flows, commodity exchanges, and racialized economic exploitation.[35]

This efflorescence of globalized southern scholarship would seem to beg the question of what explanatory value for the study of the South remains for a relatively cramped Atlantic perspective. But such a question actually rests on a false distinction: the two approaches, Atlantic and global, are not mutually exclusive and can be mutually enhancing. Alison Games understands this, claiming Atlantic history as "a *slice* of world history. It is a way of looking at global *and* regional processes within a contained unit." Games adds the crucial rider that the Atlantic World in toto and the constitutive parts of that world severally, including the American South, were never "hermetically sealed off from the rest of the world, and thus was simultaneously involved in transformations unique to the Atlantic and those derived from global processes."[36]

This seems a thoroughly sensible and productive formulation. Scholars spend a lot of their time evaluating the relative explanatory power of the many different factors that contribute to any given phenomenon; they sort out hierarchies of immediate and underlying, decisive and contributory, proximate and distant causes—and then do the same again for consequences: short-term and enduring, superficial and profound, local and far-reaching. For southernists this kind of analysis, as Coclanis rightly observes, will eventually lead them to global connections. And yet, more often than not it is the Atlantic portion of that globe that has been the most interpretatively significant zone of transnational exchange, influence, and counter-influence affecting and affected by the American South.

Complicating the Transnational Turn: Oceans, Nations, and Regions

Regardless of disciplinary affiliation, a major appeal of Atlantic and global approaches to the American South is that they promise to accommodate the complex interactions among trade, peoples, and cultures that were not wholly circumscribed by national borders or merely expressions of state and imperial power. According to Furstenburg, the principal goal of Atlantic history is "to transcend the limits imposed by national historiographies," while the editors of *The American South in a Global World* insist that the South is best considered as "taking its place in a world of regions, not simply of nation-states."[37]

Yet, this much-vaunted transnationalism has often been more evident in theory than in practice. David Armitage predicted in 2002 that Atlantic history "is unlikely to replace traditional national histories and it will compete with other forms of national and international history," and he has been broadly correct.[38] As Furstenburg tartly notes, Atlantic history "has tended to remain content sailing aboard ships or landing along coastlines, leaving the more grueling trek into continental interiors to the national historiographies it so haughtily claims to supersede."[39]

From a literary and cultural studies perspective, Sharon Monteith, a savvy advocate of global approaches to the American South, has expressed similar reservations. Although she applauds "the shift from the American South to the 'global' U.S. South" because it "begins to extricate the region from a national model," Monteith recognizes that "a dynamic 'new' Southern studies is still contained within a deterministic (sub)national framework." She asks, "Is it possible, or even productive, to overcome the idea that the history of Southern Studies continues to be a series of regional struggles in national frame?" admitting that "relatively few of us have so far extended the parameters of the discussion outside of a national framework."[40]

There are three points to be made regarding the stubborn persistence of nation-states (and empires) as key units of analysis even in avowedly transnational studies of the American South. First, with regard to Atlantic studies this obstinacy has something to do with the location and nature of source materials and the range of academic competencies among the scholars working in these fields. Most Atlantic-South scholarship has relied heavily on written evidence from American, British, Danish, Dutch, French, Italian, Portuguese, and Spanish archives or on memoirs and various forms of creative literature written in the same languages. This largely textual material, which contains relatively little direct evidence of African or Native American experiences, cultures, or opinions, has helped to sustain an emphasis on imperial and national histories along with a residual Eurocentrism within many Atlantic World projects. Contributions from those trained in historical archaeology, anthropology, and linguistics and by those whose language skills extend beyond the tongues of the major colonizing powers have only slightly moderated this tendency by offering alternatives to European and Euro-American written sources.[41]

A second, related point is that few scholars can claim the wide-ranging expertise that would enable a truly authoritative, integrated, comprehensive study of the American South in Atlantic perspective for any period or along any thematic trajectory. Jon Smith offers a puckish checklist of the qualifications required of a newly minted New Southern Studies scholar—adept in postcolonial theory, reading skills in French and/or Spanish, capacity to "talk about Texas and Cuba as easily as about Mississippi and

Virginia," willingness to teach courses on New World plantation literatures and minority southern writing beyond the African American tradition—to make a serious point about the enormous demands on those
who would hazard a truly transnational, Atlantic or global, approach to
the American South.[42]

Historians encounter similar competency deficits whenever they try to
grapple with the sheer scale and diversity of the Atlantic World. Colonialist Simon Newman admits that "it is all but impossible for a historian today to amass the language skills or to master the diverse secondary literature in a way that makes a comprehensive Atlantic history possible, for the
Atlantics of the African, Iberian, Western European, Caribbean, North
American, Central American and South American worlds were enor-
mously different."[43] Kwasi Konadu makes this point even more forcefully
in his historical-linguistic-anthropological study of the Akan diaspora in
the Americas. Konadu explains that the Akan, an ethnocultural grouping
of West Africans from the Gold Coast who generally speak Kwa languages
and include subgroups like the Ashanti, Coramantin, and Fante, "contributed in specific and integral ways to the diasporic themes of maroonage,
conspiracies and rebellions, self-help organizations and communities,
and an African spiritual-ideational-material culture in the Americas"—
including Virginia, Georgia, and South Carolina, where "a minimum of
17,000 Akan persons or persons fluent in Akan culture settled."[44]

Konadu's Akan expertise adds nuance to sweeping generalizations
about the nature of the Black Atlantic and the impact of the African diaspora in the American South and beyond. But he laments how "Africa
remains neglected in Atlantic histories because many scholars lack competency in the African histories and languages of the people they study."
As a consequence, "national historical narratives of European or North
American origin are privileged, and Africans are denied *their own* agency
in the patronizing ways they are 'founders and creators' of a culture that
ultimately flowed from Europe."[45]

Paradoxically, while technical limitations and the preeminence of certain kinds of sources have nudged both Atlantic and transnational southern studies back toward traditional, accessible, and comprehensible (to
Western-trained scholars) units of analysis such as nations and empires,
they have also encouraged renewed interest in comparative, or what
David Armitage calls "Trans-Atlantic," studies that merely require deep
knowledge of, at a minimum, two locations in the Atlantic World![46]

Of course, there has been a long tradition of comparative work involving the American South. The dean of southern historians, C. Vann Woodward, was a pioneer. Casting a comparative eye over the region in 1953, Woodward's "The Irony of Southern History" preempted the work of many contemporary southernists by puncturing the myth of southern exceptionalism and demonstrating how much the South had in common with places that had also experienced slavery, emancipation, racism, agrarianism, poverty, military defeat (a category more appropriate to white southerners than black southerners, who rarely viewed the Civil War as a defeat), occupation, and reconstruction.[47] Other distinguished postwar historians, including Frank Tannenbaum, Stanley Elkins, David Brion Davis, Carl Degler, Herbert Klein, Richard Dunn, and George Fredrickson, also probed the distinctiveness, or otherwise, of the American South in comparative, trans-Atlantic perspective, usually with issues of slavery, emancipation, and race relations again to the fore.[48] More recently, books such as Don Doyle's *Nations Divided*, Peter Kolchin's *Unfree Labor* and *A Sphinx on the American Land*, Gerald Horne's *The Deepest South*, Laird Bergad's *The Comparative Histories of Slavery in Brazil, Cuba, and the United States*, and some of the essays in collections such as *The American South and the Italian Mezzogiorno* and *Britain and the American South* testify to a continuing interest among historians in comparative approaches to the South in Atlantic contexts.[49]

If anything, southern literary scholars have been even more drawn to comparative studies to undermine exceptionalist narratives of the South and the nation. Deborah Cohn's influential *History and Memory in the Two Souths*, for example, compares the fiction of the modern South and Latin America. Cohn concludes that similar historical experiences have generated similar literary traditions exemplified by the self-conscious indebtedness to and unconscious echoes of William Faulkner's writings in the works of Gabriel García Márquez and Carlos Fuentes.[50] George Handley's *Postslavery Literatures in the Americas* also compares the work of southern fiction writers, including Faulkner, Charles Chesnutt, and Toni Morrison, with their counterparts elsewhere in the Americas such as Alejo Carpentier, Jean Rhys, Cirilo Villaverde, and Rosario Ferré, exposing multiple parallels and intersections, mostly clustered around themes of memory, genealogy, and racial identities.[51] Moving beyond the New World, Sarah Robertson has looked at representations of coal mining in Appalachian and Welsh fiction, Michael Kreyling has contrasted aspects of Italian and southern U.S. literatures, and Victoria Kennefick has placed the writings of Georgian Flannery O'Connor and Irishman Frank O'Connor in dialogue to explore two societies that share a strong religiosity, experiences of military defeat and occupation, and a powerful agrarian tradition.[52]

Most of these trans-Atlantic studies start from an assumption of significant similarities between the two sites of comparison, be they national, sub-national, or regional. Yet, as Elijah Gould has noted in the context of comparative Atlantic history, this can be problematic, since the "comparison tends to take as a given the very national boundaries that Atlantic history has long sought to complicate."[53] For some transnational partisans, this failure to dislodge the nation-state from the heart of Atlantic World analysis is a matter of regret, almost betrayal. And yet, and this is my third point on this issue, to do so would actually be perverse, misleading, and ahistorical. Distaste for the more odious and oppressive features of imperialism and nationalism is no reason to deny, ignore, or underestimate the enormous influence of state-driven economic agendas, diplomatic and military initiatives, social policies, laws, cultural imperatives, and territorial ambitions in shaping the experiences of peoples living in the American South or elsewhere around the Atlantic. Moreover, despite a tendency to hail the liberating and progressive potential of globalization, there is little to suggest that transnational manifestations of private, though often state-supported, economic and cultural power are inherently liberating and progressive. As Wanda Rushing notes in her account of the globalized economy of Memphis, Tennessee, "each new wave of development strategies tends to reproduce old patterns of inequality, generating wealth and power for a few and maintaining the structure of poverty and inequality for many."[54]

The crucial point here is that, while the American South was partly created by, and was a co-participant in, the creation of Atlantic worlds that transcended national borders, it was also a product, victim, beneficiary, and co-architect of various national histories, including that of the United States. Consequently, the key to a persuasive transnational southern studies, be it global or Atlantic in its primary orientation, is not to deny the signal importance of the nation-state, or of any other supra-state, sub-state, or aspirational state formation (Confederacy, anyone?), but rather to interrogate their reciprocal relationships with the American South.[55] We need analyses that portray the South, in Jon Smith's phrase, as "simultaneously center and margin, colonizer and colonized, global north and global south, essentialist and hybrid."[56] But we must also recognize that the American South has been concurrently part of various imperial, national, and sub-national as well as transnational configurations of power and influence.

In an effort to reconcile the centrality of national and imperial power in the early modern Atlantic World with the transnational imperatives that drive Atlantic history, Elijah Gould posits an "entangled history of the sort exemplified by the English-speaking and Spanish Atlantic worlds." Here the emphasis is on "interconnecting themes and influences" among European powers and the native and African peoples with whom they had contact.[57] Getting down to southern cases, this would enable us, for example, to better appreciate that Spanish adventures in the Americas provided the main template for English settlements in Virginia, where, as April Lee Hatfield has shown, the English initially hoped to create a Protestant version of Spanish Mexico.[58] We would also recognize that the notorious harshness of South Carolina's slave codes was connected to the proximity of Spanish power in neighboring Florida, to which many African slaves fled and swore allegiance after the Stono Rebellion of 1739.[59]

Part of Gould's agenda here is to counteract a persistent and distortive Anglocentrism within the Eurocentrism evident in many studies of the early modern Atlantic World. He stresses that although the British and Spanish New World empires "were part of the same hemispheric system or community," this system "was fundamentally asymmetric with Spain, as the senior and historically preeminent member, often holding the upper hand."[60] Iberian power and Spanish cultural influences mattered greatly across the Caribbean and the continental Americas, including Florida in the Southeast and Texas, Arkansas, and Louisiana in the Southwest.

These Spanish—and sometimes French—influences have helped to shape a distinctive hemispheric subset of the Atlantic World that yokes together the Caribbean, Latin America, and the American South in a relationship that has provided fertile grounds for the work of comparative literary scholars like Deborah Cohn and George Handley.[61] "The American South," John Lowe claims, "is in many ways the northern rim of the Caribbean—especially the coastal states of Texas, Louisiana, and Florida."[62] In a similar vein, *Just Below South*, a collection of essays on Caribbean-South cultural connections, is dedicated, in the words of coeditor Jessica Adams, to refuting the notions of southern exceptionalism which have served "to isolate the *idea* of the South from the region just below it on the map." Instead, contributors to the volume focus on the "transactions, migrations, armed struggles, casual contacts, and prolonged relationships" between the two regions.[63] Historian Edward Rugemer, meanwhile, has even placed the origins of the American Civil War—and with it the main economic, social, political, and racial coordinates of Confederate nationalism—firmly in a Caribbean context.[64]

Equally important to Elijah Gould's critique of much comparative Atlantic history is his appreciation that "analytical categories such as the nation, which comparative approaches tend to take as fixed, were (and are) themselves entangled constructs with shifting histories and borders, literal as well as figurative."[65] Here Gould makes two valuable interventions. First, not only does he refuse to abandon the nation (or the empire) as a vital unit of analysis, but he also reminds us that modern nation-states actually emerged, in a multiplicity of shifting forms, largely as a result of the commercial, political, cultural, and demographic processes that bound together the early modern Atlantic World.[66]

Paradoxically, then, one of the greatest benefits of Atlantic studies is that it can illuminate the histories and cultures of the empires and nations that have been instrumental in the creation of Atlantic worlds that transcend their imperial and national jurisdictions. Even at the putative Ur-moment in the emergence of a New Southern Studies in 2001, when Houston A. Baker and Dana Nelson called for southernists to free the objects of their inquiries from the bonds of national histories, they recognized that one consequence of placing the South resolutely in transnational context would be to deepen our understanding of the United States. All Americans, they insisted, are "always already in 'the South,' that is it is unequivocally and intricately lodged in us, a first principle of our being in the world." Indeed, they held that "'the South' is the US social, political, racial, economic, ethical, and everyday-life imaginary written as 'regionalism.'"[67]

If this was hardly a novel insight—years before, Carl Degler had insisted that the South should be examined as a crucial "co-creator of the nation's history," not as peripheral or aberrant within that history—Baker and Nelson refocused attention on the Americanness of the South and the southernness of America while urging a productive concern for the transnational contexts within which region and nation, and the critical interplay between them, might be better understood.[68] "A concept of the South is essential to national identity in the United States of America," Jennifer Rae Greeson asserts boldly in *Our South*, her study of how notions of a distinctive yet integrated South permeated American literature in the late eighteenth and nineteenth centuries.[69] As McKee and Trefzer have summarized, New Southern Studies scholars "are certain in our knowledge of the South's metonymic relation to the nation and convinced of its centrality to American Studies, but we are equally interested in the region's fascinating multiplicity and its participation in hemispheric and global contexts."[70]

Gould's second key intervention is to gesture toward the importance of figurative expressions of Atlantic identities. Economic historian and demographer David Eltis has also argued that "to make sense of Atlantic history we still have to break out of the materialist paradigm and focus on the cultural, not the economic, or to put it another way, to make sense of the economic, scholars should re-examine cultural patterns."[71] One criticism sometimes leveled at southern historians from their colleagues in literary and cultural studies is that they could show more interest in exploring the "symbolic economies" that, as Michael Bibler notes, "travelled alongside, and often influenced . . . material changes and relations in the South."[72]

It is worth pausing here to consider what appears to be a significant and deepening disciplinary fault line between literary and historical studies of the South, and not just among those adopting an Atlantic perspective. The New Southern Studies tends to focus on what Jon Smith and Deborah Cohn characterize as a "performative and situational" South and is, in Richard King's phrase, "primarily an exploration of the way the South has been thought about."[73] Southern historians, however, tend to bristle whenever they feel that their literary and cultural studies colleagues mistake the map for the road, the signifier for the signified, and, as Bibler concedes is sometimes the case, "come too close to treating representations of the South as if they were straightforward reflections of history."[74]

Yet these disciplinary tendencies are hardly absolute. Southern historians have hardly been resistant to the idea that "the South" has always been at some level an imaginary construct, or that "southern identity" has been largely performed: the best work in the field accepts that these are contested intellectual, cultural, and symbolic phenomena with complex relationships to any discernible material reality. Thus, Michael O'Brien has pronounced the South "an intellectual perception . . . which has served to comprehend and weld an unintegrated social reality"; Edward Ayers defines southern identity as "a fiction of a geographically bounded and coherent set of attitudes to be set off against a mythical non-South"; and Karen Cox describes how ideas about "the South" and "southern identity" coalesced in the late nineteenth and early twentieth centuries partly through their expression in popular cultural forms such as music, advertising, tourism, and the movies.[75]

The proliferation of southern "memory studies" by historians such as W. Fitzhugh Brundage also stresses the importance of highly contested symbolic discourses in creating competing ideas of the South—and in the process helping to define the United States.[76] Even the perennial concern among southern historians with constructions of race necessarily involves a keen interest in the circulation of racial ideologies, representations, cultures, and identities that moves far beyond a crudely empiricist fixation with the material record.[77] In other words, there have always been southern historians willing to take what Richard King calls "interpretive chances" in attempting to understand how the South has been created, how it has functioned, and how it has been perceived and represented at the level of symbol and imagination.[78]

Conversely, there have always been southern literary and cultural studies scholars whose work, while conceptually and interpretively daring, is grounded in the historical record. Patricia Yeager's article on "Circum-Atlantic Superabundance" offers a highly pertinent example of a genuinely interdisciplinary effort to explore the American South's Atlantic World relationships.[79] Yeager ambitiously tries to find the elusive "material sources of style," hoping to tether recurring thematic concerns and formal predilections in southern art and literature to concrete historical facets of the Atlantic World. For example, she reads the preoccupation with the use of black breast milk to rear southern white children in the works of Kara Walker, Alice Randall, and Margaret Mitchell as testimony to a transatlantic slave economy that was exploitative along both gender and racial lines. Even more central to southern—and to much Latin American—art is what Yeager calls an "aesthetics of excess." She asks if the luxuriant, baroque qualities evident in some of the American South's most powerful visual and literary cultures "mimics the profligate expenditure that has gone into this culture's making."[80]

This is highly suggestive, perhaps inherently speculative, scholarship. Yeager encourages us to think through the connections among economics, trade, migration, race, racism, place, and gender and important aspects of southern art and culture in a circum-Atlantic context. Moreover, by taking her "interpretive chances" she reminds us that much can be learned and retrieved about the experiential and affective aspects of the Atlantic World and the American South by paying attention to their entwined cultural and symbolic economies. Most importantly, her work implicitly challenges the value of privileging, or drawing false distinctions between, symbolic and materialist approaches to Atlantic World and southern studies.[81]

Going Granular: Particularism in Atlantic-South Studies

David Armitage dubbed the last of his trinity of Atlantic World models "cis-Atlantic" history. The term has its roots in the American South, where Thomas Jefferson coined it initially to indicate the distinctive qualities of the flora and fauna of Virginia. Armitage likes the phrase because it showed Jefferson's attentiveness to the characteristics of a world on "this"—as in the American—side of the Atlantic that was meaningfully differentiated from the Old World, yet still intimately connected to it by the Atlantic Ocean. Cis-Atlantic for Jefferson was "a badge of difference and a marker of a novel American perspective just as it was defined in relation to the Atlantic Ocean." Accordingly, Armitage defines a cis-Atlantic approach as one that "studies particular places as unique locations within an Atlantic world and seeks to define that uniqueness as the result of the interaction between the local particularity and a wider web of connections (and comparisons)." Atlantic history, he contends, "still needs to be investigated at the most intimate levels of town, village, and even household."[82]

The American South has often been construed as a site of "uniqueness" in ways that contemporary scholars tend to reject, even as they are drawn inexorably toward trying to explain when, how, and why ideas of southern exceptionalism emerged, to dissect the myths that have sustained them, and to identify who has benefited and who has suffered from their perpetuation. Notwithstanding the dangers of cis-Atlantic approaches slipping into a kind of neo-exceptionalism, however, it has its merits. "We can better understand the local through the lens of the transnational and the global," claims John Lowe; but the converse is also true.[83] We can often glean a better understanding of the significance of transnational forces by paying attention to how they have operated in particular locales and affected the lives of identifiable groups and individuals.

Before discussing how an emphasis on place and on individual and collective biography can allow us to monitor the percolation of Atlantic World influences through the American South, it is worth noting that thematically driven studies also offer a productive way to narrow the focus but enlarge the explanatory power of Atlantic approaches to the region. The possibilities are virtually endless. Here, however, three examples can illustrate the potential of thematic approaches to the South's Atlantic World relationships.

The first example is epidemiological and is related to studies of the Atlantic World's diverse yet interdependent climatic systems and natural environments.[84] J. R. McNeill's *Mosquito Empires* traces the enormous impact in the Atlantic World of malaria and yellow fever from the seventeenth century to the early twentieth century, indicating the capacity of topically driven studies to stretch the conventional chronology of Atlantic history. Both diseases were brought across the ocean from Africa by mosquitoes and in the blood of their victims aboard the same ships that bore Africans to the Americas. Regularly ravaging the subtropical South and cities like Memphis, New Orleans, and Jacksonville, these Atlantic World diseases had profound consequences for the region's economic development, health, and culture.[85]

Lawyers, lawmakers, and the law constitute another possible thematic route around the Atlantic World and in and out of the American South. Lauren Benton has proposed the idea of a transnational "legal pluralism" to describe the relationships between various legal structures emanating from the metropolitan centers of Europe and the local adjustments made on the ground by colonizers, the colonized, and the many thousands who straddled such convenient, though not wholly adequate, designations. Benton acknowledges the diversity of these statutory, practiced, and evaded legal regimes (Anglo, Iberian, Francophone, African, and later American) but still makes a compelling case that legal systems and their institutional correlates—particularly those relating to slavery and race—were crucial in helping to define "a social space for cultural difference that was present across the South Atlantic world."[86]

A third thematic strand in Atlantic studies focuses on how particular rituals, performances, and artifacts have united the Atlantic World symbolically and imaginatively as well as economically and demographically.

Joseph Roach's *Cities of the Dead* has been highly influential here, and other scholars have, much like Patricia Yeager, examined the provenance, dissemination, and consumption of specific stories, songs, dances, artifacts, and ceremonies to reveal the reciprocal relationships among different Atlantic sites and peoples, including those in the American South. Julian Gerstin, for example, has followed the footsteps of the Kalenda, a "creolized" or "neo-African" dance that spread throughout "a major part of the Caribbean and southern United States" during the late eighteenth century. Promiscuously mixing African, French, and Spanish influences, and enduring into the twenty-first century in various incarnations, including as a "tourist kalenda" in Martinique, the Kalenda illustrates how migrating cultural practices, texts, and rituals can reveal the intricate Atlantic networks of influence and counter-influence within which the American South has always existed.[87]

English mystic and poet William Blake claimed to "see a world in a grain of sand"; those studying the American South can also profit from a granular approach in which the nature and significances of the Atlantic World are revealed by close attention to a particular southern locale.[88] To give but one example, Joshua Piker's forensic study of Ofuskee, an eighteenth-century Creek town in present-day Alabama, uncovers the intersections and divergences of local, Atlantic, and to a lesser extent global influences. While warning against overgeneralization ("Ofuskee was not a Creek every-town; neither were Coweta, Okchai, Muccoulous-sus, nor any of the other approximately fifty-five Creek towns. Each had its own history"), Piker focuses on Ofuskee and its residents to see "the points in their histories where Native and Euro-American communities overlapped" but also to appreciate "the separate paths that each people took."[89]

Piker's study forms part of a vibrant new scholarship on Native American tribes and confederations in the South during the precolonial, colonial, and early republic periods, some of which explicitly invokes the idea of an Indian Atlantic.[90] More generally, the boom in southern Native American studies demonstrates how the histories of particular social groups can reveal the region's Atlantic connections. Without denying the genocidal violence, disease, and exploitation often visited upon Native Americans by Europeans, the cumulative weight of this scholarship has been to restore a greater measure of agency to the indigenous peoples of the American South, thereby affirming Daniel Usner's assertion that participation in the Atlantic economy "did not automatically reduce Indians to dependency," and recognizing their role in creating both the South and an Atlantic World.[91]

Even in the borderlands of the Southwest, far from the Atlantic shoreline, the histories of Native Americans were inextricably bound up with European economic and imperial ambitions; and those ambitions were realized, thwarted, and modified in the context of Native American power and influence. Juliana Barr and Pekka Hämäläinen, for example, have demonstrated that Native Americans, especially the Comanche, dominated the Texas borderlands long after the arrival of the Spanish, who spent much of their time clinging precariously to limited power in the region and frantically accommodating to Native Americans' concepts of diplomacy, trade, and social organization.[92] Kathleen DuVal and F. Todd Smith have described how Quapaws, Caddos, and other southwestern tribes negotiated a series of favorable agreements with the French, the Spanish, and, after the Louisiana Purchase of 1803, the United States. This demonstrates, in DuVal's phrase, both "the importance of individuals and local circumstances in determining the fate of empires" and the perils of "generalizing about the relationships among various European and Indian groups."[93] In sum, this scholarship suggests that the early history of the Southwest is only fully intelligible in terms of encounters between natives and Europeans brought together by the demands of transatlantic commerce and imperial ambitions which, from a European perspective, made the Louisiana territories resemble a "pawn on the chessboard of European politics."[94]

Away from the borderlands, in the Southeast portions of the American South closest to the Atlantic, James Merrill describes "the ebb and flow of challenge and response, crisis and calm, disintegration and reformation" among the Catawba in the Carolinas as transatlantic trade brought them into contact with Europeans and Africans. Like their counterparts in the Southwest, the Catawba fought to retain control over their cultures and destinies in the face of European intrusion. They opened formal diplomatic relations with the colony of South Carolina, for which they, like the Creeks, provided slave catching and military service and with whom they traded extensively. It was only with the inexorable rise of cotton and its attendant hunger for labor and land that there was a shift from "a world where trade was king to one where cotton would be" and a system built in large measure around diplomacy and exchange was replaced by a more brutally exploitative one.[95]

Collectively, this scholarship has shown that Native Americans in the South participated in a multiplicity of commercial, political, and social relationships with Europeans, often skillfully playing them off against each other for their own advantage. They also exerted significant influence on European lives, cultures, commerce, and diplomacy both in the Americas and, as Alden Vaughan has stressed, in the metropolitan centers of Europe.[96] Particularly during the period from the fifteenth century to the early nineteenth century, Native Americans' experiences in the American South, like those of African Americans, were forged in the context of, if never wholly defined by, European commercial, diplomatic, and military struggles for mastery over the natural and human resources of the Atlantic World.

Even more granular than collective studies of Native Americans, African Americans, or other social groups and subgroups are those that have focused on the families and individuals who co-created the relationships between the American South and the Atlantic World. It is in their histories that one can see the economic, social, and cultural impact of the Atlantic World registered in the lives of real people, here that grand theories and broad generalization assume a vital corporeality.

For example, consider the histories of Anta Majigeen Ndiaye and Zephaniah Kingsley. Born in Bristol, England, in 1765, Kingsley was a slave trader and ship captain who, as he plied his transoceanic trade, at various times swore loyalty to France, Denmark, Spain, and the United States. He also owned successful plantations, first at Laurel Grove and then at Fort George Island on the Atlantic coast of Spanish Florida. These plantations were partly administered by his remarkable wife, Anta. A Wolof slave, Anta was purchased by Kingsley in Havana, Cuba, in 1806 when she was just thirteen. Five years later, Kingsley successfully petitioned the Spanish colonial authorities to manumit Anna, as she became known after an "African" marriage to Kingsley, along with their children. When Florida became a U.S. territory, it abolished the Spanish three-caste racial system, which gave certain rights and privileges to mulatto offspring. Fearing for the future of their children in the more rigid and draconian racial environment of the southern United States, Anna and Zephaniah moved their family to Haiti in 1837. When Zephaniah Kingsley died in 1843, he left most of his estate to Anna and their family—and to several other families he had with slave women. He gave instructions that none of his remaining slaves should be separated from their families and that all of them should be allowed to purchase their freedom at half the current market rate. When Kingsley's white relatives challenged the will on racial grounds, Anna returned to Florida to defend her claim; in 1846 her rights to her inheritance were upheld by a Duval County court.[97]

The histories of Anta Majigeen Ndiaye and Zephaniah Kingsley ranged geographically from West Africa to the American South, from western Europe to the Caribbean. Topically, their story illuminates transoceanic economic links dominated by the slave trade and plantation slavery and speaks to national rivalries that were played out across the Atlantic World; it evokes the horrendous history of sexual exploitation of black women by white men which has profoundly shaped southern and Atlantic history, yet complicates that grim narrative with ample evidence of mutual affection between Zephaniah and Anna and a shared concern for their family's welfare; and it reminds us how competing legal regimes in the Atlantic World profoundly shaped the lives of southerners, especially in matters relating to race.

There are perils as well as prospects in using individual lives to examine how Atlantic forces flowed into and out of the American South, not least regarding the question of how to generalize from specific cases. In *Freedom Papers*, a fascinating account of one slave and her descendants' multiple migrations around the Atlantic over a period of more than 150 years, from Senegambia to Saint-Domingue, Cuba, New Orleans, France, and Belgium, authors Rebecca Scott and Jean Hébrard carefully disavow "any claim to typicality or representativeness for the Vincent/Tinchant family" at the center of their story.[98] Moreover, as Sharon Monteith has observed of a more general trend toward autobiography within southern studies, "At the very moment that the image of the South's exceptional status is complicated by its positioning in a global nexus, some critics are choosing to (re)connect to a more traditional nostalgic South, often with an emphasis on the autobiographical. The narrative glue remains place and ancestry."[99]

Yet Atlantic world autobiographies, biographies, and prosopographies can also work to destabilize fixed assumptions about southern identity: they reveal the sheer diversity of roots and routes that became entangled in various American Souths and help to track the reverberations from the region as they spread around the Atlantic World. Consequently, when contemporary Guinea-born writer Tierno Monénembo gives an unashamedly autobiographical account of his relationship to William Faulkner's writings, it adds not only an African dimension to our sense of that southern white writer's Atlantic, indeed global, influence, but also adds what Richard King calls a "subjective-experiential dimension to literary history, which often neglects such evidence."[100]

There are numerous autobiographical accounts of journeys—real and imagined—around, across, and through an Atlantic World, or at least through portions of that world, in which the American South looms large as a point of departure, or arrival, or transit. Spanning the centuries, travel narratives by Alvar Núñez Cabeza de Vaca, Olaudah Equiano, Alexis de Tocqueville, William Wells Brown, Frances Kemble, Mary Church Terrell, Richard Wright, James Yates, Maya Angelou, V. S. Naipaul, Nick Middleton, and Gary Younge have all placed the, or rather "their," South in transatlantic context.[101]

These personal testimonies by men and women of diverse national, racial, and ethnic provenance—some of whom were born in the American South, some who came to the region as voluntary migrants, many who were transported against their will, and some who were just visiting—help to expose the material, symbolic, and emotional cartographies of the Atlantic World. They chronicle the myriad forces that have bound together the American South, Europe, and Africa, while also expressing the ruptures and differences evident within that world, along with its relationships to other, more broadly global or narrowly national contexts. This is the tradition to which Caryl Phillips's *The Atlantic Sound* belongs. This is the condition to which any Atlantic tributary within southern studies and any southern stream within Atlantic studies should surely aspire.

Notes

1. Caryl Phillips, *The Atlantic Sound* (2000; London: Vintage, 2001).

2. Caryl Phillips, *A New World Order* (London: Secker & Warburg, 2001), 305.

3. Fred D'Aguiar, "Home," *British Subjects* (Newcastle: Bloodaxe, 1993), 14–15. The "here" and "there" aspects of the diaspora have been neatly theorized by Paul Tiyambe Zeleza, "Re-Writing the African Diaspora: Beyond the Black Atlantic," *African Affairs* 104, no. 414 (2005): 35–68.

4. Gregory D. Smithers, "Challenging a Pan-African Identity: The Autobiographical

Writings of Maya Angelou, Barack Obama, and Caryl Phillips," *Journal of American Studies* 45, no. 3 (2011): 498.

5. Phillips, *Atlantic Sound*, 221.

6. Phillips, *New World Order*, 183. For Phillips's indebtedness to Glissant's ideas, see Paul Giles, *Atlantic Republic: The American Tradition in English Literature* (New York: Oxford University Press, 2006), 351.

7. Trevor Burnard, "Only Connect: The Rise and Rise (and Fall?) of Atlantic History," *Historically Speaking* 7, no. 6 (2006): 20. Other useful attempts to define Atlantic history and Atlantic studies include David Armitage, "Three Concepts of Atlantic History," in *The British Atlantic World*, ed. David Armitage and Michael Braddick (New York: Palgrave, 2002), 11–27; Bernard Bailyn, *Atlantic History: Concept and Contours* (Cambridge: Harvard University Press, 2005) and "The Idea of Atlantic History," *Itinerario* 20, no. 1 (1996): 19–44; Toyin Falola and Kevin D. Roberts, Introduction, in *The Atlantic World, 1450–2000*, ed. Falola and Roberts (Bloomington: Indiana University Press, 2008), ix–xiv; Donna Gabaccia, "A Long Atlantic in a Wider World," *Atlantic Studies* 1 (2004): 1–27; Alison Games, "Atlantic History: Definitions, Challenges, and Opportunities," *American Historical Review* 111 (June 2006): 741–57; Jack P. Greene and Philip D. Morgan, eds., *Atlantic History: A Critical Appraisal* (New York: Oxford University Press, 2008).

8. Phillips, *New World Order*, 305.

9. Armitage, "Three Concepts," 11, 26.

10. J. H. Eliott, "Atlantic History: A Circumnavigation," in Armitage and Braddick, *The British Atlantic World*, 234.

11. Peter Linebaugh and Marcus Rediker, *The Many-Headed Hydra: Sailors, Slaves, Commoners, and the Hidden History of the Revolutionary Atlantic* (Boston: Beacon Press, 2000).

12. Peter Coclanis argues that the South began to emerge as a distinct region in North America during the mid-seventeenth century as a result of its unusual dependence on slavery and plantation agriculture, while Jennifer Rae Greeson suggests that ideas of a distinct South were already congealing in American literature by the late eighteenth century. Coclanis, "Tracking the Economic Divergences of the North and South," *Southern Cultures* 6, no. 4 (2000): 82–103; Greeson, *Our South: Geographic Fantasy and the Rise of National Literature* (Cambridge: Harvard University Press, 2010).

13. Gabaccia, "A Long Atlantic"; Falola and Roberts, *The Atlantic World*. See also Thomas Benjamin, *The Atlantic World: Europeans, Africans, Indians, and Their Shared History, 1400–1900* (Cambridge: Cambridge University Press, 2009); Douglas R. Egerton, Alison Games, Jane G. Landers, Kris Lane, and Donald R. Wright, eds., *The Atlantic World: A History, 1400–1888* (Wheeling, Ill.: Harlan Davidson, 2007).

14. Paul Gilroy, *Black Atlantic: Modernity and Double Consciousness* (London: Verso, 1993).

15. For the uses and misuses of Black Atlantic models, see Douglas B. Chambers, "The Black Atlantic: Theory, Method, and Practice," in Falola and Roberts, *The Atlantic World*, 151–74. The voluminous literature placing slavery and the emergence of African American cultures in the South within an Atlantic World framework includes Ira Berlin,

Many Thousands Gone: The First Two Centuries of Slavery in North America (Cambridge: Harvard University Press, 1998); Charles Joyner, *Down by the Riverside: A South Carolina Slave Community* (Urbana: University of Illinois Press, 1984); Gwendolyn Midlo Hall, *Africans in Colonial Louisiana: The Development of Afro-Creole Culture in the Eighteenth Century* (Baton Rouge: Louisiana State University Press, 1992); Michael Mullin, *Africa in America: Slave Acculturation and Resistance in the American South and British Caribbean, 1736–1831* (Urbana: University of Illinois Press, 1992); Phillip D. Morgan, *Slave Counterpoint: Black Culture in the Eighteenth-Century Chesapeake and Lowcountry* (Chapel Hill: University of North Carolina Press, 1998); Michael Gomez, *Exchanging Our Country Marks: The Transformation of African Identities in the Colonial and Antebellum South* (Chapel Hill: University of North Carolina Press, 1998); Jon Sensbach, *A Separate Canaan: The Making of an Afro-Moravian World in North Carolina, 1763–1840* (Chapel Hill: University of North Carolina, 1998); Lorena S. Walsh, *From Calabar to Carter's Grove: The History of a Virginia Slave Community* (Charlottesville: University of Virginia Press, 1997); Peter Wood, *Strange New Land: Africans in Colonial America* (New York: Oxford University Press, 2003); Sylvia Frey and Betty Wood, *Come Shouting to Zion: African American Protestantism in the American South and British Caribbean to 1830* (Chapel Hill: University of North Carolina Press, 1998); Daniel Littlefield, *Rice and Slaves: Ethnicity and the Slave Trade in Colonial South Carolina* (Urbana: University of Illinois Press, 1991); Stephanie E. Smallwood, *Saltwater Slavery: A Middle Passage from Africa to American Diaspora* (Cambridge: Harvard University Press, 2007); James Sidbury, *Becoming African in America: Race and Nation in the Early Black Atlantic* (New York: Oxford University Press, 2006); Douglas B. Chambers, *Murder at Montpelier: Igbo Africans in Virginia* (Jackson: University of Mississippi Press, 2005).

16. See, for example, George Fredrickson, *Black Liberation: A Comparative History of Black Ideologies in the United States and South Africa* (New York: Oxford University Press, 1995); James Meriwether, *Proudly We Can Be Africans: Black Americans and Africa, 1935–1961* (Chapel Hill: University of North Carolina Press, 2002); Mary Rolison, *Grassroots Garveyism: The Universal Negro Improvement Association in the Rural South, 1920–1927* (Chapel Hill: University of North Carolina Press, 2007); Susan Pennybacker, *From Scottsboro to Munich: Race and Political Culture in 1930s Britain* (Princeton: Princeton University Press, 2009).

17. Helen Taylor, *Circling Dixie: Contemporary Southern Culture through a Transatlantic Lens* (New Brunswick: Rutgers University Press, 2001), 163.

18. Martyn Bone, "Narratives of African Immigration to the U.S. South," *CR: The New Centennial Review* 10, no. 1 (2010): 66. See also Martyn Bone, "The Transnational Turn, Houston Baker's New Southern Studies and Patrick Neate's *Twelve Bar Blues*," *Comparative American Studies: An International Journal* 3, no. 2 (2005): 189–211.

19. Joseph Roach, *Cities of the Dead: Circum-Atlantic Performance* (New York: Columbia University Press, 1998), 4.

20. George Handley, *Postslavery Literatures in the Americas: Family Portraits in Black and White* (Charlottesville: University of Virginia Press, 2000), 146–47. For a deft analysis of how the legacies of Atlantic World slavery have been preserved, manipulated, and occluded through various cultural practices, see Alan Rice, *Creating Memorials, Building*

Identities: The Politics of Memory in the Black Atlantic (Liverpool: Liverpool University Press, 2010).

21. Armitage, "Three Concepts," 11–27. Armitage sees these approaches as complimentary, rather than exclusive, and fully accepts the instability and limitations of his own categories. "Circum-Atlantic history would seem to extend no further than the ocean's shores," he explains. "As soon as we leave the circulatory system of the Atlantic itself, we enter a series of cis-Atlantic histories. Trans-Atlantic history combines such cis-Atlantic histories into units of comparison." Armitage, "Three Concepts," 15, 26.

22. François Furstenburg, "The Significance of the Trans-Appalachian Frontier in Atlantic History," *American Historical Review* 113, no. 3 (2008): 650.

23. Linda M. Heywood and John K. Thornton, *Central Africans, Atlantic Creoles, and the Foundations of the Americas, 1585–1660* (New York: Cambridge University Press, 2008); Toyin Falola and Matt D. Childs, eds., *The Yoruba Diaspora in the Atlantic World* (Bloomington: Indiana University Press, 2004; Sheila S. Walker, ed., *African Roots/ American Cultures: African in the Creation of the Americas* (New York: Rowman and Littlefield, 2001); Linda M. Heywood, *Central Africans and the Transformations in the American Diaspora* (New York: Cambridge University Press, 2001).

24. Peter Coclanis, "Atlantic World or Atlantic/World," *William and Mary Quarterly* 63, no. 4 (2006): 727–28.

25. Peter Coclanis, "*Drang Nach Osten*: Bernard Bailyn, the World-Island, and the Idea of Atlantic History," *Journal of World History* 13, no. 1 (2002): 176.

26. Peter Coclanis, "Globalization before Globalization: The South and the World to 1950," in *Globalization and the American South*, ed. James C. Cobb and William Stueck (Athens: University of Georgia Press, 2005), 30.

27. Coclanis, "*Drang Nach Osten*," 179.

28. Simon P. Newman, "Making Sense of Atlantic World Histories: A British Perspective," *Nuevo Mundo Mondos Nuevos*, Coloquious, 2008, 3, http://nuevomundo.revues. org/index42413.html (accessed September 3, 2010).

29. J. Waties Waring, speech to naturalization class at Charleston, South Carolina, November 23, 1951, quoted in Phillips, *Atlantic Sound*, 207–9.

30. Similar evocations of a global South appear throughout *The Atlantic Sound*. For example, the young black and white people Phillips sees dancing to African-derived music in Charleston are wearing Nike apparel, an internationally produced and marketed brand that has become convenient shorthand for globalization. Ibid., 211.

31. Marko Maunula, *Guten Tag, Y'all: Globalization and the South Carolina Piedmont, 1950–2000* (Athens: University of Georgia Press, 2009); James Peacock, *Grounded Globalism: How the U.S. Embraces the World* (Athens: University of Georgia Press, 2007); Wanda Rushing, *Memphis and the Paradox of Place* (Chapel Hill: University of North Carolina Press, 2009), 197; Cobb and Stueck, *Globalization and the American South*, xii.

32. For the transnational and post-national turns in American studies, see John Carlos Rowe, ed., *Post-Nationalist American Studies* (Berkeley: University of California Press, 2000); Robert Gross, "The Transnational Turn: Rediscovering American Studies in a Wider World," *Journal of American Studies* 34, no. 3 (2001): 373–93; Shelley Fisher Fishkin, "Crossroads of Cultures: The Transnational Turn in American Studies,"

American Quarterly 57, no. 1 (2005): 17–57; Emory Elliott, "Diversity in the United States and Abroad: What Does It Mean When American Studies Is Transnational?" *American Quarterly*, 59, no. 1 (2007): 1–22; Paul Giles, *Transnationalism in Practice: Essays on American Studies, Literature and Religion* (Edinburgh: Edinburgh University Press, 2011).

33. Kathryn McKee and Annette Trefzer, "Preface: Global Contexts, Local Literatures: The New Southern Studies," *American Literature* 78, no. 4 (2006): 683.

34. Melanie R. Benson, *Disturbing Calculations: The Economics of Identity in Postcolonial Southern Literature, 1912–2002* (Athens: University of Georgia Press, 2008), 18.

35. Annette Trefzer and Ann J. Abadie, eds., *Global Faulkner* (Jackson: University of Mississippi, 2009); Frank Cha, "Remapping the 38th Parallel in the Global South: Korean Immigration in Southern Spaces," *The Global South* 3, no. 2 (2009): 32–49; Scott Hicks, "Rethinking King Cotton: George W. Lee, Zora Neale Hurston, and Global/Local Revisions of the South and the Nation," *American Quarterly* 65, no. 4 (2009): 63–91.

36. Games, "Atlantic History," 748. See also Newman, "Making Sense," 5; Jorge Cañizares-Esguerra and Erik R. Seeman, eds., *The Atlantic in Global History, 1500–2000* (Upper Saddle River, N.J.: Pearson Prentice Hall, 2007).

37. Furstenburg, "Significance of the Trans-Appalachian Frontier," 648; James L. Peacock, Harry L. Watson, and Carrie R. Matthews, eds., *The American South in a Global World* (Chapel Hill: University of North Carolina Press, 2005), 2–3.

38. Armitage, "Three Concepts," 26.

39. Furstenburg, "Significance of the Trans-Appalachian Frontier," 648.

40. Sharon Monteith, "Southern Like US?" *The Global South* 1, nos. 1–2 (2007): 66, 68–69. McKee and Trefzer also champion scholarship that "embeds the U.S. South in a larger transnational framework" and promises to "unmoor the South from its national harbor." McKee and Trefzer, "Preface," 678.

41. See, for example, Kathleen Deagan, *Spanish St. Augustine: The Archaeology of a Colonial Creole Community* (New York, Academic Press, 1983) and "Colonial Origins and Colonial Transformation in Spanish America." *Historical Archaeology* 37, no. 4 (2003): 3–14.

42. Jon Smith, "Postcolonial Theory, the U.S South and New World Studies," *Society for the Study of Southern Literature Newsletter* 36, no. 1 (2002): 11.

43. Newman, "Making Sense," 6–7.

44. Kwasi Konadu, *The Akan Diaspora in the Americas* (Oxford: Oxford University Press, 2010), 22, 183.

45. Ibid., 22.

46. Armitage, "Three Concepts," 18, 21.

47. C. Vann Woodward, "The Irony of Southern History," *Journal of Southern History* 19, no. 1 (1953): 3–19. In this essay Woodward actually endorsed an exceptionalist view of America, claiming that "from a broader point of view it is not the South but America that is unique among the peoples of the world." See also C. Vann Woodward, ed., *The Comparative Approach to American History* (New York: Basic Books, 1968).

48. Frank Tannenbaum, *Slave and Citizen: The Negro in the Americas* (New York: Vintage, 1946); Stanley M. Elkins, *Slavery: A Problem in American Institutional and Intellectual Life* (Chicago: University of Chicago Press, 1959); David Brion Davis, *The Problem*

of Slavery in the Age of Revolution, 1770–1823 (Ithaca: Cornell University Press, 1966); Carl N. Degler, *Neither Black nor White: Slavery and Race Relations in Brazil and the United States* (New York: Macmillan, 1971); Herbert S. Klein, *Slavery in the Americas: A Contemporary Study of Virginia and Cuba* (Chicago: University of Chicago Press, 1967); Richard Dunn, "A Tale of Two Plantations: Slave Life at Mesopotamia in Jamaica and Mount Airy in Virginia, 1799 to 1828," *William and Mary Quarterly* 34, no. 1 (1977): 32–65; George Fredrickson, *White Supremacy: A Comparative Study in South African and American History* (New York: Oxford University Press, 1982).

49. Don Doyle, *Nations Divided: America, Italy, and the Southern Question* (Athens: University of Georgia Press, 2002); Peter Kolchin, *Unfree Labor: American Slavery and Russian Serfdom* (Cambridge: Harvard University Press, 1990) and *A Sphinx on the American Land: The Nineteenth-Century South in Comparative Perspective* (Baton Rouge: Louisiana State University Press, 2003); Gerald Horne, *The Deepest South: The United States, Brazil, and the African Slave Trade* (New York: New York University Press, 2007); Laird W. Bergad, *The Comparative Histories of Slavery in Brazil, Cuba, and the United States* (New York: Cambridge University Press, 2007); Enrico Dal Lago and Rick Halpern, eds. *The American South and the Italian Mezzogiorno: Essays in Comparative History* (Basingstoke: Palgrave, 2002); Joseph Ward, ed., *Britain and the American South: From Colonialism to Rock and Roll* (Jackson: University of Mississippi Press, 2003).

50. Deborah Cohn, *History and Memory in the Two Souths: Recent Southern and Spanish American Fiction* (Nashville: Vanderbilt University Press, 1999). See also Jana Evans Braziel, "Antillean Detours through the American South: Édouard Glissant's and Jamaica Kincaid's Textual Returns to William Faulkner," in *Just Below South: Intercultural Performance in the Caribbean and the U.S. South*, ed. Jessica Adams, Michael P. Bibler, and Cécile Accilien (Charlottesville: University of Virginia Press, 2007), 239–64.

51. Handley, *Postslavery Literatures in the Americas.*

52. Sarah Robertson, "The Green, Green Hills of Home: Representations of Coal Mining in Appalachian and Welsh Fiction," in *Transatlantic Exchanges: The American South in Europe—Europe in the American South*, ed. Richard Gray and Waldemar Zacharasiewicz (Vienna: Austrian Academy of the Sciences Press, 2007), 503–18; Michael Kreyling, "Italy and the United States: The Politics and Poetics of the 'Southern Problem,'" in *South to a New Place: Region, Literature, Culture*, ed. Suzanne W. Jones and Sharon Monteith (Baton Rouge: Louisiana State University Press, 2002), 285–302; Victoria Kennefick, "Lonely Voices of the South: Exploring the Transnational Dialogue of Flannery O'Connor and Frank O'Connor" (Ph.D. diss., National University of Ireland, Cork, 2009). There has been a recent proliferation of work on the relationships between Ireland and the American South from a range of disciplinary perspectives and across several centuries. See the special Irish issue of *Southern Cultures* 17, no. 1 (2011) guest-edited by Bryan Gymza. Also, David O'Connell, *The Irish Roots of Margaret Mitchell's "Gone with the Wind"* (Decatur, Ga.: Claves & Petry, Ltd., 1996); David T. Gleeson, *The Irish in the South, 1815–1877* (Chapel Hill: University of North Carolina Press, 2001); Kieran Quinlan, *Strange Kin: Ireland and the American South* (Baton Rouge: Louisiana State University Press, 2005); Peter D. O'Neill and David Lloyd, eds., *The Black and Green Atlantic: Cross-currents of the African and Irish Diasporas* (Basingstoke: Palgrave

Macmillan, 2009); Kathleen M. Gough, "Whose 'Folk' Are They Anyway? Zora Neale Hurston and Lady Augusta Gregory in the Atlantic World," in this volume.

53. Elijah H. Gould, "Entangled Histories, Entangled Worlds: The English-Speaking Atlantic as a Spanish Periphery," *American Historical Review* 112, no. 3 (2007): 785.

54. Rushing, *Memphis*, 85. See also Michael O'Brien, "Epilogue: Place as Everywhere: On Globalizing the American South," in *Creating Citizenship in the Nineteenth-Century South*, ed. William A. Link, David Brown, Brian Ward, and Martyn Bone (Gainesville: University Press of Florida, 2013), 271–89.

55. See also Paula M. L. Moya and Ramón Saldívar, "Fictions of the Trans-American Imaginary," *Modern Fiction Studies* 49, no. 1 (2003): 1–18.

56. Jon Smith, "Postcolonial, Black and Nobody's Margin: The US South and New World Studies," *American Literary History* 16, no. 1 (2004): 144.

57. Gould, "Entangled Histories," 785, 767.

58. Ibid., 769; April Lee Hatfield, *Atlantic Virginia: Intercolonial Relations in the Seventeenth Century* (Philadelphia: University of Pennsylvania Press, 2004), 8, 16–18.

59. Gould, "Entangled Histories," 775. See also John K. Thornton, "African Dimensions of the Stono Rebellion," *American Historical Review* 96, no. 4 (1991): 1101–13.

60. Gould, "Entangled Histories," 765. See also J. H. Elliott, *Empires of the Atlantic World: Britain and Spain in America, 1492–1830* (New Haven: Yale University Press, 2006). For historical accounts of Spanish power and encounters with other Europeans, indigenous peoples, and Africans in the colonial American South, see Jane Landers, *Black Society in Spanish Florida* (Urbana: University of Illinois Press, 1999); Paul E. Hoffman, *Florida's Frontiers* (Bloomington: Indiana University Press, 2002); Juliana Barr, *Peace Came in the Form of a Woman: Indians and Spaniards in the Texas Borderlands* (Chapel Hill: University of North Carolina Press, 2007).

61. For French Atlantic influences on the American South see Bill Marshall, *The French Atlantic: Travels in Culture and History* (Liverpool: Liverpool University Press, 2009); Bradley G. Bond, ed., *French Colonial Louisiana and the Atlantic World* (Baton Rouge: Louisiana State University Press, 2005). Cohn, *History and Memory*; Handley, *Postslavery Literatures in the Americas*; Jon Smith and Deborah Cohn, eds., *Look Away! The US South in New World Studies* (Durham: Duke University Press, 2004).

62. John Lowe, "'Calypso Magnolia': The Caribbean Side of the South," *South Central Review* 22, no. 1 (2005): 54.

63. Jessica Adams, "Introduction: Circum-Caribbean Performance, Language, History," in Adams, Bibler, and Accilien, *Just Below South*, 2–3.

64. Edward Rugemer, *The Problem of Emancipation: The Caribbean Roots of the American Civil War* (Baton Rouge: Louisiana State University Press, 2008). Thanks to David Brown for alerting me to this book, and for his many invaluable comments on an earlier draft of this essay.

65. Gould, "Entangled Histories," 785.

66. Paul Giles makes a complementary point when discussing the emergence of a fluid and contested "transatlantic imaginary" in the fictions of the Atlantic World. Giles describes how a complex process of comparison, attachment, and insularity in the literature emanating from sites around the Atlantic Ocean helped to define national

identities, rather than to negate them. Giles, *Virtual Americas: Transnational Fictions and the Transatlantic Imaginary* (Durham: Duke University Press, 2002), 1. Historian Paul Quigley also contends that Confederate nationalism emerged at a time when the nature of nation-states, national identities, and citizenship rights was neither fixed nor uniform in the Atlantic World, but was subject to a good deal of transatlantic scrutiny, influence, and counterinfluence. Quigley, *Shifting Grounds: Nationalism and the American South, 1848–1865* (New York: Oxford University Press, 2012).

67. Houston A. Baker Jr. and Dana Nelson, "Preface: Violence, the Body, and 'The South,'" *American Literature* 73, no. 2 (2001): 243, 235.

68. Carl N. Degler, "Thesis, Anti-Thesis, Synthesis: The South, the North and the Nation," *Journal of Southern History* 53 (February 1987): 6.

69. Greeson, *Our South*, 1. See also Leigh Anne Duck, *The Nation's Region: Southern Modernism, Segregation, and U.S. Nationalism* (Athens: University of Georgia Press, 2006).

70. McKee and Trefzer, "Preface," 677, 683.

71. David Eltis, "Atlantic History in Global Perspective," *Itinerario* 23, no. 2 (1999): 143–44.

72. Michael P. Bibler, "Teaching Historians about the Real (By Which I Mean Symbolic) South," *Society for the Study of Southern Literature Newsletter* 44, no. 1 (2010), 6.

73. Jon Smith and Deborah Cohn, "Introduction: Uncanny Hybridities," in Smith and Cohn, *Look Away!* 10; Richard H. King, "Allegories of Imperialism: Globalizing Southern Studies," *American Literary History* 23, no. 1 (2010): 148.

74. Bibler, "Teaching," 6.

75. Michael O'Brien, *The Idea of the American South, 1920–1941* (Baltimore: Johns Hopkins University Press, 1979), xiv; Edward L. Ayers, "What Do We Talk About When We Talk About the South," in *All Over the Map: Rethinking American Regions*, ed. Edward L. Ayers, Patricia Nelson Limerick, Stephen Nissenbaum, and Peter S. Onuf (Baltimore: Johns Hopkins University Press, 1996), 65; Karen L. Cox, *Dreaming of Dixie: How the South Was Created in American Popular Culture* (Chapel Hill: University of North Carolina Press, 2010).

76. W. Fitzhugh Brundage, ed., *Where These Memories Grow: History, Memory, and Southern Identity* (Chapel Hill: University of North Carolina Press, 2000); W. Fitzhugh Brundage, *The Southern Past: A Clash of Race and Memory* (Cambridge: Harvard University Press, 2005). See also David Blight, *Race and Reunion: The Civil War in American Memory* (Cambridge: Harvard University Press, 2001); David R. Goldfield, *Still Fighting the Civil War: The American South and Southern History* (Baton Rouge: Louisiana State Press, 2002); Renee C. Romano and Leigh Raiford, eds., *The Civil Rights Movement in American Memory* (Athens: University Press of Georgia, 2006).

77. For the centrality of race in southern history and historiography, see David Brown and Clive Webb, *Race in the American South* (Gainesville: University Press of Florida, 2007).

78. King, "Allegories of Imperialism," 157.

79. Patricia Yeager, "Circum-Atlantic Superabundance: Milk as World-Making in Alice Randall and Kara Walker," *American Literature* 78, no. 4 (2006): 769–98.

80. Ibid., 774, 771.

81. For other exemplary efforts to ground readings of southern expressive culture in the historical record, see Michael P. Bibler, *Cotton's Queer Relations: Same-Sex Intimacy and the Literature of the Southern Plantation, 1936–1968* (Charlottesville: University of Virginia Press, 2009); Martyn Bone, *The Postsouthern Sense of Place in Contemporary Fiction* (Baton Rouge: Louisiana State University Press, 2005)—Bone deploys what he calls "a historical-geographical-materialist approach to the capitalist production and literary representation of 'place'" (vii); Patricia Yeager, *Dirt and Desire: Reconstructing Southern Women's Writing: 1930–1990* (Chicago: University of Chicago Press, 2000).

82. Armitage, "Three Concepts," 22, 21, 25.

83. Lowe, "'Calypso Magnolia,'" 54. For other endorsements of the value of localism in Atlantic studies, see Don E. Walicek, "Farther South: Speaking American, the Language of Migration in Samaná," in Adams, Bibler, and Accilien, *Just Below South*, 116; Jonathan Elmer, "The Black Atlantic Archive," *American Literary History* 17, no. 1 (2005): 166.

84. Geologically speaking, the Appalachians, Scottish Highlands, and the Atlas Mountains in North Africa are the same mountain chain, testament to a time about 480 million years ago when the lands that surround the Atlantic Ocean were contiguous. Furstenburg, "Significance of the Trans-Appalachian Frontier," 647.

85. J. R. McNeill, *Mosquito Empires: Ecology and War in the Greater Caribbean, 1620–1914* (New York: Cambridge University Press, 2010). For the Memphis Yellow Fever epidemic of 1878 see Molly Caldwell Crosby, *The American Plague: The Untold Story of Yellow Fever, the Epidemic That Shaped Our History* (New York: Berkeley, 2006). See also Josh Russell's novel of antebellum New Orleans, *Yellow Jack* (New York: Norton, 2000).

86. Lauren Benton, "The Legal Regime of the South Atlantic World, 1400–1750: Jurisdictional Complexity as Institutional Order," *Journal of World History* 11, no. 1 (2000): 29. See also Lauren Benton, *Law and Colonial Cultures: Legal Regimes in World History, 1400–1900* (New York: Cambridge University Press. 2002); Martha S. Jones, "The Case of Jean Baptiste, un Créole de Saint-Domingue: Narrating Slavery, Freedom, and the Haitian Revolution in Baltimore City," in this volume; and Eric L. Wong, *Neither Fugitive nor Free: Atlantic Slavery, Freedom Suits, and the Legal Culture of Travel* (New York: New York University Press, 2011).

87. Julian Gerstin, "The Allure of Origins: Neo-African Dances in the French Caribbean and the Southern United States," in Adams, Bibler and Accilien, *Just Below South*, 133, 140.

88. William Blake, "Auguries of Innocence," 1863, in *The Norton Anthology of Poetry*, rev. ed. (New York: Norton, 1975), 555.

89. Joshua Piker, *Ofuskee: A Creek Town in Colonial America* (Cambridge: Harvard University Press, 2004), 6–7.

90. For the idea of an Indian Atlantic, see Tim Fulford and Kevin Hutchings, eds., *Native Americans and Anglo-American Culture, 1750–1850* (Cambridge: Cambridge University Press, 2009).

91. Daniel Usner, "American Indians in Colonial History: A Review Essay," *Journal of American Ethnic History* 11, no. 2 (1992): 82. Among the works that place southern Native Americans, explicitly or implicitly, in an Atlantic World context are Allan Gallay, *The*

Indian Slave Trade: The Rise of the English in the American South, 1670–1717 (New Haven: Yale University Press, 2002); Theda Purdue, *Mixed Blood Indians: Racial Construction in the Early South* (Athens: University of Georgia Press, 2003); Jerald T. Milanich, *Laboring in the Fields of the Lord: Spanish Missions and Southeastern Indians* (Washington, D.C.: Smithsonian Institution Press, 1999); Claudio Saunt, *A New Order of Things: Property, Power and the Transformation of the Creek Indians, 1733–1816* (Cambridge: Cambridge University Press, 1999); Helen C. Rountree, *The Powhatan Indians of Virginia* (Norman: University of Oklahoma Press, 1989); Peter H. Wood, Gregory A. Waselkov, and M. Thomas Hatley, eds., *Powhatan's Mantle: Indians in the Colonial South East* (Lincoln: University of Nebraska Press, 1976); Daniel H. Usner, *Indians, Settlers, and Slaves in a Frontier Exchange Economy: The Lower Mississippi Valley before 1783* (Chapel Hill: University of North Carolina Press, 1992); Bernard W. Sheehan, *Savagism and Civility: Indians and Englishmen in Colonial Virginia* (Cambridge: Cambridge University Press, 1980); James Axtell, *The Indians' New South: Cultural Change in the Colonial Southeast* (Baton Rouge: Louisiana State University Press, 1997); Tom Hatley, *The Dividing Paths: Cherokees and South Carolinians through the Era of Revolution* (New York: Oxford University Press, 1995).

92. Barr, *Peace Came in the Form of a Woman*; Pekka Hämäläinen, *The Commanche Empire* (New Haven: Yale University Press, 2008).

93. Kathleen DuVal, "The Education of Fernando de Leyba: Quapaws and Spaniards on the Borders of Empire," *Arkansas Historical Quarterly* 60, no. 1 (2001): 1–29, quote on 2; F. Todd Smith, "A Native Response to the Transfer of Louisiana: The Red River Caddos and Spain, 1762–1803," *Journal of the Louisiana Historical Association* 37, no. 2 (1996): 163–85.

94. George Herring, *From Colony to Superpower: U.S. Foreign Relations since 1776* (New York: Oxford University Press, 2008), 99.

95. James H. Merrell, *The Indians' New World: Catawbas and Their Neighbors from European Contact through the Era of Removal* (Chapel Hill: University of North Carolina Press, 1989), x; see also Joshua Piker, "Colonists and Creeks: Rethinking the Pre-Revolutionary Southern Backcountry," *Journal of Southern History* 70, no. 3 (2004): 503–4.

96. Alden T. Vaughan, *Transatlantic Encounters: American Indians in Britain, 1500–1776* (New York: Cambridge University Press, 2006).

97. Daniel L. Schafer, *Anna Madgigine Jai Kingsley: African Princess, Florida Slave, Plantation Slave Owner* (Gainesville: University Press of Florida, 2003); Mark J. Fleszar, "The Atlantic Mind: Zephaniah Kingsley, Slavery and the Politics of Race in the Atlantic World" (master's thesis, Georgia State University, 2009), http://digitalarchive.gsu.edu/history_theses/33 (accessed September 27, 2011).

98. Rebecca J. Scott and Jean M. Hébrard, *Freedom Papers: An Atlantic Odyssey in the Age of Emancipation* (Cambridge: Harvard University Press, 2012), 5.

99. Monteith, "Southern Like US?" 67.

100. King, "Allegories of Imperialism," 152.

101. Álvar Núñez Cabeza de Vaca, *The Narrative of Cabeza De Vaca*, translation of *La Relacion* (1542), ed. Rolena Adorno and Patrick Charles Pautz (Lincoln: University of Nebraska Press 2003); Olaudah Equiano, *The Interesting Narrative of the Life of Olaudah*

Equiano or Gustavus Vassa, the African Written by Himself (1789), ed. Vincent Caretta (New York: Penguin Classics, 2003); Alexis de Tocqueville, *Democracy in America* (1835/1840), trans. and ed. Harvey C. Mansfield and Delba Winthrop (Chicago: University of Chicago Press, 2000); Frances Anne Kemble, *Journal of a Residence on a Georgian Plantation in 1838–1839* (New York: Knopf, 1961); William Wells Brown, *The Travels of William Wells Brown* (1852), ed. Paul Jefferson (Edinburgh: Edinburgh University Press, 1991); Mary Church Terrell, *A Colored Woman in a White World* (1940; New York: G. K. Hall, 1996); Richard Wright, *Pagan Spain* (London: The Bodley Head, 1960); James Yates, *Mississippi to Madrid: A Memoir of a Black American in the Abraham Lincoln Brigade* (Seattle: Open Hand, 1989); Maya Angelou, *All God's Children Need Travelling Shoes* (London: Virago, 1987); V. S. Naipaul, *A Turn in the South* (New York: Knopf, 1989); Nick Middleton, *Ice Tea and Elvis: A Saunter through the Southern States* (London: Weidenfield & Nicolson, 1999); Gary Younge, *No Place Like Home: A Black Briton's Journey Through the American South* (Picador, 1999). Two important anthologies of Black Atlantic writings are Vincent Carretta, ed., *Unchained Voices: An Anthology of Black Authors in the English-Speaking World of the 18th Century* (Lexington: University of Kentucky Press, 1996), and Alasdair Pettinger, ed., *Always Elsewhere: Travels of the Black Atlantic* (London: Cassell, 1998). See also Vincent Carretta and Philip Gould, eds., *Genius in Bondage: Literature of the Early Black Atlantic* (Lexington: University of Kentucky Press, 2003), and Alan J. Rice, *Radical Narratives of the Black Atlantic* (New York: Continuum, 2003).

2

....

Early Southern Religions in a Global Age

JON SENSBACH

In 1831 an African-born slave in Fayetteville, North Carolina, put his life story to paper. Most slaves in the antebellum South could not read or write, but this author had been raised and schooled a Muslim, and his narrative ran to fifteen pages of Arabic script. Like any autobiography, it captures a piece of the world in miniature, but the world this narrator knew was perhaps more expansive than most.

"My name," he wrote,

> is Omar ibn Said. My birthplace was Fut Tur, between the two rivers. . . . Before I came to the Christian country, my religion was the religion of Mohammed, the Apostle of God—may God have mercy upon him and give him peace. . . . I sought religious knowledge under the instruction of a Sheikh called Mohammed Seid, my own brother, and Sheikh Soleimon Kembeh. . . . I walked to the mosque before daybreak, washed my face and head and hands and feet, I prayed at noon, prayed in the afternoon, prayed at sunset, prayed in the evening. I went every year to the holy war against the infidels. I went on pilgrimage to Mecca, as did all who were able. . . . I continued my studies twenty-five years, and then returned to my home where I remained six years.
>
> Then there came to our place a large army, who killed many men and took me, and brought me to the great sea, and sold me into the hands of the Christians, who bound me and sent on board a great ship and we sailed upon the great sea a month and a half, when we came to a place called Charleston in the Christian language. There they sold me to a small, weak, and wicked man named Johnson, a complete infidel who had no fear of God at all. Now I am a small

man, and unable to do hard work, so I fled from the hand of Johnson and after a month came to a place called Fayd-il [Fayetteville].
When I left my country I was thirty-seven years old; I have been in
the country of the Christians for twenty-four years.[1]

From this brief narrative we can reconstruct some of the essentials of
Omar ibn Said's life. He would have been born in about 1770 in present-
day Senegal, between the Senegal and Gambia Rivers in West Africa. He
was evidently the son of a well-to-do family that could afford to send
him to a Muslim academy, perhaps even to the great Malian University
at Timbuktu. Without a doubt the dominant aspect of this early part of
his life would have been the *hajj*, the pilgrimage to Mecca that he mentions almost casually, one of the five pillars of Islam that involved an extraordinarily arduous journey lasting years and from which not everyone
returned. From West Africa, long caravans of the faithful made their way
by camel slowly across the Sahara, tracking Muslim trade routes and commercial towns, more than three thousand miles to Cairo and down the
Arabian peninsula to the holy city. "The point of a pilgrimage, of course,"
according to historian Richard Wunderli, "is *movement*: from the mundane to the mysterious, from normal time and space to enchanted time
and space, from homes and familiar surroundings to the unfamiliar 'light'
of a holy place." In Mecca, the shrine of sacred renewal, Said would have
mingled with thousands of pilgrims from around the Muslim world, all
"temporarily freed from their worldly bonds of rank and status." Perhaps
he stayed in Mecca for weeks or months, resting and basking in this holy
light before turning north and west again across the desert, his duty to
Allah fulfilled. The perilous journey home took many months, and Said
was fortunate to survive it, as few did.[2]

Once returned, and newly snared in the slaving wars that still plun-
dered West Africa in the early nineteenth century, this former pilgrim
would have been thrust into exactly the opposite experience during the
Middle Passage to America. The stinking hold where he was shackled
with hundreds of captives for six weeks was a desolate, unholy place, a
desacralized conveyor of imprisonment and death, utterly profane except
for whatever spark of the sacred the enslaved Africans could keep alive
amid the blasphemy around them. And so, having moved from enchanted
to disenchanted time and space, Omar ibn Said emerged from the slave
ship in Charleston in 1807, the last legal year of the slave trade to North

America, his faith intact, a onetime supplicant in Mecca destined to live out his life in Fayetteville, North Carolina.

This remarkable life story introduces us to the subject of religion in the region where Said now found himself enslaved, the American South. His narrative seems so uncharacteristic of what we consider the normative cultural and religious experience of the South, for which very reason I want to use it to challenge our perception of the reigning paradigm of southern religious history. Until his arrival in the South, Said's life was international, cosmopolitan, polyglot, mobile, worldly; it had encompassed the most extreme polarities imaginable of spiritual exaltation and despair; Said had crossed divides of land and sea, of body and spirit, of belonging and exile. By no means did his experiences reflect those of all Africans enslaved in the Americas—probably few, indeed, were veterans of the hajj—but still, among the millions of captives taken in the trade were many thousands of Africans, Muslim and otherwise, who had traveled widely along West African trade corridors, engaging in commerce with an array of African and European customers, acquiring what we might call an expansive international outlook.

By contrast, the conventional image of the South, at least as it came to be in the nineteenth century, is of a provincial, hidebound region, held fast in the narrow, monolithic grip of Protestant evangelicalism—in other words, the Bible Belt. This South, memorably described as "Christ-haunted" by Flannery O'Connor, has long occupied a position in the popular and scholarly imagination as a place where fundamentalism has traditionally gone hand in hand with steadfast social and political conservatism. In posing such a stark contrast between images of globalism and provincialism as those categories apply to the South, I am of course simplifying things considerably. But the dichotomy gives us a vehicle to examine critically the reigning paradigm of "southern religion" as synonymous with Christian fundamentalism. And it provides a way to situate the multiple religious histories of the region in larger geographic and historical contexts. These might include those vast continents commonly thought to constitute the "Atlantic World"—the Americas, Europe, and Africa—as well as zones not conventionally thought to have much bearing on southern history, such as the Middle East and Asia. The South has its own unique past, to be sure, but by enfolding the region in larger global narratives the very nature of southern distinctiveness—and, in particular, the notion of southern religion—becomes altered considerably.

Protestant evangelicalism has often been identified as the defining characteristic of what historians have called the "distinctiveness" of southern religion and of the continued vitality of religion in southern culture. Religion and the American South, historian Donald Mathews has written, "belong together"; they are "fused in our historical imagination in an indelible but amorphous way." Indeed, scholars have concluded that "the central theme of southern religious history is the search for conversion, for redemption from innate human depravity." In *Religion in the Old South*, his landmark study from 1977, Mathews explained that his purpose was not to give "a history of the churches, nor of the denominations, nor of the theology, nor of the religious culture of the Old South," but rather to explore "how and why Evangelical Protestantism became the predominant religious mood of the South." According to Samuel Hill, one of the pioneers of southern religious historiography, so pervasive has been the grip of evangelicalism that "the impact of a single coherent way of understanding Christianity is extensive and tenacious in the South," rendering the region's religious outlook a "limited-options culture." In "hardly any other aspect," Hill has written, "has the limitation of choices been more pronounced than in religion." In such views, then, "southern religion" *is* evangelical Protestant religion, and a figure like Omar ibn Said seems very much out of place in this spiritual landscape.[3]

The image of a fundamentalist South no doubt has much basis in fact, but it is also in part the creation of late-nineteenth- and early-twentieth-century observers who looked for and found a South they wanted to see. As Mary Beth Mathews has explained in her 2006 book, *Rethinking Zion: How the Print Media Placed Fundamentalism in the South*, evangelical religion was part of a package of negative stereotypes fastened on the South around the turn of the century by journalists and authors who saw the region as a national problem, an embarrassment—poverty-stricken, violent, provincial, ignorant, a cultural wasteland. In this scenario, close-minded Christian fundamentalism—what H. L. Mencken called "Baptist and Methodist barbarism"—the enemy of progress, found its "natural" home in a benighted South resistant to change. His term "Bible Belt" became a convenient marker for political observers commenting on what we now call the red state/blue state divide.[4]

This fundamentalist South has occupied the journalistic, literary, and academic imagination for the better part of a century. Historians likewise have devoted a great deal of attention to explaining the origins of southern evangelical Protestantism and its tenacious hold on the region. From Rhys Isaac in the 1980s to Christine Heyrman in the 1990s to a host of scholars in the new millennium such as Jewel Spangler, Charles Irons, and Monica Najar, historians have studied and re-studied that crucial period in the mid- to late eighteenth century and early nineteenth century when evangelical religion crossed the Atlantic from the British Isles, came to the South, and took root. This scholarship has left us with a series of unforgettable images of plainly clad itinerant Baptist "New Lights" preachers from New England and the mid-Atlantic condemning the licentious lifestyles of the southern planter elite; of black and white "brothers" and "sisters" forgetting worldly distinctions to embrace each other in the thrall of the holy spirit; of camp meetings where religious seekers waded into rivers by scores for baptism.[5]

But the need to explain the origins and durability of Protestant evangelicalism has inadvertently imposed what we might call "the burden of southern religious history" on the study of the region. The problem becomes acute when we try to define what and where "the South" is and when it came to be, as the editors of a 2007 issue of the *Journal of Southern History* on the colonial South point out. They quote historian Carl Bridenbaugh's observation that "in 1776 there was no South; there never had been a South. It was not even a geographical expression." And yet historians have considered the region anachronistically as "the land of plantations and slavery in the region of the Chesapeake and Lowcountry . . . project[ing] this convenient geographic and social definition back in time, resulting in a colonial South that emphasizes the English-settled eastern seaboard almost exclusively and in which one seeks the origins of features dominant in 1830 or 1860." Accordingly, "the South," in this intellectual project, refers to the Anglophonic southern states that incubated and nourished evangelicalism, and in following the documentary trail the revivalists left, we risk reducing earlier centuries of southern history to a kind of foreshortened prelude to the rise of the "Bible Belt." The early South can easily become reduced to a time and place that explains the evangelical moment, overwhelming what was, in fact, the riotous heterogeneity of early southern religious history. The weight of an apparent fundamentalist destiny overpowers the narrative of southern history, suggesting that the South was always evangelical in orientation, always

Protestant and English-speaking. In this framework, the indigenous religions of the pre-Columbian South, or the Catholic orientation of the Gulf South, for example, is simply written out of the story.[6]

I propose, in fact, that our focus on the modern South has obscured a sharper focus on the most volatile and dynamic period in southern religious history, the sixteenth through eighteenth centuries, when the South contained more forms of spiritual expression and saw more cataclysmic changes in religious practice than perhaps any other region at any point in American history. At no other time was the South so much a part of the transatlantic religious world and receptive to so many international influences from the British Isles, France, Spain, the German lands, and a huge swath of West Africa from Senegambia to Kongo. As newcomers both willing and unwilling funneled into the vast region from across the Atlantic to collide and intermingle with native southerners, the unprecedented combination of European, African, and Native American religions made the South a cultural crossroads to compare in diversity and combustible energy with any in world history. These diverse elements gave an extraordinary cosmopolitanism to the region as Mecca pilgrims rubbed shoulders with Scots Highlanders, Lutheran Salzburgers, Choctaw mound builders, and Castilian Catholics. The presence of so many often-discordant faiths made for a landscape of raucous spiritual competition while at the same time underscoring the South's immersion in overlapping, and jarring, international religious communities. The South was no isolated religious backwater at the remote margins of European empire but the stage for creative fusion and re-visioning of ancient faiths.

In this regard, the narrative of the Atlantic pilgrim Omar ibn Said, while perhaps out of place in 1830s Fayetteville, North Carolina, is much more characteristic of the early South, far less an anomaly. Whatever it became later, the South in the eighteenth century was hardly a limited-options culture. Rather, it was a kind of precursor to what we now call the "global South"—a term designating, in our own time, the challenges of modern development and poverty in Africa, Latin America, and much of Asia. Somewhat differently, I use the term to refer to the immersion of the American South in broader processes of globalization in the early modern period. That is, between the sixteenth and early nineteenth centuries the South, like the rest of North America, Latin America, Africa, and Asia, was the site of European economic and imperial expansion that wrought multiple, often violent, encounters between colonizers and indigenous people. It also resulted in the migration, both voluntary and involuntary, of millions of people, a demographic redistribution that redefined huge portions of the globe. While the South was shaped most directly by economic, ideological, demographic, and imperial forces at work within the Atlantic World, the imprint of those forces on the region bears comparison with the rest of the world.[7]

From this perspective, the colonial South was more than a cultural appendage to the northern colonies, more than an isolated afterthought on the fringes of empire, more than a prelude to the evangelicals. From the British colonies through Florida, Louisiana, and Texas, the early South was a place of imperial rivalry and profound international influences, continually remade by free immigrants, transformed by the trade in African and Indian slaves, deeply implicated in European politics, linked by transatlantic, and occasionally even global, networks of communication, culturally connected to Europe and West Africa as well as to the greater French, British, and Spanish Caribbean. At no other time in its history has the South been shaped by such a heterogeneous mix of people espousing a medley of beliefs, from its many Native American traditions to several kinds of Catholicism, many varieties of Protestantism, as well as Islam and Judaism. This web of forces calls into question the very notion of "southern religion," a term that seems evocative of southern regionalism, of fixity in time and place, of rootedness in a "southern" identity shaped by the geopolitics of slavery in the early national United States—forces that connote a certain cultural and geographic insularity to the South.

However insular the nineteenth- and early-twentieth-century South may have been, a few examples underscore the extent to which the South was integrated into worldwide religious cultures in earlier periods. Consider, for instance, the missions of colonial Spanish Florida, which were the dominant imperial and ecclesiastical presence in the colony from the late sixteenth through the early eighteenth centuries. On one hand, Spanish authorities considered Florida an unprofitable, even uninteresting outpost on the northern edge of the empire in America, and with its tiny Spanish population, the colony received little military protection from the Crown. On the other hand, the missions were of a strategic piece with Spanish missions throughout the Americas as vehicles to pacify Indians and absorb them into royal hegemony through Christianity rather than violent conquest—though of course the latter option remained more than an implied threat. It is unlikely that the Timucua, Apalachee, and Guale Indians of northern Florida ever achieved complete "conversion" to Christianity. Strong evidence suggests that, like native people throughout Spanish America, they retained elements of traditional belief that mingled or coexisted with Catholicism in overlapping and parallel ways. Nonetheless, at their height in the mid-seventeenth century, the long chain of missions in Florida stretched from coastal Georgia to present-day Tallahassee, numbered perhaps twenty thousand converts, and stood as visible reminders that Catholicism, not Protestantism, was the dominant form of Christianity in the American Southeast until the very end of the seventeenth century. In that sense, the missions were Spain's way of drawing southern North America into its continuing war of the Counter-Reformation that encompassed a global evangelical effort from Japan, China, and the Philippines to the Caribbean, South America, New Mexico, and eventually California. Through networks of communication, Jesuit and Franciscan missionaries knew about and followed the efforts of their brethren elsewhere in the world.[8]

The missions illustrate the international connections between religion and trade that enfolded the South. A key feature of the currency used by Spanish and Indians in the spiritual economy of the missions was glass beads, which the friars supplied and which Indians used for ritual, adornment, and mortuary purposes and to trade for deerskins with Indians far in the interior. Excavations from the mission site at St. Catherine's Island, Georgia, which dates from the late sixteenth century, have uncovered thousands of beads produced in Spain, Venice, Bohemia, France, the Netherlands, the Baltic region, and China, most likely via the Philippines. "The pattern of the bead sources for St. Catherine's reflects that of the larger pattern of trade between Spain and her American colonies," concludes one scholar, adding: "Who would have imagined that a small, isolated mission on the edge of a great empire would yield so much information about the rest of the globe?"[9]

As the life of the missions was connected to a larger economic and geopolitical world, so was their death. When South Carolina governor James Moore led a series of devastating raids on the Florida missions by an allied force of Carolina militia and Creek Indians in 1702 and 1704, he opened up a southern front in the War of Spanish Succession between Britain and other powers concerned about the union of Spain and France. With theaters in Europe, the Caribbean, and North America, that war had strong Atlantic reverberations. Moore's raids destroyed almost all the missions, killed hundreds of Catholic Indians, and took thousands more as slaves. The British Empire in the early eighteenth century was driven ideologically by a militant effort to advance international Protestantism and roll back Catholicism on all fronts, and though Florida lingered on as a Spanish colony, the destruction of the Catholic Indian population opened the southeastern frontier for Protestant expansion in the eighteenth century.

These events illustrated in one deep corner of the Southeast dramatic and tragic processes at work throughout the broader South as indigenous populations, numerically dominant in much of the region through the 1760s, declined sharply through disease, warfare, and slavery. As Indians were decimated in what anthropologist Robbie Ethridge calls the "shatter zone" of these overpowering forces, native religions retreated, retrenched, died out. Although Indians did not disappear altogether from the land, the rapid spread of white and black populations into Indian lands doomed native inhabitants to cultural and territorial dispossession, making them a tiny fragment of the population in a region they once dominated. And therein lay perhaps the most profound change in southern religious history: the virtual replacement of Indian religions by Christianity and African-Christian faiths.[10]

The mission wars also reaffirm Catholicism's powerful presence in the colonial Deep South, a presence long dismissed by historians of British America who perceived North America's Latin world to be on the exotic margins of colonial history. More recent work has begun to bring southern Catholicism into the mainstream of scholarship on both early America and southern religion by connecting the church to developments in France, Spain, and Rome, to the broader Spanish and Francophone Atlantic and Caribbean, and to the wider colonial South. As historians such as John Thornton and Linda Heywood have demonstrated, the Catholicism of enslaved Kongolese and Angolans, converted to the faith in the sixteenth and seventeenth centuries by Capuchin missionaries in Africa, was an essential feature of African Atlantic culture in early Virginia, Bermuda, low-country Carolina, and Florida. Enslaved escapees from South Carolina who reached St. Augustine received their freedom if they joined the Catholic Church and promised to fight for the Spanish. The offer proved attractive for hundreds of runaways, many of whom were already Catholic, including the Kongolese or Angolan rebels whose attempt to flee south to Florida failed near the Stono River in South Carolina in 1739. And in colonial New Orleans, the sisters of the Ursuline convent helped educate enslaved Africans and prepare their entry into the church, giving rise to a nascent Afro-Catholic community from which the city's famous Creole population of color would germinate. Such connections reaffirm the immersion of the American South in Atlantic and global Catholic networks.[11]

Unlike the conventional image of a narrow-minded, inward-looking South in the grip of monochromatic fundamentalism, thousands of European immigrants in the early South, whatever their beliefs, considered themselves members of extended international church networks. Recent work, for example, has repositioned the Huguenots in the Reformation politics of sixteenth-century France and tracked their expulsion and dispersal around the Atlantic rim in the late seventeenth century, from the Netherlands to Britain to the Caribbean and North America, including South Carolina and Virginia. From this perspective, the Huguenot world of the American South was not a remote, self-contained outpost but part of an international, well-connected diasporic community.[12] Likewise, intricate German Pietist networks marshaled elaborate coordination and planning to organize immigration, often by entire villages and congregations, to Maryland, Virginia, the Carolinas, and Georgia. Many of these German communities in the early South considered themselves members of a transatlantic spiritual web, maintaining contact with church administrators in their homeland. In parts of the eighteenth-century South, then, to speak of religion is to speak of settlers whose language was not English and whose faith was not Anglican, Baptist, or Methodist.[13]

Along with the violence and chaos that characterized so many colonial encounters, scholars have found cross-cultural cooperation, accommodation, and hybridity. The geographic and cultural frontiers among Indians, Europeans, and Africans in the eighteenth-century South represented real and symbolic zones of encounter in trade, diplomacy, gender relations, and religion. The complex interactions between Indians and Africans on a fluid southeastern frontier, for example, yielded mutual influences on often compatible belief systems, sometimes leading to the creation of unsanctioned, and sometimes surprising, forms of prophetic spirituality. In the 1730s, for example, the German mystic Gottlieb Priber attempted to establish a multiracial utopia of Indians, runaway African slaves, and European dissenters in Cherokee country, which he called "Paradise." For his efforts, he was arrested by South Carolina authorities and died in prison on St. Simon's Island, Georgia. Priber was a singular figure, but he represented the way radical beliefs could threaten colonial religious and governmental authorities. Some of Priber's contemporaries, the early evangelical Protestant itinerants in the Georgia and Carolina low country and in the Chesapeake, aroused the same kind of opposition with their attempts to preach the doctrine of Christian spiritual equality among enslaved Africans.[14]

As the African presence swelled in the colonial South, the mix of African religions with various forms of Christianity produced a flourishing of spiritual hybrids. Across the Gulf South, the fusion of African and Catholic beliefs produced dynamic new forms of worship, and people of African descent used the church to solidify families, gain protection against abuse, and establish fictive kinship ties through godparenthood. Likewise, African Americans' embrace of Christianity in the Protestant South served as a nexus between white and black worshipers in a surprising variety of settings. By the mid-eighteenth century, Baptist and Methodist revivals from Maryland to Georgia produced scores of interracial congregations that became experimental laboratories where co-religionists tested the meanings of race, slavery, and spiritual inclusion. But as white evangelicals gradually retreated from the socially and spiritually egalitarian implications of their practices in the Revolutionary era, they moved black parishioners to the back of the church, erected wooden barriers down the center aisle for segregated seating, or excluded them altogether to separate churches supervised by white preachers. And whereas for African American Christians religion served as a promise of deliverance and a prophetic critique of slavery, evangelical religion for white southerners by the 1820s became an unequivocal ideological support for the enslavement of others, including fellow Christians.[15]

As immigrants both willing and unwilling streamed into the South, the region received many new religious philosophies from Europe and Africa, but it also transmitted religious ideas to other destinations. For example, black Christians from the South—some enslaved, some free—evacuated with British troops and American loyalists after the American Revolution to found new congregations in the Caribbean, Nova Scotia, and elsewhere. Many black lay evangelicals in this reverse diaspora came from the Silver Bluff, South Carolina, Baptist Church, the first black congregation in the early South and one of exceptional importance in the history of African American Christianity. George Liele went to Jamaica, Moses Baker to the Bahamas, David George to Nova Scotia and Sierra Leone.

White Methodists like Thomas Coke, Francis Asbury, and William Hammett also regarded the South and the greater Anglophonic Caribbean as a linked region, shuttling back and forth between them to preach to slaves. In this way, the late-eighteenth-century South was an important connector node for religious ideas and people in constant motion.[16]

The rise of the evangelicals to power in the late-eighteenth-century South is in some ways a triumphant story—of the ascension of "New Light" upstarts, itinerant preachers taking the word directly to the people, urgently preaching a regenerate religion of the heart, scorned and feared by the authorities for witnessing to the people, finally gaining a foothold in the slave quarters and the plain folks' homes in the southern backcountry far from any established church or seat of power. But it is also a tragic narrative of declension—of the turning away from the radical social possibilities that the democratic people's religion heralded as experimentation and flexibility gave way to conformity. And it is a story that probably has something to do with the receding of the global South. By the early nineteenth century many immigrants from the British Isles and Germany had shed their transatlantic connections, Americanized, and assimilated into the South. Newer immigrants tended to settle in the North. The Gulf South maintained its Latin feel and Caribbean connections, but as the century progressed those too grew more faint. On the eve of the Civil War only an estimated 5 percent of the southern population was born abroad, making the region culturally more homogeneous, less shaped by, and engaged with, internationalism, and more inwardly focused in its religious expression. That profile accords with the notion of a South increasingly drawn in on itself in its "search for conversion, for redemption from innate human depravity," which, we are told, is "the central theme of southern religious history."[17]

In sum, the religious lives of the South before the early nineteenth century were more integrated into, and shaped by, Atlantic, and even global, forces than was the case later in the nineteenth century, which we associate more with the rise of "southern religion." Beginning in the sixteenth century, imperial expansion by Spain, Britain, and France into the Americas, subjugation and displacement of native peoples, religious warfare, and the African slave trade permanently marked the region. All of this marked the South's religious cultures as deeply immersed in those of the early modern world. Those cultures left a permanent imprint on the region. But by the early nineteenth century much of the South's cultural and religious pluralism was receding in the face of the evangelical advance.

The evangelical ascendancy appears not so much as the beginnings of southern religion but as one among multiple competing and often overlapping narratives of religious expression in the early South. The region before the demise of indigenous populations, before the triumph of Anglo-American Protestantism, before the South became more culturally uniform, was a different world altogether, although still recognizable for all its difference. Amid severe hierarchies of worldly power, native people, Europeans, and Africans sought to make sense of each other through the idiom of religion and, in doing so, produced syncretic religious cultures that reshaped the South. Historians have long pointed out that the dividing line between sacred and secular was not so neatly drawn in early modern societies. In like fashion, for most early southerners, to exist was to be religious in some form. Religion lay at the heart of the early South, but the manifestation of religious identities changed markedly by the early nineteenth century as evangelical Protestantism became the region's dominant discourse.

Evangelicalism embodies so much that seems quintessentially southern—the preoccupation with sin and guilt, the emotional search for redemption, the plainspoken directness of the faith of ordinary folk, the twining of race and religion. The ironies brood over the southern religious landscape: the tension between an egalitarian religion of the heart and the undemocratic compromises it made on race, slavery, and gender; the paradox that the same language of sin and freedom that inspired white evangelicals also fueled the radical moral vision of the black church. Evangelicalism helped shape the emergence of the modern South. Fittingly, in a region awash in tragedy, pathos, and squandered opportunities, the triumph of evangelicalism reaped its share of those harvests; it also brought a message of hope and redemption to the South. When we consider the terms "evangelical" and "religious revival," for example, do we include early-nineteenth-century Native American religious renewal movements in the Deep South that sought to regenerate native people spiritually and fortify them for armed struggle in a last attempt to save their land?

Arriving in the South just as the legal slave trade was about to end, the Saharan and Atlantic pilgrim Omar ibn Said straddled these worlds, witnessing and taking part in the dramatic transition. He reportedly lived in Fayetteville until his death at almost one hundred after the Civil War. In his memoir he wrote that he clung fast to Islam for a long time, aided by a Koran that someone gave him, but that gradually he began attending church and was baptized a Presbyterian. "When I was a Mohammedan," he wrote, "I prayed thus: 'Thanks be to God, Lord of all worlds, the merciful, the gracious, Lord of the Day of Judgment, thee we serve, on thee we call for help. Direct us in the right way, the way of those on whom thou hast had mercy, with whom thou hast not been angry and who walk not in error.' But now I pray 'Our Father, etc.' in the words of our Lord Jesus the Messiah."[18] It is as though he had become a pilgrim again in this new land, this new South, embarking on a journey to a new self, his sanctified Christian identity a remodeled version of his Muslim spirit. His long-ago trek across the desert, a world away in physical and emotional distance, was but a distant memory.

Notes

1. "Autobiography of Omar ibn Said, Slave in North Carolina, 1831," ed. John Franklin Jameson, *American Historical Review* 30 (1925): 787–95, quotes on 792–94.

2. J. Richard Wunderli, *Peasant Fires: The Drummer of Niklashausen* (Bloomington: Indiana University Press, 1992), 61. On the trans-Saharan pilgrimage see J. S. Birks, *Across the Savannas to Mecca: The Overland Pilgrimage Route from West Africa* (London: Frank Cass, 1978); Umar al-Naqar, *The Pilgrimage Tradition in West Africa* (Khartoum: Khartoum University Press, 1972); Ghislaine Lydon, *On Trans-Saharan Trails: Islamic Law, Trade Networks, and Cross-Cultural Exchange in Nineteenth-Century Western Africa* (New York: Cambridge University Press, 2009); Simon Coleman and John Elsner, *Pilgrimage: Past and Present in World Religions* (Cambridge: Harvard University Press, 1995), 67–68; Michael Wolfe, ed., *One Thousand Roads to Mecca* (New York: Grove Press, 1997).

3. Donald G. Mathews, "Forum: Southern Religion," *Religion and American Culture* 8 (Summer 1998): 147; Donald G. Mathews, *Religion in the Old South* (Chicago: University of Chicago Press, 1977), xiii–xiv; Martin Marty, foreword to Mathews, *Religion in the Old South*, xi; Samuel S. Hill, "Religion," in *Encyclopedia of Southern Culture*, ed. Charles Reagan Wilson and William Ferris (Chapel Hill: University of North Carolina Press, 1989), 1269–70. See also Donald G. Mathews, "'We Have Left Undone Those Things Which We Ought to Have Done': Southern Religious History in Retrospect and Prospect," *Church History* 67 (1998): 305–25; and Jon Sensbach, "Indians, Africans, and the New Synthesis of Eighteenth-Century Southern Religious History," in *Religion in the American South: Protestants and Others in History and Culture*, ed. Beth Barton Schweiger and Donald G. Mathews (Chapel Hill: University of North Carolina Press, 2004), 5–29.

4. Mary Beth Swetman Mathews, *Rethinking Zion: How the Print Media Placed Fundamentalism in the South* (Knoxville: University of Tennessee Press, 2006); H. L. Mencken, "Sahara of the Bozart," in *The American Scene: A Reader*, ed. H. L. Mencken and Huntington Cairns (New York: Knopf, 1977), 157–68.

5. Rhys Isaac, *The Transformation of Virginia, 1740–1790* (Chapel Hill: University of North Carolina Press, 1982); Christine Heyrman, *Southern Cross: The Beginnings of the Bible Belt* (Chapel Hill: University of North Carolina Press, 1998); Monica Najar, *Evangelizing the South: A Social History of Church and State in Early America* (New York: Oxford University Press, 2008); Jewel L. Spangler, *Virginians Reborn: Anglican Monopoly, Evangelical Dissent, and the Rise of the Baptists in the Late Eighteenth Century* (Charlottesville: University Press of Virginia, 2008); Charles F. Irons, *The Origins of Proslavery Christianity: White and Black Evangelicals in Colonial and Antebellum Virginia* (Chapel Hill: University of North Carolina Press, 2008); Randolph Scully, *Religion and the Making of Nat Turner's Virginia: Baptist Community and Conflict, 1740–1840* (Charlottesville: University Press of Virginia, 2008).

6. "Redefining and Reassessing the Colonial South," *Journal of Southern History* 73 (2007): 523; Carl Bridenbaugh, *Myths and Realities: Societies of the Colonial South* (1952; New York: Atheneum, 1963), vii.

7. See, for example, James L. Peacock, *Grounded Globalism: How the U.S. South Embraces the World* (Athens: University of Georgia Press, 2007); James C. Cobb, *Globalization and the American South* (Athens: University of Georgia Press, 2005).

8. The Spanish missions of Florida have an extensive bibliography, but for an incisive introduction see Jerald D. Milanich, *Laboring in the Fields of the Lord: Spanish Missions and Southeastern Indians* (Washington, D.C.: Smithsonian, 2000). See also Stuart B. Schwartz, *All Can Be Saved: Religious Tolerance and Salvation in the Iberian Atlantic World* (New Haven: Yale University Press, 2008); J. H. Elliott, *Empires of the Atlantic World: Britain and Spain in America, 1492–1830* (New Haven: Yale University Press, 2007); Liam M. Brockey, *Journey to the East: The Jesuit Mission to China, 1579–1724* (Cambridge: Harvard University Press, 2008); Florence C. Hsia, *Sojourners in a Strange Land: Jesuits and Their Scientific Missions in Late Imperial China* (Chicago: University of Chicago Press, 2008); Andrew Ross, *A Vision Betrayed: The Jesuits in Japan and China, 1542–1742* (New York: Orbis, 2003); Vicente Rafael, *Contracting Colonialism: Translation and Christian Conversion in Tagalog Society under Early Spanish Rule* (Durham: Duke University Press, 1993).

9. Peter Francis Jr., "Significance of St Catherines' Beads," in *The Beads of St. Catherines' Island*, by Elliott H. Blair, Lorann S. A. Pendleton, and Peter Francis Jr. (New York: American Museum of Natural History Anthropological Papers no. 89, 2009), 180, 182. Also see David Weber, *The Spanish Frontier in North America* (New Haven: Yale University Press, 1994), 94–97, on global aspect of Spanish missions.

10. Robbie Ethridge, *From Chicaza to Chickasaw: The European Invasion and the Transformation of the Mississippian World, 1540–1715* (Chapel Hill: University of North Carolina Press, 2010); Robbie Ethridge and Sheri M. Shuck-Hall, eds., *Mapping the Mississippian Shatter Zone: The Colonial Indian Slave Trade and Regional Instability in the American South* (Lincoln: University of Nebraska Press, 2009); Joel W. Martin, "Indians,

Contact and Colonialism in the Deep South: Themes for a Post-colonial History of American Religion," in *Retelling U.S. Religious History*, ed. Thomas Tweed (Berkeley: University of California Press, 1997).

11. Recent work on Atlantic Catholicism in the early South includes Linda M. Heywood and John K. Thornton, *Central Africans, Atlantic Creoles, and the Foundation of the Americas, 1585–1660* (New York: Cambridge University Press, 2007); Jason R. Young, *Rituals of Resistance: African Atlantic Religion in Kongo and the Lowcountry South in the Era of Slavery* (Baton Rouge: Louisiana State University Press, 2007); Jane Landers, *Black Society in Spanish Florida* (Urbana: University of Illinois Press, 1999); Emily Clark, *Masterless Mistresses: The New Orleans Ursulines and the Development of a New World Society, 1727–1834* (Chapel Hill: University of North Carolina Press, 2007).

12. Jon Butler, *The Huguenots in America: A Refugee People in New World Society* (Cambridge: Harvard University Press, 1983); Bertrand Van Ruymbeke and Randy J. Sparks, eds., *Memory and Identity: The Huguenots in France and the Atlantic Diaspora* (Columbia: University of South Carolina Press, 2003); Bertrand Van Ruymbeke, *From New Babylon to Eden: The Huguenots and Their Migration to Colonial South Carolina* (Columbia: University of South Carolina Press, 2006).

13. A. G. Roeber, *Palatines, Liberty, and Property: German Lutherans in Colonial British America* (Baltimore: Johns Hopkins University Press, 1993); Aaron Fogleman, *Hopeful Journeys: German Immigration, Settlement, and Political Culture in Colonial America, 1717–1775* (Philadelphia: University of Pennsylvania Press, 1996); Jon Sensbach, *A Separate Canaan: The Making of an Afro-Moravian World in North Carolina, 1763–1840* (Chapel Hill: University of North Carolina Press, 1998).

14. Verner W. Crane, "A Lost Utopia of the First American Frontier," *Sewanee Review* 27 (1919): 48–61; Knox Mellon Jr., "Christian Priber and the Jesuit Myth," *South Carolina Historical Magazine* 61 (1960): 75–81.

15. Essential overviews remain Albert Raboteau, *Slave Religion: The "Invisible Institution" in the Antebellum South* (New York: Oxford University Press, 1978); and Sylvia Frey and Betty Wood, *Come Shouting to Zion: African American Christianity in the American South and British Caribbean to 1830* (Chapel Hill: University of North Carolina Press, 1998). See also Sylvia Frey, "The Visible Church: Historiography of African American Religion since Raboteau," *Slavery and Abolition* 29 (2008): 83–110.

16. John W. Catron, "Evangelical Networks in the Greater Caribbean and the Origins of the Black Church," *Church History* 79 (2010): 77–115.

17. Heyrman, *Southern Cross*, remains the standard work on this transition. Quotation from D. G. Mathews, *Religion in the Old South*, xiii–xiv.

18. "Autobiography of Omar ibn Said," 794.

"A Most Unfortunate Divel . . . without the Prospect of Getting Anything"

A Virginia Planter Negotiates the Late Stuart Atlantic World

NATALIE ZACEK

In recent years, historians have increasingly sought to understand the connections between the British colonies established in the American South and those of the West Indies, and in particular to develop an explicitly Atlantic framework by which to link the histories of both of these regions to one another, as well as to Africa and the European imperial powers. This essay analyzes the story of one individual, Daniel Parke, in order to explore those relationships as they played out in the career of a Virginia planter turned West Indian colonial governor.[1] Specifically, Parke's experience suggests that, for all of the evidence of common ground, parallels, and continuities between the colonial Americas, broadly conceived, local circumstances sometimes varied tremendously between the constituent parts of the first British Empire. Parke's tragic history reveals that approaches to imperial government that worked well within the American South were not always successful elsewhere in the Anglo-American world, and reminds us that, within the broad sweep of Atlantic World histories, local contexts mattered a great deal.

"A Brutal and Licentious Despot"

On the morning of December 7, 1710, a mob estimated to have consisted of four to five hundred men assembled in the streets of St. John's, the capital of the island of Antigua, and advanced upon the mansion of the governor of the federated Leeward Islands colony (comprising the islands of

Antigua, Montserrat, Nevis, and St. Kitts), demanding that Daniel Parke dismiss the regiment of British regular soldiers with whom he had garrisoned his residence, resign his post, and depart the island immediately. When Parke refused to "quit the Government with which he had been entrusted by his Royal Mistress," Queen Anne, his opponents formed themselves into two assault squads. Captain John Piggott and his men attacked the governor's mansion from the front, and those commanded by Captain Painter advanced upon it from the rear.[2] Parke ordered that the soldiers fire upon the attackers, but the mob, which outnumbered the defenders by at least six to one, soon overwhelmed the grenadiers and broke into the house, where they found that Parke had locked himself in his bedchamber. Piggott and his men broke down the door, at which point Parke shot and killed Piggott, but was almost immediately felled by a bullet wound to his leg.

At this point, the story becomes murky. The more sober accounts assert that Parke's injury was mortal and that Piggott's men permitted some of the governor's defenders to transport him to the nearby house of a Mr. Wright, where Gousse Bonnin, a Huguenot physician, bandaged the wound, but these ministrations apparently came too late to prevent the governor's death from shock and blood loss shortly thereafter.[3] However, a number of alternate versions claim that Parke met a considerably more violent end. One account concurs that Parke died in Wright's home under the care of Dr. Bonnin but states that after the governor was wounded the crowd did not immediately permit his friends to evacuate him, but instead stripped him of his clothes "with such violence that only the wrist and neckbands of his shirt were left on him," and dragged him down the steps of Government House and into the street, where his assailants, after getting their fill of insulting and reviling him, left him to die of his wounds and of thirst in the heat of the afternoon, at which point Wright and Bonnin were able to ease his end.[4] Other variants of the story depict the attackers as rending apart not only Parke's clothes but his body as well; they "dragged him by the members about his house, bruised his head, and broke his back with the butt end of their pieces."[5] Other versions of the story are still gorier, maintaining that after Parke was felled by his leg wound he was "then torn into pieces and scattered in the street," and that "some, whose Marriage-Bed, 'tis thought he had defiled, revenged themselves on the sinning Parts, which they cut off and exposed."[6]

In the words of the Jamaican planter and historian Bryan Edwards,

Thus perished, in a general insurrection of an insulted and indignant community, a brutal and licentious despot, than whom no state criminal was ever more deservedly punished. He was a monster in wickedness, and being placed by his situation beyond the reach of ordinary restraint, it was as lawful to cut him off by every means possible, as it would have been to shoot a wild beast that had broke its limits, and was gorging itself with human blood. . . . [His] was an avowed and unrestrained violation of all decency and principle. He feared neither God nor man; and it was soon observed of him, as it had formerly been of another detestable tyrant, *that he spared no man in his anger, nor woman in his lust.*[7]

This last phrase referred originally to the perceived depredations of Henry VIII. In his multivolume history of the British West Indies, which went through five editions between 1793 and 1818, Edwards reserves some of his sharpest invective for Parke, who at that point had been dead for nearly a century; he functions in Edwards's text as a sort of bogeyman representing a vicious and unprincipled form of tyranny which, in Edwards's view, destabilized the political and social life of these island colonies and undercut their efforts to transplant British values and practices of government into the context of tropical plantation societies. Edwards's judgment echoed that which appeared in a London journal just three months after Parke's death, which expressed the hope that "the Tragical End of this Gentleman may be a Warning to all the Governours of our American Plantations, not to abuse the large Power with which they are entrusted."[8]

According to Richard Dunn, "the murder of Governor Parke . . . was not an isolated or accidental event. It summed up many long years of life on the tropical firing line." In Dunn's view, Parke's murder was just another example, albeit an exceptionally bloody one, of the "disastrous social failures" of the West Indies, as precipitated by the supposedly violent and uncivilized people who populated them.[9] In reality, though, the murder *was* in important ways an isolated event within the history of the English West Indian colonies, and in that of colonial British America more generally. Many royal governors, perhaps the majority, came into some sort of serious conflict with the colonists over whom they were sent to govern, and the seventeenth and eighteenth centuries witnessed numerous instances in which these disagreements over the nature and limits of imperial authority devolved into outright conflict.

As we will see, these tensions were epitomized by the career of Daniel Parke's friend and patron, Sir Edmund Andros. In general, English colonists throughout North America and the West Indies were strongly predisposed to dislike and mistrust their governors, to see them as unwelcome interlopers who were often grievously ill-prepared to cope with the challenges that they and their communities faced. But the Parke incident was the sole instance in which disgruntled colonists actually took up arms against an unpopular governor; not even in the course of the American Revolution would such a situation recur. Although Parke, almost alone among British American royal governors, was himself a colonial, it appears that his upbringing and political service in Virginia, rather than rendering him more aware of and sensitive to the concerns of his West Indian subjects, instead encouraged him to develop a willful blindness to these people's claims to what they considered the natural rights of Englishmen, whether at home or abroad. If the residents of the Leewards initially may have welcomed his appointment, believing that a fellow colonist would rule them in a more egalitarian and consensual manner than his English-born predecessors, they were doomed to disappointment.

To the Antiguan planters and merchants of the early eighteenth century, what was unusual about Daniel Parke, and what led directly to his death at their hands, was that he appeared to be bent upon denying these colonists many of what they conceived of as the natural rights of Englishmen, especially those connected to the security of persons and property. From the islanders' point of view, every aspect of Parke's life history, and of his personal and official conduct as governor, proved that he was intent upon subjugating the Leeward Islands to his arbitrary rule and denying them the exercise of their much-vaunted English rights. His veneration of the authoritarian imperial governor Andros, his ardent and fulsomely expressed royalism, and his involvement, in the form of a bribery scandal, in an attempt to undermine the integrity of the House of Commons all seemed to show him to be a man who would in every instance uphold royal prerogative or personal empowerment over the rights of those he governed.

In the course of his four years as leader of the Leewards, Parke had, according to the articles of impeachment the Antiguans presented against him in 1708, threatened his subjects' rights to their property, by questioning long-established land titles, and had interfered with their jealously guarded right to trial by jury. He had attempted to intimidate them by wandering in disguise through the streets of St. John's, allegedly listening at the windows of the taverns and private houses in which he believed that his opponents met to conspire against him. He had employed royal troops, which had been sent to the Leewards to protect them from attack by French vessels during the War of the Spanish Succession, as a sort of private standing army charged to do his bidding and, in the last extremity, to serve as his personal bodyguard against the aggrieved locals. He had, in the face of vitriolic local opposition, ordered the erection of the grandiose and costly governor's mansion, and it was widely rumored that he had taken the island's seal, a crucial symbol of imperial authority, and had it melted down and transformed it into a drinking vessel for his personal use, a shocking act of personal arrogance and, possibly, treason. Most menacingly, to the minds of many of his subjects, he had employed all possible means by which to undercut the power of the individual islands' houses of assembly, which the residents of Antigua and Montserrat, Nevis and St. Kitts viewed as the principal safeguards of their liberty and as bulwarks against the threat of gubernatorial and imperial tyranny.

By ridding themselves of Parke, Leeward colonists believed that they were rescuing themselves from the clutches of an unprincipled tyrant who clearly held no respect for them either as individuals or as a community. The governor appeared to the governed as an immovable obstacle standing between Queen Anne and her loyal colonial subjects, and as a would-be despot who seemed to fear neither man nor God. When Parke, despite his sworn commitment to follow the commands of his "Royal Mistress," refused to obey her order that he "leave those Islands and return into Our Presence prepared to make your Defence before us in Council," his subjects concluded that nothing short of brute force would rid them of his "Oppression and Maladministration."[10]

The articles of complaint that the Antiguan colonists presented against Parke provide fascinating reading for the historian. While some of the offenses cited seem quite trivial, and others amount to little beyond hearsay evidence, the document also levels against the governor allegations as serious as attempting to intimidate witnesses in a criminal case, interfering in local elections, ordering the commission of illegal searches and seizures, and using imperial troops in "the highest Act of Violence, Force, and Injustice."[11] Why, then, did Parke, a stranger in a strange land, a man who had no family or friends in the West Indies, who had never visited the islands before taking up his governorship, and whose dependence for his salary and perquisites on the goodwill of a notably fractious and uncooperative local legislature prevented him from reaping favor through the disposal of patronage, seem convinced that he would be able to get away with such obviously controversial and antagonistic behavior towards local society? The answers to these questions throw light on the social and political history not only of the Leeward Islands but of the broader Atlantic World, in which the colonies of the mainland South were embedded and in which Parke was raised.

"Overbearing Self-Assurance"

In order to answer these questions, it is vital to delve into both Parke's personal history and that of the late-seventeenth-century Virginia social and political milieu in which he came to maturity. As the only son of one of the Tidewater region's most successful planters—his father had accumulated vast landholdings in several counties and had served as a member of the Council and of the House of Burgesses, as well as treasurer and secretary of the colony—Parke was born into a position of considerable wealth and privilege. He significantly augmented his status by a youthful marriage to Jane Ludwell. His bride's father, Philip Ludwell, was not only one of the colony's richest planters but also "perhaps the most prominent citizen in Virginia," a former governor of both North and South Carolina, as well as having served as the speaker of Virginia's House of Burgesses between 1695 and 1698.[12] He was also the third and last husband of Lady Frances Berkeley, the widow of two previous governors, one of the richest women in colonial America, and the undisputed matriarch of Virginia society in the late seventeenth century. Moreover, Parke's father had died when the former was very young and, as he was from the age of ten the only male in his immediate family, he had "every opportunity to mature and feel his independence at an early age," rather than having been brought up under the control of a strict patriarch; indeed, the historian Clifford Dowdey claimed that, "as the only male heir to his father's estate and position, the young Parke had matured early and arrogantly," becoming a youth of "overbearing self-assurance."[13]

In late-seventeenth-century Virginia, fathers, especially those who numbered among the colony's elite, were expected to exert strict control over their children, particularly the boys.[14] Sons, it was hoped, would grow up to be assertive and self-reliant young men, but this sense of personal independence and self-confidence needed to be constrained within definite limits—unruly sons were frequently threatened with disinheritance, and many planters were reluctant to send their boys to be educated in England, as they would return not only without essential experience in the management of plantations and slaves but possessed of a self-willed spirit which meant that they would not be likely to easily "Submit himselfe to the Paternall or Maternall Yoke."[15]

As a young man possessed of both great wealth and respected lineage, as well as being the son-in-law of a very powerful political leader, Daniel Parke, despite his youth, rapidly climbed the ladder of officeholding in Virginia. By the time he turned twenty-four he had taken a seat in the House of Burgesses; the following year he had joined the vestry board of Williamsburg's Bruton Parish Church; and by 1695 he was appointed to the colony's governing council, while simultaneously occupying the posts of collector, naval officer, escheator of lands, and, in an especially prestigious position, governor of the newly established College of William and Mary, Virginia's first institution of higher education, and, after Harvard, the second college established in the Anglo-American colonies.[16]

In these pursuits, Parke soon acquired both loyal friends and virulent opponents. As a young man, and perhaps seeking both political patronage and a father figure, he came to idolize Sir Edmund Andros, who served as governor of Virginia between 1692 and 1698. Andros, the son of a staunchly Royalist English family, was a man of long-standing military experience both in England and the colonies, and had acquired a transatlantic reputation as an aggressive proponent of a strong and consolidated imperial administration.

Although Andros's service as governor first of the colony of New York (1674–80) and later of the short-lived Dominion of New England, an abortive and much-resented attempt by James II to unify New York, New Jersey, and the New England colonies (1686–89), resulted in his recall from the former and his ejection from the latter, William and Mary were sufficiently impressed by his military and administrative experience that they rewarded him with the prestigious Virginia post, in which he again made himself extremely unpopular to the colonists, primarily in relation to virulent controversies regarding the proper relationship between the Church of England and the colonial government. In 1698, aging, in poor health, and worn out from his ongoing combat with the far younger and more vigorous James Blair, commissary of the bishop of London, Andros was successful in his petition to the King that he be allowed to resign his governorship and return to England. His final years were spent in yet another governorship, of the island of Jersey, allowing him to come to the end of his life in a position of authority and prestige.

If Andros was Parke's great friend and mentor, Blair was for many years the latter's nemesis. Not only were the two men encouraged in their hostilities against one another through their respective support for and opposition to Governor Andros, but both had notably stubborn and aggressive personalities. Parke preferred to resolve interpersonal conflict with physical violence, if he was unable to gain satisfaction otherwise—he famously threatened to horsewhip Francis Nicholson, then governor of Maryland, when the latter had publicly accused him of lying—but, as a member of the clergy, Blair was immune from challenges to duel.[17] Frustrated, Parke compensated by striking at the commissary through his wife, creating a shocking public scandal when he marched into Bruton Parish Church in the midst of Blair's sermon, seized Sarah Blair by the arm, and dragged her from the Ludwell family pew, in which she sat as a guest, and out of the building, a "ruffianly & profane action" that rendered those present "extremely scandalized."[18] Yet, perhaps surprisingly, the enmity between Parke and Blair did not last forever; by 1703 the two men had bonded over their shared opposition to Nicholson, now governor of Virginia, in his attempts to limit the power of the colony's entrenched institutions and its self-confident governing elite.[19]

Considering Parke's career in imperial politics, it is worthwhile to speculate about the lessons he may have learned from his experiences in Virginia. The example of Andros may have encouraged him not only to subscribe to an aggressive and fulsomely expressed idea of royal prerogative but also to believe that even particularly notorious political misdeeds, of the sort that had inflamed public opinion against a royal governor throughout the Anglo-Atlantic world, could be forgiven by Whitehall, and their perpetrator rewarded with further prestigious posts. Parke's relationship with Blair, moving as it did from naked and public hostility to relative amity and political cooperation, could have led him to believe that such a climate of interpersonal hatred should not be a subject of particular anxiety, as even seemingly serious and deeply rooted disagreements might well in time be ameliorated by a more pressing need for collaboration against a common opponent. These lessons, taken in combination, may well have encouraged Parke, as governor of the Leewards, to dismiss as unimportant the public opposition his controversial behavior generated, believing that such matters could be finessed at both the local and the imperial level. Trevor Burnard has asserted that men who came to maturity in colonial societies dominated by slavery often "found it difficult not to be tyrants in all their relationships," and Parke's experiences as a member of the highest circles of the Virginia planter elite no doubt encouraged such tendencies.[20]

While Parke's personal background and youthful experiences in relation to both local and imperial politics may have encouraged him to feel confident in his ability to succeed in any situation, and to assume that he could avoid the consequences of even the most flagrant misdeeds, it is also important to acknowledge his impressive ability to ingratiate himself with ever more powerful individuals. While men such as Ludwell and Andros, and women such as Lady Berkeley, stood at the apex of political and social power in Parke's native Virginia, his relocation in 1697 to England saw him developing ties of friendship and patronage within far more exalted circles. Shortly after his arrival in the metropole, he initiated a close friendship with Charles Mordaunt, the third Earl of Peterborough, a former member of the Privy Council and a Surrey neighbor of the Evelyn family, Parke's maternal kinfolk. Upon enlisting in the army in 1702, Parke was appointed aide-de-camp to John Churchill, the future Duke of Marlborough and a leader of the English forces in the War of the Spanish Succession. Although Parke failed to gain any particular distinction as a soldier, he made the most of the opportunity presented by Churchill's great victory at the battle of Blenheim in August 1704. It was Parke whom Churchill asked to travel to England to give the good news to Queen Anne, and Parke did so in flamboyant style, rushing across the Low Countries without sleep, changing horses whenever he could, crossing the Channel, and rushing to Anne's side at Windsor Castle, to present her with the glad tidings.

His actions gained the approbation not only of the Duke and of his influential wife, Sarah (who so treasured her husband's brief note about the victory which Parke brought to her that she took care to preserve it, and it remains on display at Blenheim Palace, the Churchill family estate, named to honor the famous battle), but also of the Queen, who was so impressed not only by the welcome news of the English triumph at Blenheim but by Parke's charm and physical attractiveness that he soon became one of her favorites at court. The monarch was apparently particularly delighted by the fact that Parke refused the five hundred pounds with which the bearers of great news to the sovereign were traditionally rewarded, requesting instead a likeness of Anne; she responded with a purse of a thousand guineas, as well as a miniature set in a gold locket studded with diamonds, which Parke wore at all times for the rest of his life.[21] With friends such as these, Parke felt confident that it would always be he, rather than the disgruntled inhabitants of distant imperial possessions, who would gain and retain metropolitan favor and be empowered to uphold imperial authority.

It is also important to note that, up until the moment at which the crowd of disaffected Antiguans launched their attack against him, Parke had invariably managed to get away with numerous instances and varieties of political and personal misbehavior, whether in Virginia, in England, or in the islands. Having feuded bitterly with Blair, Nicholson, and many others among the Virginia elite, he had moved to England, where the accusation that he had been involved in a bribery scandal in an attempt to gain a seat in the House of Commons failed to forestall his emergence as a loved and trusted intimate not only of some of the most powerful figures at court but of the Queen herself. Although his conflicts with influential fellow Virginians, in combination with the fact that he essentially abandoned his wife and their two daughters (even forcing Jane to adopt his illegitimate son by another woman, and leaving her and the children in a very difficult financial position), might have been assumed to have made him an unlikely candidate to serve as that colony's governor, Parke himself certainly believed that, upon Governor Nicholson's recall in 1705, Whitehall gave him serious consideration as Nicholson's replacement. This confidence was not entirely misplaced, although it was extremely unusual for any "colonial" to be appointed to a royal governorship in this era; despite his various misdeeds, Parke seems to have been expert in charming, and appealing to the vanities of, influential courtiers, who may have interpreted his more egregious behavior as stemming from his colonial birth and upbringing. Taken in combination, these various personal and political factors gave Daniel Parke a strong impression that, however outrageous his words and actions appeared to the Leeward settlers, he would be able to continue to behave as he pleased, with little threat that he would suffer any serious consequences as a result.

But beyond the issues of Parke's personal character and life experience, it is also worthwhile to consider the relationship between late-seventeenth- and early-eighteenth-century Virginia and other parts of the Anglo-Atlantic world, particularly the West Indian colonies. Why, in a nutshell, might the political and personal lessons that Parke had learned in his youth and young manhood turn out not to be applicable elsewhere in the empire? In seeking to answer this question, we may be able to gain a more nuanced understanding about the relationship that has historically existed between the South and the rest of the Atlantic World.

"Villain and Victim of the Imperial System"

Perhaps the most basic, yet most important, difference between Virginia and the Leeward Islands was that of size, in terms of both geography and population. Virginia has an area of more than 40,000 square miles, whereas Antigua, the largest of the four Leewards, is a mere 108. Of course, during Parke's lifetime, much of the former colony, particularly the western half, was very thinly populated by white colonists, but even the long-settled Tidewater region was significantly larger in physical terms than any of the Leewards. At least as noteworthy was the disparity in population: circa 1700, Virginia was home to approximately 45,000 whites, whereas the four Leewards, taken together, had less than one-fifth of that number. These differences are central to Parke's story because, however seriously his private and public behavior might have outraged community opinion in his native colony, the stage upon which he moved was considerably wider than that upon which he found himself in the islands, and many Virginians who lived outside the circle of the Williamsburg-centered elite were almost certainly unaware of and/or unconcerned by Parke's words and actions. However, in colonial societies as small, in both physical and human terms, as the Leewards, flagrant misbehavior, particularly by such a visible public figure as the colony's royal governor, could be neither hidden nor ignored.

Helen Hill Miller, the author of the only scholarly biography of Daniel Parke, has described her protagonist as possessed of "all the vices of a Restoration rake."[22] These "vices"—licentiousness, quarrelsomeness, arrogance, vanity—make Parke an interesting, if perhaps not terribly admirable, historical character, and one who might seem, both to metropolitan observers of his own era and to more modern historians, well suited to rule over tropical plantation colonies. In both Parke's era and our own, commentators and scholars have frequently depicted these colonies as social failures, places in which fortunes were soon won and sooner lost, in which slaves labored under worse conditions and their owners lived in greater luxury than elsewhere in colonial British America, and where highly uneven sex ratios, a challenging and unpredictable physical environment, and perpetual anxieties regarding slave rebellion and foreign attack combined to prevent the development of most of the institutions that were considered to have had a calming and civilizing effect elsewhere in Anglo-America. Moreover, the most prevalent image of the island colonies was as places of sexual license: West Indian colonists, encouraged by a sultry climate, the allegedly low origins of many settlers, and the absence of church courts and other bodies regulating sexual behavior, supposedly dedicated themselves to the pursuit of every kind of pleasure. But, while pamphleteers might claim that the very air of the West Indies "so changes the constitution of its inhabitants that if a woman land there chaste as a vestal, she becomes in forty-eight hours a perfect Messalina," and "it is grown a Proverb with the English Merchants, that tho a Man goes over never so honest . . . the very Air there does change him in a short time," in reality, by the onset of the eighteenth century the "vices of a Restoration rake" were beginning to fall from metropolitan fashion, and in the Leewards the small size of the islands and their white populations largely discouraged such flamboyant and self-indulgent actions.[23]

As Henry Hulton, a Liverpudlian who spent several years in Antigua as deputy collector of customs in the 1750s, noted, when the marriage between the son of Colonel Leslie, the president of the Council, and the daughter of Stephen Blizard, the island's chief justice, went sour, "the unhappiness of this marriage caused a breach between the families . . . and it was difficult in so small a society to maintain an intercourse with both of them." Private romantic or sexual scandals could not easily be contained in such inescapably intimate societies, and those who precipitated them often found themselves judged quite harshly by local white society.[24] Therefore, it is hardly surprising that Parke's embarkation, upon his arrival in Antigua, on a series of liaisons with married women, most notably with Catherine, the wife of Edward Chester, the Royal African Company's local factor, would seriously unsettle local social life and generate tremendous hostility toward the new governor, encouraging the Antiguans to interpret not only his personal but also his political activities with great suspicion.

In comparison with the Chesapeake, the Leeward Islands, and the English West Indian colonies more generally, were much more socially tense places, in which, as Richard Pares noted, the settlers "lived on their nerves" at all times.[25] As well as laboring under the ongoing threat of natural disasters such as floods, droughts, and especially hurricanes, and of attack from the nearby French islands, the Leeward colonists were in much more of a minority in relation to the enslaved population than were the Virginians: circa 1700 there were 45,000 Anglo-Virginians and a mere 15,000 slaves and free people of color, while the Leewards, home to around 8,000 whites, had approximately 22,000 slaves. Under these stressful circumstances of life, island residents might at least at some moments welcome a strong and assertive governor, but, should tensions either increase or subside, they were liable to resent his authority and do their utmost to undermine it. The colony's governors were obligated to walk a very thin line between being perceived as a dictator and developing a reputation as a weakling; few were entirely successful in finding this balance, but Parke's character and actions proved to be particularly provocative to local sensibilities.

Although his character and behavior undoubtedly rendered him unpopular among some of those who encountered him in his early life, as long as he remained in Virginia Daniel Parke possessed significant social and political legitimacy, as his lineage granted him membership in what was by the final decades of the seventeenth century already an entrenched colonial elite, that of the self-mythologizing "First Families of Virginia." In the Leewards, however, Parke's family background was either unknown to the settler community or dismissed by them as inconsequential. Rather than appearing as a man whose heritage rendered him inherently worthy of trust and respect, the governor struck many of the local planters and merchants as not having any real merits of his own. Instead he was viewed merely as a court favorite, a protégé of Queen Anne and of the Marlboroughs who, despite the Duke's undeniable military triumphs, were far from universally popular throughout the empire; the Duchess, in particular, was execrated by many metropolitans and colonials alike as a vulgar, scheming harlot.[26]

By the time of his arrival in the islands, Parke himself had been forced to realize that even these friendships in the highest places had their limitations. They had, for example, been insufficient to secure for this rather unremarkable American-born colonist the more prestigious imperial office of the governorship of Virginia, which Parke most coveted. Despite Parke's energetic lobbying for this post, it was awarded to George Hamilton, the Earl of Orkney. Not only had Hamilton played a much more active and important military role than Parke had in the war in Flanders, including a crucial performance at Blenheim, but, and more importantly, Whitehall considered the former, as an influential Scots aristocrat, to be ideally placed to ensure enthusiasm among Glasgow's large community of powerful transatlantic merchants, a number of whom were already involved in the lucrative commerce of Virginia tobacco, for the forthcoming Act of Union. It is not surprising that, when Parke learned that his substitute for the longed-for prize of the governorship of the Old Dominion was that of the Leeward Islands, he pronounced himself "a most unfortunate Divel here to be roasted in the sun, without the prospect of getting anything."[27]

Parke was particularly despondent as he insisted that Churchill "promised me the Government of Virginia at the Battle of Blenheim, but for some Reasons of State that was given to my Lord Orkney," but the fact remains that, although Parke, like many men of the Chesapeake elite, hoped to "become not just a colonial member of the British ruling class but an English country gentleman with influence in British politics," in reality, "he rated as only a very minor figure in Augustan England."[28] Parke's failure to attain the longed-for prize of the governorship of Virginia, and his reward with the lesser one of the Leewards, illustrates the extent to which dynamics of class, status, and interpersonal relations across the Anglo-Atlantic world decisively shaped patterns of political preferment and policy, and with them the history, of the colonial South, the West Indies, and the metropole.

In the end, the friendship and patronage of the Marlboroughs was almost certainly far more of a hindrance than a help to Parke in the Leewards. While John and Sarah Churchill maintained their influence at court, the Leeward settlers believed, Parke, however repugnant he made himself to the island colonists, was politically unassailable; one of the "Articles of Complaint" against him alleged that he "did frequently and publicly declare, That he had Assurance from . . . the Duchess of Marlborough, that he should be supported and protected, let him do what he would."[29] But, by the summer of 1710, it was apparent to Londoners in the know that both the Duke and the Duchess were losing their influence at court, and they thus could no longer continue to defend and promote Parke to Queen Anne. Moreover, despite the distance and unreliability of communications between England and the West Indies, Parke found that the Antiguans, whom he viewed as unsophisticated and disconnected from metropolitan developments, soon learned from their London-based family, friends, and business associates that the governor's chief patrons were fast losing their influence, an alteration that quite likely encouraged the islanders to become more aggressive in their attempts to rid themselves of him.

Elite Virginians of Parke's era tended to have a very high opinion of themselves both individually and communally, considering themselves to be socially and culturally superior to all other colonial leadership groups in the Anglo-Atlantic world. However, the planters of the English West Indies were just as convinced that it was their settlements, not any of those in North America, that were the real jewels in the imperial crown. Although Chesapeake tobacco was a lucrative colonial commodity, West Indian sugar far outranked it in both real and perceived economic importance within the empire. By the beginning of the eighteenth century the richest Caribbean sugar growers were, both in reality and by reputation, far wealthier than the leading Virginia tobacco planters. In addition, the West Indian colonies were considered in England to possess far greater geopolitical value than any of the settlements located on the North American mainland. Although at the beginning of the eighteenth century absenteeism among West Indian colonists had not reached the levels evident later in the century, these colonists tended to have notably closer economic, familial, and social connections to the metropole than was true of the Virginians.[30]

Parke's son-in-law, William Byrd, a self-consciously cultured man who possessed one of the colony's greatest fortunes, was shocked and humiliated to find, upon his arrival in London in the 1710s, that high society assigned rather little value to even the richest and most socially polished Virginia planter, and that the parents of "fine ladys" were happy to see their daughters "chain'd to a Booby with a great Estate" as long as that estate was in England rather than in the colonies.[31] Even the most lurid tales of the alleged decadence, luxury, cruelty, and sexual misdeeds attributed in popular culture to West Indian planters provide evidence that metropolitan readers were simply far more interested in the island colonies than they were in the Chesapeake, a fact of which island colonists were well aware.

Finally, Parke's career in the Leewards was significantly undermined by his failure to comprehend the serious differences between local political culture and that with which he had become familiar in Virginia. Although many scholars, most notably Edmund Morgan, have concurred that, in the wake of Bacon's Rebellion, the Virginia elite realized that, in order to maintain racial unity and continue their political and social dominance within the colony, it was necessary that they accord poorer white settlers greater respect, nonetheless "deference to authority was expected all down the line," and less-elite whites were very much expected to know their place.[32] In sharp contrast, West Indian colonial society was marked, in Bryan Edwards's words, by "a display of conscious equality . . . the poorest white person seems to consider himself nearly on a level with the richest, and, emboldened by this idea, approaches his employer with extended hand." According to Edwards, this phenomenon stemmed from "the preeminence and distinction which are necessarily attached even to the complexion of a white man . . . the blacks outnumber the whites in the proportion of seven to one . . . a sense of common safety therefore unites the latter in closer ties than are necessary among men who are differently situated, so the same circumstance necessarily gives birth among them to reciprocal defence"—a very different set of social relations than that which governed Parke's Virginia.[33]

Parke made himself notorious wherever he went for his rakish mode of life, yet simultaneously subscribed enthusiastically to the code of patriarchism and its concomitant emphasis on personal virtue so valorized by the Virginia elite. For example, when his daughter Frances came of age, he wrote her a long letter from London in which he attempted to impress upon her of the type of behavior expected by a woman of her social position, and of the obligations that the gentry held toward their alleged inferiors.[34] To a Virginian of Parke's time and background, the West Indian planters, despite their tremendous wealth, were mere parvenus (although metropolitan elites expressed the same view of even the richest Virginians, such as Parke's son-in-law, William Byrd), whose claim to elite status rested solely upon their financial success, and whom he was quick to accuse of myriad forms of misbehavior, ranging from smuggling to brawling to indulging their "unnaturall and monstrous lusts," which inevitably gave rise to a "slaveish sooty race" of mixed-race children.[35]

In Virginia, to be one of those great planters who viewed themselves as the natural leaders of society meant that one had been born to a great estate, as had Parke, rather than having acquired it through one's own efforts, as was true of the great majority of the members of the Leeward elite in Parke's time.[36] Thus, Parke did not feel obligated to accord even the wealthiest Antiguans what they considered their due respect, and simultaneously they were profoundly unimpressed by his lineage, and by the fact that his fortunes were, by the time of his arrival in the islands, seriously depleted; Edward Chester, the factor of the Royal African Company for the Leewards, and one of Parke's leading local opponents, apparently both responded to and inflamed their mutual hostility by boasting in public that his salary from the company was far more substantial than that which the Crown allotted the governor. Such conflicts in individual and communal values show just how much attitudes toward politics and society differed between the Chesapeake and the Caribbean, and throughout the Anglo-Atlantic world in the late seventeenth and early eighteenth centuries. Clearly, Parke's apprenticeship in Virginia politics had failed to school him effectively for his later endeavors in the islands. As the imperial historian Ruth Bourne observed, "seen in focus against his late Stuart background, none more startlingly than Parke illuminates the struggle of the colonial placeman, aristocrat though he was, villain and victim of the imperial system, whether in the Old Dominion of Virginia, at 'home' in England, or in the far-off 'Charibee Islands.'"[37]

Conclusion

As Patricia Bonomi has asserted,

> the abuses suffered by [New York governor Lord] Cornbury, Parke, and other royal governors at the hands of provincials in the late seventeenth and early eighteenth centuries reflected the seething volatility of imperial relations in a time of political innovation, administrative transformation, and pervasive anxiety. Only in the past quarter-century have scholars come to appreciate fully the dizzying series of changes that overtook England in late Stuart times. Political nerves were chronically exposed in an Anglophone society still rocking from a half-century of upheaval that began and ended with revolution.[38]

As Brendan McConville has observed, "the Civil Wars marked partici-pants with an indelible imprint of blood and trauma still visible in all areas of British America decades, even a century, later."[39] It was Daniel Parke's great misfortune that his own character and behavior were of the sort so likely to inflame both provincial and metropolitan opinion against him, to the extent that his murder literally at the hands of his fellow co-lonials represents, in Gabriel García Márquez's phrase, a chronicle of a death foretold.

The story of Daniel Parke's life and death shows the great diversity of personal and communal experiences and expectations that constituted and reflected the colonial British Atlantic world. Viewing Parke's seri-ous missteps, deliberate or unintended, as he attempted to negotiate a world encompassing Virginia, England, and the Caribbean encourages acknowledgment of this diversity, which can and, in some instances, has been flattened in scholars' understandable drive to theorize connections and similarities between the often highly socially, economically, politi-cally, and culturally disparate constituent parts of this Atlantic system. Parke's history also works to display the importance of concepts of rank and status, and of familial connections, within the administration of co-lonial British America. While Parke's personal excesses and lurid end may appear to be sui generis, his life and death allow us to better understand the place of the American South in the Atlantic World, and to speculate about the extent to which the South is Atlantic, and the Atlantic southern.

Notes

1. I have explored other aspects of Parke's imperial career in *Settler Society in the English Leeward Islands, 1670–1776* (Cambridge: Cambridge University Press, 2010), 189–95 and 219–35, and in "A Death in the Morning: The Murder of Daniel Parke, Antigua, 1710," in *Cultures and Identities in Colonial British America*, ed. Robert A. Olwell and Alan Tully (Baltimore: Johns Hopkins University Press, 2005), 223–43.

2. Algernon E. Aspinall, "The Fate of Governor Parke," in Aspinall, *West Indian Tales of Old* (New York: Negro Universities Press, 1969), 44.

3. Vere Langford Oliver, *The History of the Island of Antigua* (London: Mitchell and Hughes, 1894), 1:lxxxi.

4. Aspinall, "Fate," 45–46.

5. Quoted in Richard S. Dunn, *Sugar and Slaves: The Rise of the Planter Class in the English West Indies, 1624–1713* (Chapel Hill: University of North Carolina Press, 1972), 146.

6. Bryan Edwards, *The History, Civil and Commercial, of the British Colonies in the West Indies* (Philadelphia: J. Humphreys, 1806), 2:166; *The Political State of Great Britain*, March 31, 1711, quoted in Edward W. Greenfield, "The Life of Colonel Daniel Parke, Jr., Virginia Gentleman-Adventurer, 1669–1710" (master's thesis, Columbia University, 1946), 255.

7. Edwards, *History*, 2:166; italics in original.

8. *The Political State of Great Britain*, quoted in Greenfield, "Life of Parke," 255.

9. Dunn, *Sugar and Slaves*, 118.

10. Aspinall, "Fate," 44; *Some Instances of the Oppression and Male-Administration of Col. Parke, late Governor of the Leeward Islands* (London: n.p., 1713).

11. Oliver, *History of Antigua*, 1:95, 101, 120, 155.

12. Nancy Ehrich Martin, "Lucy Parke Byrd: Inside the Diary and Out" (master's thesis, University of Rochester, 1994), 11; Edward W. Greenfield, "Some New Aspects of the Life of Daniel Parke," *Virginia Magazine of History and Biography* 54 (1946): 308.

13. Greenfield, "Some New Aspects," 307; Clifford Dowdey, *The Virginia Dynasties: The Emergence of "King" Carter and the Golden Age* (Boston: Little, Brown, 1969), 216.

14. See Michael Zuckerman, "Penmanship Exercises for Saucy Sons: Thoughts on the Colonial Southern Family," *South Carolina Historical Magazine* 84 (1983): 252–66; and Holly Brewer, *By Birth or Consent: Children, Law, and the Anglo-American Revolution in Authority* (Chapel Hill: University of North Carolina Press, 2005).

15. "Speeches of Students of the College of William and Mary Delivered May 1, 1699," quoted in Anthony S. Parent, *Foul Means: The Formation of a Slave Society in Virginia, 1660–1740* (Chapel Hill: University of North Carolina Press, 2003), 217, 220.

16. Greenfield, "Some New Aspects," 309.

17. Parke Rouse Jr., *James Blair of Virginia* (Chapel Hill: University of North Carolina Press, 1971), 106.

18. Helen Hill Miller, *Colonel Parke of Virginia: "The Greatest Hector in the Town": A Biography* (Chapel Hill: Algonquin Books, 1989), 84.

19. Kevin Hardwick, "Narratives of Villainy and Virtue: Governor Francis Nicholson and the Character of the Good Ruler in Early Virginia," *Journal of Southern History* 72 (2006): 39–74.

20. Trevor Burnard, "Theater of Terror: Domestic Violence in Thomas Thistlewood's Jamaica, 1750–1786," in *Over the Threshold: Intimate Violence in Early America*, ed. Christine Daniels and Michael V. Kennedy (New York: Routledge, 1999), 244.

21. Miller, *Colonel Parke*, 223, 146. In John Closterman's 1706 portrait of Parke, in the collections of the Virginia Historical Society, Parke wears this miniature.

22. Ibid., xviii.

23. William Pittis, *The Jamaica Lady, or, The Life of Bavia* (London: Thomas Bickerton, 1720), 35; Thomas Hodges, *Plantation Justice* (London: A. Baldwin, 1701), 10. On the figure of the rake in eighteenth-century Britain, see Erin Skye Mackie, *Rakes, Highwaymen, and Pirates: The Making of the Modern Gentleman* (Baltimore: Johns Hopkins University Press, 2009).

24. Henry Hulton, "Account of Travels," Codex Eng. 74, John Carter Brown Library, Providence, Rhode Island. On sexuality and social control in the eighteenth-century

Leewards, see Zacek, *Settler Society*, and Zacek, "'Banes of Society' and 'Gentlemen of Strong Natural Parts': Attacking and Defending West Indian Creole Masculinity," in *New Men: Manliness in Early America*, ed. Thomas A. Foster (New York: New York University Press, 2011).

25. Richard Pares, *A West-India Fortune* (London: Longmans, Green, 1950), 25.

26. See William Laws, *Distinction, Death, and Disgrace: Governorship of the Leeward Islands in the Early Eighteenth Century* (Kingston: Jamaican Historical Society, 1976), 77.

27. Quoted in Dunn, *Sugar and Slaves*, 144.

28. Oliver, *History of Antigua*, 1:lxxviii; Trevor Burnard, *Creole Gentlemen: The Maryland Elite, 1691–1776* (New York: Routledge, 2002), 241.

29. Oliver, *History of Antigua*, 1:91.

30. See Julie Flavell, *When London Was Capital of America* (New Haven: Yale University Press, 2010).

31. Michal Rozbicki, *The Complete Colonial Gentleman: Cultural Legitimacy in Plantation America* (Charlottesville: University Press of Virginia, 1998), 77, 79.

32. Edmund Morgan, *American Slavery, American Freedom: The Ordeal of Colonial Virginia* (New York: Norton, 1975); A. G. Roeber, "Authority, Law, and Custom: The Rituals of Court Day in Tidewater Virginia, 1720 to 1750," *William and Mary Quarterly*, 3rd ser., 37, no. 1 (1980): 51.

33. Edwards, *History*, 2:205.

34. Louis B. Wright, *The First Gentlemen of Virginia: Intellectual Qualities of the Early Colonial Ruling Class* (Charlottesville: Dominion Books, 1964), 80; Parent, *Foul Means*, 200.

35. Dunn, *Sugar and Slaves*, 145.

36. Parent, *Foul Means*, 210. On the aristocratic pretensions of the "second generation" of Anglo-Virginians, see Martin H. Quitt, "Immigrant Origins of the Virginia Gentry: A Study of Cultural Transmission and Immigration," *William and Mary Quarterly*, 3rd ser., 45, no. 4 (1988): 629–55.

37. Ruth Bourne, "John Evelyn, the Diarist, and His Cousin Daniel Parke," *Virginia Magazine of History and Biography* 78 (1970): 6.

38. Patricia Bonomi, *The Lord Cornbury Scandal: The Politics of Reputation in British America* (Chapel Hill: University of North Carolina Press, 1998), 186–87.

39. Brendan McConville, *The King's Three Faces: The Rise and Fall of Royal America, 1688–1776* (Chapel Hill: University of North Carolina Press, 2006), 100.

4

....

Revolutionary Refugees

Black Flight in the Age of Revolution

JENNIFER K. SNYDER

As the American Revolution drew to a close, British Loyalists and their slaves fled the newly freed southern colonies to coastal cities. Looking out onto the vast expanse of the Atlantic Ocean, the evacuating population must have felt apprehension facing a journey into an unfamiliar world. Unbeknownst to these revolutionary refugees awaiting ships on the edge of the British Empire, this evacuation would begin a new series of migrations in and around the Atlantic World. One Loyalist, Lieutenant Colonel James Moncrief, the chief engineer for Georgia and South Carolina, migrated his property three times, transporting both free black laborers and his own "considerable estate" of slaves from East Florida into Jamaica and then to the Mosquito Coast.[1] Using Moncrief and his retinue as a focal point, this essay follows the path of a few thousand southern refugees into the British Caribbean, on to the Mosquito Coast, and then traces their dispersal to Honduras and the Bahamas.[2]

This essay considers what these journeys reveal about how those expelled from the southern colonies navigated the perilous waters of the Revolutionary Atlantic World, creating, encountering, and responding to various kinds of freedom and enslavement. A related theme examines the extent to which the lives of white Loyalists and the blacks they conveyed into the Caribbean were intimately intertwined. The relationships between owners and slaves were neither simple nor static, and power dynamics varied across the Atlantic World. Nevertheless, the story of the slaves who accompanied Loyalists out of the colonial South reminds us that celebratory histories of black resistance and agency in the Revolutionary era need to be tempered by an appreciation that white legal, economic, social, and military power, as racialized instruments of exploitation and oppression, remained preeminent features of most black lives.[3]

Perhaps most importantly, this saga of recurring flight and settlement allows us to revisit themes of mobility, transnationalism, and diasporic identities close to the heart of much Atlantic World and Black Atlantic scholarship. In the American Revolution and its aftermath, the vast majority of blacks, especially those in the South, remained enslaved and subject to the movement of their masters, be they Loyalists or revolutionaries. However, refugee slaves belonging to southern Loyalists, unlike the slaves of Patriots, were invariably forced from the North American continent into the British Caribbean. Tracking their travels adds a new, distinctive chapter to the story of "great migrations or *passages*," which, as Ira Berlin and others have emphasized, has been the central motif of the African American experience.[4] Indeed, mobility has been the unifying factor in the lives of Africans and their descendants, in various stages of freedom and enslavement, across the Atlantic World.

In several respects, however, the travels of Moncrief, his slaves, and the nominally free blacks he quickly subsumed within his human estate fit rather uneasily into dominant conceptions of the Atlantic World. For example, their eastern and southern migrations from the American South run counter to the westward thrust of most Atlantic studies. At a most basic level, this reminds us of the sheer volatility and complexity of the Atlantic World and of the fact that Atlantic World models are useful in explaining thousands of atypical transoceanic experiences only to the extent that they can accommodate such counter-narratives and nuances.

These kinds of multidirectional Atlantic World migrations repeatedly transcended the boundaries of nation-states and empires. One attraction of Atlantic World—and of even broader global—approaches is that they can help to identify and explain precisely these kinds of transnational historical processes.[5] Yet, Atlantic World experiences were also profoundly shaped by national, tribal, and imperial political and economic interests, legal jurisdictions, and military conflicts such as those that engulfed continental North America and the Caribbean during the late eighteenth century. Juggling these twin interpretive perspectives can be challenging, and for all its insights and utility, Atlantic history has sometimes struggled to move past traditional national and imperial categories. Certainly, much of the literature on free and enslaved Black Atlantic migrants is still largely conceived in terms of nation-states and other traditional geopolitical and political economic units, such as empires. A pioneering exception here is the work of Maya Jasonoff, which demonstrates how a transnational perspective on the Loyalist diaspora reveals a migration of peoples that simultaneously disrupted and reinforced, transcended and affirmed, the power of the British Empire.[6]

In general, however, sweeping Atlantic World studies have not always generated enough "bandwidth" to focus on the smaller, chaotic, multidirectional, sometimes atypical migrations that occurred throughout the Revolutionary era and doubtless in other eras, too. It is only by close examination of how and why identifiable individuals and groups moved, or were moved, across imperial and state boundaries, while also recognizing that those traditionally understood political configurations still had power to shape their experiences, that historians can truly understand the nature and meaning of mobility in the Atlantic World.

The imperative to explore the Atlantic World mobility and the significance of successive departures and arrivals has been especially marked in Black Atlantic and diasporic studies. Here there are highly politicized discussions around the extent to which early generations of forcibly transported Africans retained their traditional cultures or acculturated to Euro-American host societies that were themselves in flux and being indelibly marked by contact with Africans as well as indigenous populations. Paul E. Lovejoy's concept of a diaspora "requires the recognition of a boundary; those on one side are associated with the homeland, if there is one, and those on the other side are in the diaspora." Thus Lovejoy defines a diasporic cultural group in opposition to "host societies," as these groups tend to define themselves differently.[7] By this definition, however, the diaspora is, according to Christine Chivallon, "certainly the only contemporary concept which manages to be so completely out of sync with the theoretical rudiments of power relations."[8] Distinctions between a diaspora that permanently and successfully rejected the influence of powerful Euro-American forces and those that adjusted to those forces risk oversimplifying a highly intricate relationship between peoples of African descent and their host societies in the Americas.

The scholarly concern to identify and celebrate African retentions in the New World can be similarly distortive. Of course, acknowledging the persistence of African traditions represents a legitimate and necessary corrective to older claims that African culture and sensibilities were wiped out during the Middle Passage, that Africans succumbed readily to enslavement and completely accepted the values of slaveholders, contributing nothing except their forced labor to American and New World development. Yet, this should not obscure the extent to which Africans inevitably and necessarily accommodated themselves to their New World predicament and even came to identify with and adopt certain attitudes and practices of their host societies. Without denying the importance of African retentions, or the ways in which generations of African Americans continued to incorporate real and inherited memories of Africa into their personal and shared histories, the tendency to privilege the idea of a diaspora forever looking backwards to Africa and African traditions can come at the expense of studying how diasporic and various host communities interacted with and endlessly reshaped each other. The point here is to recognize that all Atlantic World migrations, encounters, and settlements eventually played out in a series of compromises and fusions, victories and defeats, as reluctant and willing migrants sought to survive and, as best they could, prosper in the New World. Amid the crisis of the Revolutionary era, James Moncrief's black retinue was engaged in a rapid series of forced and voluntary moves, all the while seeking to make the best of their situation and working, whether by flight or accommodation, to keep families and communities together. In this respect, for all its other idiosyncrasies, the episode offers a particularly dramatic microcosm of a very familiar story of the Black Atlantic.

Attracting American Loyalists and Their Slaves to the Mosquito Coast

The American Revolution expelled thousands of white Loyalists and their willing (if the word is appropriate given the constraints of slave status) and unwilling human chattel from the southern section of the nascent United States. Many settled in Canada and England, but the majority of whites who wanted to retain human property moved into the British Caribbean, hoping to rebuild their personal fortunes on the backs of the slaves they brought with them. Plans for the Loyalist resettlement circulated as different islands attempted to woo the disaffected population. Islands like Jamaica, Bahamas, and, central to this essay, even outposts like the Mosquito Coast issued recruitment plans complete with tax breaks, free land, and governmental assistance. This was a potentially devastating proposition for the transported enslaved population. Blacks were faced with a terrible choice: flee from the British and risk breaking up already tenuous kinship and community networks, or confront the hardships of the voyage and resettlement in the Caribbean.

Robert White, the British agent and mediator for the Mosquito Coast, saw the Loyalist evacuation as a way to expand the British Empire into sparsely populated Spanish territory in Central America. White "presented to both Secretaries of State, a plan for the Mosquito Coast's future population and settlement." Often underrepresented in histories of the Atlantic World, the Mosquito Coast occupied a parlous and consistently shifting position in relation to British and Spanish New World ambitions. Located on the far western side of the Caribbean in present-day Nicaragua and Honduras, the Mosquito Coast stretched down the shore of the Yucatán Peninsula occupying the westernmost edge of the British Empire and the unfortified middle of the Spanish Empire. Although never an official colony, the Coast had long been a small outpost of the British Empire. The few Spanish conquistadores who had ventured into the area a century earlier met fierce native resistance, dense mangroves, swamps, torrential rain, and, of course, mosquitoes.[9] In 1630, John Pym and a few Puritans, tired of the ungodly behavior of their neighbors in Barbados, chartered the Company of Adventurers to lead an expedition to the island of Providence, 140 miles off the Mosquito Coast, claiming more land for the British Empire.[10] Operating under a policy of benign neglect, the coastal region became a haven for adventurers and small-time traders who founded settlements on this unprotected and isolated Central American Caribbean coast.

Olaudah Equiano, arguably the most famous Black Atlantic personality, was among those who helped to settle the Mosquito Coast in the 1770s. His narrative is famous for its portrayal of the horrors of the Middle Passage; his plantation adventure in the Mosquito Coast is less well known but no less compelling.[11] As the first shots of the American Revolution rang out, Equiano was embroiled in a plan to ship Jamaican slaves to the Mosquito Coast to capitalize upon the European demand (and high prices) for exotic woods such as mahogany. Equiano and a few other enterprising British citizens paved the way for the migrants who would flee there from wartorn America a decade later, several hundred of whom were enslaved blacks from the South Carolina region where Equiano sometimes claimed he was born.[12]

In the wake of the American Revolution, Robert White hoped to build the Mosquito Coast outpost into a colony by enticing well-established southern planters. He proposed the "most liberal provision" specifically "for the loyal Americans."[13] White believed that granting land to Loyalists would be beneficial for planters and the empire. By rewarding "loyal Americans," the empire would reinforce Loyalist attachment to the "Parent State; and, in consequence, advance, in the highest degree, its commercial interests and naval power." Rewarded for their loyalty, Loyalists who traveled with their enslaved property would be welcomed into the mosquito-infested coast in the proverbial backyard of the Spanish Empire. This backwater colony was "being erected into a British Government," which would "supply to this nation, in far greater perfection, the loss of whatever was most precious and valuable in all the southern colonies of North America, such as indigo, cotton, rice, tobacco, &c; as well as numberless (many of them hitherto unknown) plants, shrubs, and trees, useful in medicine and for dying of colours."[14] Thus, the Mosquito Coast became a viable destination for Loyalist refugees because it was envisioned as an alternative source for many of the raw materials lost to Britain from the southern colonies as a result of the Revolution. A few thousand Loyalists were wooed by the description of a new "southern colony" in Central America.

Moncrief oversaw the removal of hundreds of runaway slaves, some of whom had previously defected from Patriot owners. During the war he transported "eight hundred negroes in the engineer and ordnance departments to Florida."[15] Claiming he was worried over the "crueltys which would have been inflicted upon them by their former Masters," he was able to send four hundred of these previously enslaved men and women into the West Indies as a protection from angry owners.[16] If Moncrief was, as he claimed, motivated by concern for the well-being of these former bondsmen, it is also true that his intervention proved personally very lucrative. In 1784 he applied to General Campbell, then governor of Jamaica, requesting permission to move these blacks to the Mosquito Coast for the "purpose of cutting mahogany." Campbell approved his application, whereupon Moncrief registered these nominally free blacks as his slaves, increasing his own wealth exponentially. Along with other Loyalists,

Moncrief thus began the process of re-creating the slave society they had fashioned in the colonial American South on the Mosquito Coast. However, just a few short years after their arrival, they would be faced with yet another evacuation.

The political situation in the Mosquito Coast was perilous at best. The British and the Spanish interpreted the 1783 Treaty of Paris, which ended the American Revolutionary War, in vastly different ways. The sixth article of the treaty restricted British subjects "from any other parts [than those expressly given to them by the said article] whether on the Spanish Continent, or in any of the islands."[17] In essence, Spain retained undisputed sovereignty over areas inhabited by Spanish settlers in Central America, including the Mosquito Coast. But the treaty also implied that areas under British control would remain so, thus, in British eyes, keeping the Mosquito Coast "under the domination of his [British] Majesty."[18] The Spanish, however, disagreed.

In September 1785 the British and the Spanish entered into discussions over the Mosquito Coast and Honduras Bay colonies. A key part of the negotiations was the British requirement that "all runaway negroes and others should be returned from the Spanish to the English settlements."[19] Clearly, many nominally free and legally enslaved African Americans, irritated at their forced migration and their treatment by the British, had fled to the backcountry. While there is no record of any concerted Spanish effort to harbor these runaways, it seems likely that enough blacks had previously "disappeared" from British holdings to warrant an official clause stipulating that in the future the Spanish should return any fugitive British slaves.

Reverend Stanford, an evangelical Episcopal chaplain stationed in the Mosquito Coast and later Belize, certainly believed that the Spanish offered blacks incentives to flee the British. Writing back to his archdiocese in England, he explained that blacks in the Mosquito Coast fled to the Spanish because they claimed to treat their slaves much better than did the British. Rumors and tales tempted blacks, who, according to Stanford, were apparently promised that "two days of the week are his own, on which days, he may work for his master at a stated price; and when his tally of those days that he has worked for his Master, returned by him to the office and compared with his Masters plantation Book . . . untill his freedom is accomplished."[20] It was well known on the colonial plantations of Georgia and Florida, where many of the slaves transported to the

Mosquito Coast originally lived, that the Spanish gave special privileges to those who escaped to their jurisdictions in the Floridas. This knowledge, coupled with inconsistent British policies toward slavery in the Americas, encouraged many enslaved to flee to Spanish-controlled areas or to the undeveloped backcountry.

On July 14, 1786, British and Spanish representatives in London signed a convention to prevent "even the Shadow of Misunderstanding which might be occasioned by Doubt, Misconceptions, or other causes of Disputes between the Subjects on the Frontiers of the two Monarchies, especially in distant Countries, as are those in AMERICA."[21] British citizens agreed to evacuate the Mosquito Coast; in return, Spain extended Belizean forestry boundaries, agreed to permit mahogany cutting and fishing, and conceded the right to occupy St. George's Key and other islands to the British. To complicate matters further, the Spanish governor of Guatemala "was instructed to dislodge the Shoremen by force if they did not leave within the treaty's eighteen-month grace period."[22]

The Convention of 1786 prevented British citizens from "raising, by cultivation, the smallest article of produce." The Spanish government interpreted this article so strictly that Captain Don Juan Bautista Gual, a Spanish commissary sent to oversee the British evacuation of the Mosquito Coast in May 1787, ordered plantations of plantain trees and other "excellent vegetables" burned and destroyed "in conformity to the convention and his instructions." In his letters back to Britain, the superintendent of the Mosquito Coast, Colonel Edward Despard, rationalized the captain's actions. Despard claimed that Bautista Gual did not carry out his duty "wantonly, or from malice for he did it with the greatest reluctance, and passed by many plantations that he knew of, which not being in fight he did not consider himself obliged to take notice of, but merely in conformity to the convention and his instructions."[23] Despite Bautista Gaul's "moderation," most British settlers did not view his actions as a conscientious execution of the convention but rather as a blatantly aggressive assault on British property and, therefore, an act of war. Believing that the treaty allowed them to grow enough food for consumption, British colonists began to take matters into their own hands—or in this case their slaves' hands. British settlers "privately furnished their negroes with arms, and in an underhand manner told them to defend their plantations."[24] Arming enslaved blacks only fueled hostilities between the British and Spanish soldiers. Rumors circulated that Bautista Gual would destroy the "little plantations of these people." Feeling angry and attacked, the white inhabitants "made the most threatening declarations, in so open and pub-lick a manner, as to reach through the whole of the Province and particu-larly to myself." On the eve of evacuation, the Mosquito Coast erupted in violence.[25]

The British government once again gave American Loyalists little choice but to abandon their homes and communities, this time leaving the Mosquito Coast for destinations either in Honduras or elsewhere in the British Caribbean. As Moncrief did not actually reside in the Mos-quito Coast himself and would die shortly before the evacuation was com-pleted, he charged a Lieutenant McCerras with the sole task of moving his slaves and his ostensibly free blacks to Jamaica and then "discharg-ing them as he saw fit." McCerras traveled to the Mosquito Coast from where he reported back that it was "governed by no Law." He complained "that the greatest confusion and disorder everywhere prevail'd—All the valuable Negroes taking advantage of the general confusion, deserted and never could be recovered." Moncrief incurred heavy losses during this chaotic time, when 350 enslaved men and women ran off into the countryside. Moncrief's claim, recorded in the British Parliament's *Com-mission of Enquiry into the Losses and Services of the American Loyalists*, describes how McCerras was forced to make three dangerous voyages back and forth between Jamaica and the Coast but was only able to "bring away with him 51 of the Negroes consisting of Women and Young Chil-dren with the exception of 4 or 5 old Men." The 51 recovered blacks were sold in Jamaica for £2,000. Historians have no way of knowing if any of these 51 enslaved blacks had once been free in continental North America prior to the Revolution and evacuation. However, it seems likely that the 350 blacks who fled from Moncrief and evaded McCerras to stay on the Coast did so to improve their lot; they could have carved out a variety of spaces between the moderately more benign slave regime of the Spanish, the precarious freedom afforded by joining with natives, or starting their own independent communities.[26]

Obviously, not all the African Americans who joined the Loyalist exo-dus from the South were able to find even this modicum of freedom. The patchy historical record means that it is sometimes impossible to be de-finitive about the fate of these exiles. Still, the evidence suggests that even many of the southern blacks who had been granted or promised their freedom by Loyalists like Moncrief in return for military service, some of whom migrated willingly from the American South at the conclusion of the war, lost that freedom in the transition. This pattern is also suggested by the case of Robert English, another white British Loyalist exile.

English was the son of an Irish Quaker in Camden, South Carolina, who became a colonel commanding the First Camden Regiment of Loyalist Militia. By 1782 he was banished by the rebel General Assembly for his Loyalist tendencies. The American government confiscated his property. English fled South Carolina and migrated to East Florida with his movable possessions—including twenty-six slaves—and accompanied by nine free blacks. These nine free blacks might have earned their freedom by laboring for English, or they could have been free or enslaved deserters who joined English on his escape down the Georgia coast. English reappeared in the historical record at Black River, Belize, in 1786 with six white persons and "thirty-one Negroes." The document lists slaves but does not mention any free blacks. It is possible that the net gain of five slaves under English's ownership during these four years was the result of births. However, it is more likely that some or all of the free blacks who were traveling with English were subsumed into enslaved families. On November 29, 1804, Robert English requested that he "be granted a portion of his deceased fathers confiscated Estate." James English, his father, died during the Revolution, leaving his estate to be confiscated by the South Carolina government. English's petition was registered nineteen years after he left the American continent. Interestingly, English concurrently requested that he be able to move his property back to the American continent, provided he gain custody of his deceased father's estate and remain "unmolested."[27]

In the migrations of the Revolutionary era, African Americans who had been promised freedom by the British often found themselves returned to a slave system that was deemed particularly harsh and inflexible. It was not surprising, therefore, that so many should eventually try to escape the clutches of slaveholding British Loyalists like English and Moncrief. Yet decisions to run or to stay were never easy. There was always the threat of lethal retribution for fugitives who got caught. Even more important were concerns about breaking the community and familial ties that helped African Americans survive slavery and preserve their humanity. Most African Americans made every effort to remain with friends and, especially, families. It was a sense of priorities that could play out in quite unpredictable ways during the post-Revolutionary migrations when white Loyalists also made efforts to preserve their extended, multiracial families, albeit ones that rested on slavery and the sexual exploitation of black women. As the experiences of Sarah Keeffe within the household of Andrew Cunningham illustrate, African Americans sometimes accepted a place within white-headed families in order to keep kinship networks intact.

Andrew Cunningham was a South Carolinia Loyalist who evacuated from Charleston in mid-December 1782 for East Florida. He brought along with him his wife, two children, and his three black female slaves, including Sarah Keeffe, who was also his mistress. Cunningham took his dependents to Jamaica, where he became an officer in the Duke of Cumberland's Regiment in Kingston, and then to the Mosquito Coast. In 1787 Cunningham petitioned the local magistrate to move his family once more, this time to Honduras Bay. His petition described how his wife had died during childbirth in the Mosquito Coast, leaving Cunningham to raise his children with his black slaves, including Sarah Keeffe, who, it was revealed, had borne Cunningham seven more children.[28] Another child, named after Cunningham's previous wife, Sarah Cunningham, was baptized on September 26, 1807. In 1810, Samuel Cunningham was baptized as the "property of Miss Sarah Kee[f]fe." In the 1816 census Keeffe was even listed as the owner of all Cunningham's property, including twenty-eight slaves. What is striking here is that Keeffe may have been Cunningham's mistress and eventually inherited all his property, yet she is always referred to as a slave, never as a free woman. Although Keeffe probably had more leverage in her relationship with Cunningham than most slaves, she could not extricate herself legally from slavery. Still, she chose to stay with her family and remain a slave rather than escape to freedom like those who fled into the backcountry to avoid relocation from the Mosquito Coast under Moncrief's plan.[29]

Belize

Evacuation of the Mosquito Coast began in March 1787 and was completed smoothly and efficiently under the direction of Superintendent William Pitt Lawrie and his assistant, Captain Marcus Hunter, with the support of men and ships from Jamaica. Lawrie was the last to leave Black River and arrived at Belize aboard HMS *Camelia* on July 7, 1787. Of the 2,650 people evacuated, the vast majority, 537 whites and freedmen and

1,677 slaves, went to Belize. The remainder elected to travel by English warships to Jamaica, Grand Cayman, and Roatan. Lawrie delivered formal possession of the Coast to Spain on August 29, 1787, and the Spanish flag was unfurled at Black River.[30]

Evacuating Mosquito Coast residents found Belize less than inviting. The superintendent of Honduras received instructions from the British government to help and accommodate the large influx of refugees, but infighting within the colony and the land claims of previous inhabitants made this request difficult to grant. Colonel Despard sent reports back explaining the "insurmountable difficulties" of the social situation in the bay. The older settlements were "claimed by one or other of the Baymen; but even the additional territory ceded by the Convention, was every spot of it claimed as the property of some of them." Older settlers, many the descendants of a failed British colony on Providence Island, were unwilling to share land with the new settlers, consisting "chiefly [of] American loyalists" who found their situation crowded and ultimately unbearable. Despard agreed that these "old settlers claimed immense tracts of country, and combined to prevent new settlers, either from the Mosquito Coast, or elsewhere, from having any benefit in the produce and trade of the district, which was this monopolized by a very few individuals, styling themselves the principal inhabitants."[31] As a result, new migrants from the Mosquito Coast moved to the outskirts of towns, technically onto Spanish land.

Despard's "laudable attemps to accommodate the new settlers" might explain the intense hatred toward him expressed by older inhabitants, who were convinced that the newcomers received preferential treatment from the British government.[32] Loyalists Robert English and Samuel Harrison, a native of Lynch Creek, South Carolina, and a member the South Carolina British Rangers, who arrived in Belize having initially been evacuated from Charleston to East Florida with his five slaves, complained to the local British superintendent about "ill treatment of the Mosquito Coast refugees by the older settlers."[33]

While exiled southern white British Loyalists did not always fare well in Belize, such was the diversity of Atlantic World migratory experience that some American blacks, as well as "mixed peoples," benefited from the move. One Belize inhabitant, Alfred Clarke, observed that there were a "great number of People of mixed colour" in the colony.[34] The Treaty of 1786 had forced white Loyalists and their black charges out of their homes on the Mosquito Coast and in the process deprived them "of many Previleges common to His Majesty's other subjects," but in Belize the British government would, upon "application grant such Previliges and Immunities to Persons of this description, as their Conduct and situation in Life intitle them."[35] Consequently, some "free people of mixed color" were bestowed with "priviliges and Immunities as may to them appear proper, according to the Behaviour, Character, property or Station of such Person of colour who may make application to His Majesty's Superintendent and the Committee for such privileges."[36] These privileges included the right to own property and participate in the local government—a very different experience for these particular "persons of colour" than that endured by the majority of people of African descent in the Americas.

James Yarborough's slaves never enjoyed such privileges. Nor did they have a stable life either in the Mosquito Coast or Belize as his relatives fought over them for more than thirty years. In November 1781 a "Major" Yarborough and his party drove cattle off the estate of Eliza Pinckney's son for British army use without compensation. In 1782, Yarborough was banished from America for being a Loyalist and his property was confiscated before he set sail for Jamaica. He managed to recover only part of his enslaved property, later claiming losses of £2,995. He appears to have either moved to the Mosquito Coast and later evacuated to Belize or gone directly to Belize, as he registered at Black River with one white dependent and thirty black slaves. Sarah Yarborough, possibly James Yarborough's second wife or perhaps a mistress, was the guardian of Mary Amelia, the first of James's children. In 1800, after James died, Sarah announced her intention to leave Belize and claim land and property in South Carolina.[37] This was by no means uncommon. For decades after the American Revolution began, American Loyalists and their widows and heirs attempted to claim the land, possessions, and human property that they believed had been wrongfully taken from them in the war or which had been lost in the forced migrations that followed it.[38]

The court records do not indicate if Sarah Yarborough was ever able to secure ownership of the slaves. Nevertheless, it is clear that the evacuation of the Mosquito Coast had generated multiple claims for personal damages, including lost and runaway slaves. One complexity of the Atlantic World was the overlapping legal jurisdictions that Yarborough, Moncrief, and Robert White, the agent for the Mosquito Coast settlers, each tried to negotiate and manipulate to their benefit. White estimated £1,009 in

Jamaican currency for all the lost slaves. While Colonel Moncrief died before the evacuation occurred under Lieutenant McCerras's supervision, his estate claimed a loss of "70 Negroes, more or less, on evacuating the Mosquito Coast" as part of that loss. Lacklan McGillivray, Tomas Clark, John Nicholson, and David Lamb each requested compensation for lost wages, homes, and slaves. Unfortunately, these records do not contain any information about who these slaves were, their location, or the migrations they made.[39] Robert Douglas, attorney to John Davidson and to the estate of James Grant, and formerly of Black River on the Mosquito Coast, placed the most detailed claim. His notice requested compensation for "two slaves who ran away at evacuating that Country in 1787 the one named, Caesar, 60 and the other named Deptford ,40, Jamaica currently making together."[40]

In Belize, many blacks fled to the woods rather than face the prospect of yet another migration into the British Indies, a prospect that loomed large in the summer of 1797 when rumors circulated suggesting that the Spanish intended to attack the remaining British colony. This prompted white slave owners to call an emergency assembly. Rather than risk the potential loss of property, life, or limb, residents voted to abandon Belize. John Nicholson, a militiaman from Georgia who owned thirteen slaves and had moved to the Mosquito Coast after the evacuation of Savannah, was one of those who voted to leave. Once the slave community heard about the potential attack, black men and women began to desert for the local friendly native tribes rather than endure the unpredictability and hardships of life on the sugar plantations of the British Caribbean.

The fact that the British settlement in Belize was so close to both Spanish outposts and friendly native tribes gave its slave system a distinctive dynamic. According to one Belize resident, Lieutenant Colonel Alfred Clarke, British citizens believed that blacks were enslaved in the towns "by choice only."[41] If this was an exaggeration, the British did feel the need to adapt laws and customs because blacks had rather more, if still sorely limited, options than elsewhere in the New World. For example, the Spanish openly encouraged blacks to flee to their settlements, where, by embracing the Roman Catholic religion, they could enjoy many privileges under Spanish law. This tempted many enslaved American blacks "to elope from their owners." Unfortunately, Clarke complained, "many of the settlers of this Country have been entirely ruined from these circumstances, and all experience great and heavy losses" from their slaves fleeing to the Spanish.[42]

Letters back to England explained how the British addressed this situation by adopting more benign practices toward their slaves. On the account of "very great laborer attending this business, more care and attention is paid to their health than in other parts of the West Indies," reported Clarke. By this account blacks were healthy and happy, as they were "better fed and clothed and live more comfortably than the laboring People of any other country whatever."[43] Dependent upon black labor, the British were willing to negotiate, at least indirectly, with the enslaved population. Although they doubtless greatly exaggerated the creature comforts enjoyed by those they kept in bondage, there does appear to have been an effort to partially alleviate their day-to-day situation, knowing that in so doing British slaveholders might prevent a black exodus to the Spanish and personal ruination.

By May 1789, many Loyalists were increasingly frustrated by the worsening situation in Belize, particularly when a mixture of Spanish intervention and "some regulations made by the old inhabitants" prevented them from engaging in logging. Concerned about the "hardship which the poor people here have sustained from the conduct of the old inhabitants," a number of the migrant Loyalists began to request permission to "be removed to some other country, and particularly mentioning the Bahaman Islands."[44] Others even suggested a return to the Mosquito Coast, a prospect that caused considerable alarm in British government circles.

For white Loyalists, the specter of any major transplantation raised the possibility of more slave desertions. Meanwhile, there were great fears among British officials and observers that those who moved back to the Mosquito Coast would soon be subsumed within the Spanish Empire. Alfred Clarke even wanted to send a warship to prevent the possibility of a re-migration to the Coast. Despard, however, thought the British government could placate these Loyalist settlers by providing them with "lands" and "six months provisions." He added that since the Loyalists were relatively wealthy, as they each "possess[ed] from three to thirty slaves each" and are well "fit for the culture of cotton," the government ought to do all it could to retain the loyalty of these productive citizens.[45]

Clarke was also concerned about the prospect of an increased slave population fleeing to the Spanish should Loyalists return to the Mosquito

Coast. He jokingly proposed to the governor of Jamaica, John Dalling, a plan to free any British slaves on the Coast, ship them to the Bahamas, and provide them with six months' provisions—a proposal that betrayed an appreciation that the only way to prevent large-scale desertion was through the offer of freedom, just as it affirmed that any such emancipation was out of the question. Clarke flattered himself that he was "particularly informed of the intentions of the people of colour" but conceded that "in my present situation I know but of one way to prevent it [large-scale desertion], which would be to declare their negroes free, and assure them of lands in the Bahama Islands and six months provisions; but I should not be warranted to give them any such assurance, neither is it a measure which I could in humanity adopt in any case."[46]

Although Clarke could not "in humanity adopt" such a radical measure, his concerns over whether Loyalists would remain loyal to the Crown and whether their slaves could be kept in British hands on the Mosquito Coast encouraged him to urge that migrant Loyalists and their enslaved property should be offered land in the Bahamas. The governor of Jamaica "received an application from the inhabitants . . . on the coast of the Mosquito Coast, which by the late convention with Spain is now to be evacuated, requesting that I will remove them to your government." These refugees were

> chiefly employed in the cultivation of cotton, of which they had favourable accounts from the Bahamas, and if you have room for them, may become valuable settlers; but I do not wish to encourage them to go there with their slaves and effects, until I hear from you that they can be easily accommodated with lands suited to their purposes, and upon what terms. They consist of about three or four hundred persons of *all descriptions and complexions* and they will be supplied from home with provisions for a few months after their arrival.[47]

On February 23, 1787, the governor of Jamaica wrote to the newly established governor of the Bahamas, Lord Dunmore, to discuss the possibility of the islands becoming the latest Caribbean refuge for displaced southern Loyalists and their black charges. Dunmore had his own history with American blacks. By issuing a proclamation in 1775 offering freedom to any blacks enslaved by rebel Americans, Dunmore had earned the nickname the "Great Liberator."[48] After evacuating Virginia during the war, Dunmore had fled to England. Subsequently, he was appointed governor of the Bahamas, where he inherited a problem partly of his own making. Thousands of enslaved blacks, some legally owned and some stolen by Loyalists, had been transported to the islands after the war. A few of them had been promised freedom but were then, in a familiar story, reenslaved at the war's end.

On March 15, 1787, Dunmore concluded that several islands within the Bahamas could be used as a "comfortable asylum." It was "impossible at present to point out a particular situation for them, it would be advisable that three or four of the most intelligent and respectable of those people . . . visit and inspect these islands in order that they may be enabled to fix on a proper spot." On September 11, 1787, the governor and Council of the Bahamas, having received a favorable account of the Island of Andros, commissioned the ship *Commoreo* to convey Loyalists and their slaves to St. Andro. In 1788, Daniel M'Kinnen toured the island, by this time known as San Andreas, possibly because some of the British Loyalists who went there migrated from St. Andreas Island off the Mosquito Coast of Nicaragua, and found "twenty-two white heads of families, and seven planters, with 132 slaves."[49] While not the numbers Clarke promised, 132 enslaved blacks had apparently moved, no doubt with varying degrees of enthusiasm, from the Mosquito Coast to San Andreas. In 1833 they would finally be emancipated under the Slavery Abolition Act.

While James Moncrief never had to deal with the legal ramifications of increasing his property holdings by essentially enslaving once-free blacks amid the legal and migratory flux of the Revolution, Dunmore was forced to deal with many blacks who felt cheated out of their freedom. In 1787, Dunmore judged a court case where "Loyalists had been hijacking free Blacks from America and were selling them to the French at Hispaniola."[50] Among free blacks, anger at this practice turned into violent protest as small groups began to act out, "disturb[ing] the peace in Nassau." Soon discontent spread from the capital into the "Out Islands." Finally gathering behind the courthouse in Nassau, enslaved blacks claiming to have been freed during the American Revolution built a makeshift camp. Fortified by growing numbers, the members of this illegal camp flaunted their newly declared freedom. Blacks also established another small illegal camp near Fort Charlotte as an asylum for runaways where "no white person dares make his appearance . . . but at risk of his life." Lord Dunmore, having arrived in the Bahamas only two days previously, attempted to deal with the problem of this very forthright black bid for freedom by issuing a proclamation bestowing pardons upon any fugitive blacks who surrendered themselves. Those who came forward would have their story heard in court. Dunmore's attempt to reconcile conflicts over property claims for runaway slaves resulted in the reenslavement of twenty-nine of the thirty slaves who appeared before his Negro Court. Despite his earlier emancipationist rhetoric in Virginia and apparent moderation toward fugitive blacks in the Bahamas, Dunmore clearly decided in favor of white slave owners and their property rights, not least his own: the reenslaved blacks were not returned to their former masters but became Dunmore's property, "legally stolen from their loyalist 'owners' only to be enslaved by one of the gouvernour's friends."[51] Just as Moncrief had acquired more human property under the guise of helping displaced and vulnerable blacks, so the contradictory rhetoric and self-serving actions of the "Great Liberator" exposed the fragility of black freedom and the potency of white power in the Revolutionary Atlantic.

Conclusion

Overshadowed in much of the historiography of the Revolutionary era by events in the northeastern theater, what happened in the American South—and in the Caribbean to which it was so intimately and intricately connected—has often been pushed to the very edges of British Empire and American history. By focusing on the experiences of southern Loyalists as they and their slaves abandoned continental North America for a series of other locations in the Americas, this essay refocuses attention on the region's myriad Atlantic connections. Fragmentary though the historical record often is, in the particulars of this story we can see a multidirectional movement of peoples that spanned multiple empires, colonies, islands, and communities within the Atlantic World, revealing the larger imperial, social, legal, economic and political networks in which particular groups and individuals were implicated and ensnared.

Most important, however, the story of the men and women of African descent embroiled in the Loyalist exodus from the South, of their struggles to maintain familial and communal ties and to claim, or reclaim, various kinds of freedom, reminds us of the sheer diversity of Black Atlantic experiences. Indeed, these particular stories raise much broader issues relating to how power, agency, and mobility operated during the

Revolutionary era. Moncrief and other white Loyalists traveled around the Atlantic World searching for personal advancement and economic opportunity. Blacks also moved around the Atlantic, but in very different circumstances. As we have seen, faced with yet another move when the Mosquito Coast was evacuated a few years after their arrival, approximately 350 of Moncrief's enslaved blacks sought refuge in the Spanish backcountry rather than be subjected to another move and possible separation from family and communal ties. In this context, mobility allowed them to exercise a modicum of control over their destinies and personal advancement.

And yet, while "mobility"—forced, voluntary, opportunistic, and planned—seems to connect black and white experiences, the term implies a kind of freedom, a degree of volition and power that does not reflect historical realities: choices to move or not move were made but, especially for blacks, rarely made freely. If mobility, the traversing of traditional boundaries of state and empire, is one of the central themes of Atlantic history, the story of the southern black and white Loyalist migrations after the American Revolution reminds us that Atlantic World mobility worked in many ways and ran in many directions.

Notes

1. James Moncrief American Loyalist Claim, Treasury Records [hereinafter T], The National Archives, Kew, England [hereinafter NA], 1/688/241–42. While these slaves earned freedom by laboring on southern military fortifications, the majority remained on American and Loyalist plantations, choosing familial networks over an uncertain and dangerous promise of freedom. While the historical record is unfortunately silent on the treatment of these nominally free slaves, Moncrief probably considered them his personal holdings, while, at the same time, the enslaved men and women might have acted, and felt, otherwise. Moncrief's decision to remove blacks who were not his property seems unusual for the southern evacuation. However, when considered in the context of how many opportunities American blacks had to flee in the revolutionary chaos, black decisions to keep families together must have been paramount. However, either choice— to flee or to stay—generally concluded with the same outcome. The majority of southern Loyalist blacks remained enslaved and were shipped into the Caribbean.

2. Many historians have made references to the number of migrating enslaved Africans during the American Revolution. See Herbert Aptheker, *The American Revolution, 1763–1783* (New York: International Publishers, 1960); Richard B. Morris, *The American Revolution Reconsidered* (New York: Harper & Row, 1967); Benjamin Quarles, *The Negro in the American Revolution* (Chapel Hill: University of North Carolina Press, 1961);

Sylvia R. Frey, *Water from the Rock: Black Resistance in a Revolutionary Age* (Princeton: Princeton University Press, 1991). For a summary of the debate, see Cassandra Pybus's "Jefferson's Faulty Math: The Question of Slave Defections in the American Revolution," *William and Mary Quarterly*, 3rd ser., 62, no. 2 (2005): 243–64.

3. Recent historical scholarship on northern blacks who escaped to Nova Scotia and later Sierra Leone depicts their difficult experiences. In New York the British recorded the names of three thousand formerly enslaved black Loyalists in the "Book of Negroes" just before they boarded ships for a life of freedom in Nova Scotia. This group, some of whom went on to found the first free black colony in Sierra Leone in 1789, has been studied thoroughly. See Mary Louise Clifford, *From Slavery to Freetown: Black Loyalists after the American Revolution* (Jefferson, N.C.: McFarland, 1999); Sidney Kaplan, *The Black Presence in the Era of the American Revolution 1770–1800* (Washington, D.C.: New York Graphic Society Ltd., 1973); James W. Walker, *The Black Loyalists: The Search for a Promised Land in Nova Scotia and Sierra Leone, 1783–1870* (New York: Africana Publishing Company, 1976); Ellen Gibson Wilson, *The Loyal Blacks* (New York: Capricorn Books, 1976); Carole Watterson Troxler, "The Migration of Carolina and Georgia Loyalists to Nova Scotia and New Brunswick" (Ph.D. diss., University of North Carolina–Chapel Hill, 1974). Simon Schama, *Rough Crossings* (London: Oberon Books, 2007), and Cassandra Pybus, *Epic Journeys of Freedom: Runaway Slaves of the American Revolution and Their Global Quest for Liberty* (Boston: Beacon, 2006), trace the black refugees' flight and resettlement in parts of the British Empire as distant as Botany Bay, Australia.

4. Ira Berlin, *The Making of African America: The Four Great Migrations* (New York: Viking, 2010), 9.

5. Martin W. Lewis and Karen Wigen, *The Myth of Continents: A Critique of Metageography* (Berkeley: University of California Press, 1997).

6. Maya Jasonoff, *Liberty's Exiles: American Loyalists in the Revolutionary World* (New York: Knopf, 2011).

7. Paul E. Lovejoy, "The African Diaspora: Revisionist Interpretations of Ethnicity, Culture and Religion under Slavery," *Studies in the World History of Slavery, Abolition and Emancipation* 2, no. 1 (1997): 3–4; James H. Sweet, "Mistaken Identities? Olaudah Equiano, Domingos Álvares, and the Methodological Challenges of Studying the African Diaspora," *American Historical Review* 114, no. 2 (2009): 279–306; Paul Gilroy, *The Black Atlantic: Modernity and Double Consciousness* (Cambridge: Harvard University Press, 1993); D. B. Chambers, "Ethnicity in the Diaspora: The Slave-Trade and the Creation of African 'Nations' in the Americas," *Slavery and Abolition* 22, no. 3 (2001): 25–31.

8. Christine Chivallon, *Black Diaspora of the Americas: Experiences and Theories out of the Caribbean* (Miami: Ian Randle, 2011). Chivallon points out the perils of homogenizing the diaspora by "by putting under the umbrella of the same concept those who move motivated by expansionist intentions and those who are moved and subjected to the expansionist intentions of others" (188).

9. Captain Nathaniel Uring, who wrote an early description of the area, remarked that "neither Mouth, Nose, Eyes or any part of us was free of" the pesky insect. Olaudah Equiano, *The Interesting Narrative of the Life of Olaudah Equiano, or Gustavus Vassa, the*

African, Written by Himself, 1789, in The Project Gutenberg EBook, http://www.guten-berg.org/ebooks/15399 (accessed Mary 10, 2009). B. Potthast-Jutkeit, "Indians, Blacks and Zambos on the Mosquito Coast, 17th and 18th Century," *América Negra* 6 (1993): 53–65. More than a hundred years later, Equanio ventured into the area and still complained of the swarms of "musquito flies, and they proved troublesome to us." However, this area was not named after the insect but rather the Miskito Indians, who refused to acknowledge nominal Spanish control over the region. The word "mosquito" is apparently of North American origin and dates back to about 1583. See Marston Bates, *The Natural History of Mosquitoes* (New York: Macmillan, 1949).

10. Pym and his fellow Puritans imported Africans to perform difficult plantation labor in their "godly" community. However, the lawless, tropical frontier proved irresistible to rogues, pirates, and prostitutes, and the island became one of the more famous pirate lairs of the Caribbean. The Company of Adventurers opened trade with the Miskitos, leading the way for a small migration to occur from the island to the mainland.

11. Vincent Carretta, *Surprising Narrative: Olaudah Equiano and the Beginnings of Black Autobiography* (Westport, Conn.: Greenwood Press, 1987).

12. Vincent Carretta, "Olaudah Equiano or Gustavus Vassa? New Light on an Eighteenth-Century Question of Identity," *Slavery and Abolition* 20, no. 3 (1999): 96–105.

13. It also included a provision for the distressed Baymen of Honduras, who had been unceremoniously run out of Honduras by the Spanish in 1779. Spain burned down Belize City in a surprise attack in 1779. Robert White, *The case of the agent to the settlers on the coast of Yucatan: and the late settlers on the Mosquito-Coast. Stating the whole of his conduct, in soliciting compensation for the losses, sustained by . . . His Majesty's injured and distressed subjects,* November 18, 1793 (London: printed for T. Cadell, 1793), 70–85. Robert White, *The case of His Majesty's subjects having property in and lately established upon the Mosquito Coast in America: Most humbly submitted t [sic] the King's most excellent Majesty in Council, . . . Parliament, and the nation of Great-Britain at large* (London: printed for T. Cadell, 1789), 135–80. John Alder Burdon, *Archives of British Honduras . . . Being Extracts and Précis from Records, with Maps* (London: Sifton, Praed & Co. Ltd, 1931).

14. White, *The case of the agent,* 76–78.

15. Wilbur H. Siebert, "The Slavery in East Florida, 1776 to 1785," *Florida Historical Society Quarterly* 10, no. 3 (1932): 153.

16. Moncrief, Loyalist Claim, T1/688/241–42.

17. "The Definitive Treaty of Peace 1783," Our Documents, http://www.ourdocuments .gov/doc.php?flash=true&doc=6&page=transcript (accessed April 3, 2008); Thomas Southey, *Chronological History of the West Indies* (London: Longman, Rees, Orme, Brown, and Green, 1827), 550.

18. White, *The case of the agent,* 74.

19. Ibid., 82–83.

20. W. Stanford to Bishop Porteus, Westmorland, July 22, 1788, Fulham Papers, NA, volume 18, 65–70.

21. White, *The case of the agent,* 76–78.

22. Frank Griffith Dawson, "William Pitt's Settlement at Black River on the Mosquito Shore: A Challenge to Spain in Central America, 1732–87," *Hispanic American Historical Review* 63, no. 4 (1983): 677–706.

23. James Bannantine, *Memoirs of Edward Marcus Despard By James Bannantine* (London: printed for J. Ridgway, 1791), 20.

24. Ibid., 20–22.

25. British subjects in the Mosquito Coast were able to secure a seven-month reprieve from their slated relocation to the Bay of Honduras so that arrangements could be made to move the "little plantations at Convention town, where the greatest number of the poor people are settled." These poor people might have included a few free blacks. These evacuations concerned British officials; General Clarke believed that this mass departure would be the first of many until not a single "article of British property will be left in this Country a twelve month hence." Ibid.

26. Moncrief, Loyalist Claim, T1/688/241–43.

27. St. John Robinson, "Southern Loyalists in the Caribbean and Central America," *South Carolina Historical Magazine* 93, nos. 3–4 (1992): 205–20.

28. The Memorial of the Loyalists residing at Black River, November 5, 1786, Mosquito Coast, Colonial Office [hereinafter CO], 137/86, 166–70.

29. Robinson, "Southern Loyalists," 211–13.

30. "Disposal of Mosquito Shore Settlers" (July 1787), CO 123/6, 18–19.

31. Bannantine, *Memoirs of Edward Marcus Despard*, 24.

32. Ibid.

33. Memorial, CO 137/86, 166–70.

34. Alfred Clarke to Lord Lyndsey, May 30, 1790, Jamaica CO 137/88, No. 7.

35. Ibid., No. 7.

36. Ibid., No. 6.

37. Robinson, "Southern Loyalists," 223–24.

38. See Arnett G. Lindsay, "Diplomatic Relations between the United States and Great Britain Bearing on the Return of Negro Slaves," *Journal of Negro History* 4 (1920): 391–419.

39. White, *The case of the agent*, 177. Lacklan McGillivray, of Black River, claimed "Houses, Plantations, Negroes, Craft, and Mahogany" that amounted to £665. Tomas Clark, of Great River, claimed "Houses, Plantations, cattle, Mahogany, and a Negro," for a total of £509. John Nicholson, of Black River, claimed "Mahogany, Craft, Provisions, and Negroes" amounting to £655. David Lamb, of Black River, claimed "Provision grounds and Negroes," totaling £270.

40. White, *The case of the agent*, 178.

41. Alfred Clarke to Lord Lyndsey, May 30, 1790, Jamaica CO 137/88 No. 12.

42. Ibid., 179.

43. Ibid., 180–82.

44. Bay of Honduras, May 26, 1789, CO 137/88, 52. Those few who stayed received special dispensation from the Spanish government as local ambassadors to the natives.

45. Bay of Honduras, May 27, 1789, CO 137/88, 53.

46. Ibid., 47.

47. *Proceedings of the Royal Geographical Society and Monthly Record of Geography* (London: Edward Stanford, 1879–92), 134. Emphasis in original.

48. Benjamin Quarles, "Lord Dunmore as Liberator," *William and Mary Quarterly* 15, no. 4 (1958): 494–507.

49. Daniel M'Kinnen, *A Tour through the British West Indies, In the Years 1802 and 1803* (London: Printed for J. White, 1804), 255. See also R. W. Burchfield and Roger Lass, *The Cambridge History of the English Language: English in Britain and Overseas* (Cambridge: Cambridge University Press, 1994), and, for legends surrounding the settling of San Andreas, see *Washington Daily News*, October 13, 1937.

50. Sandra Riley, *Homeward Bound: A History of the Bahama Islands to 1850 with a Definitive Study of Abaco in the American Loyalist Plantation Period* (Miami: Riley Hall, 2000), 169.

51. Ibid.; Proclamation, CO 23/27, 76–79.

5

The Case of *Jean Baptiste,*
un Créole de Saint-Domingue

Narrating Slavery, Freedom,
and the Haitian Revolution in Baltimore City

MARTHA S. JONES

It was November of 1796 when eight-year-old Jean Baptiste and the other members of the household of the widow Jeanne Drouillard de Volunbrun gathered on the waterfront of Saint-Domingue's western capital, Port-au-Prince. They were preparing to board the brig *Mary and Elizabeth*, a party of persons black, white, enslaved, free, adults but mostly children.[1] Shortly, they would put themselves under the care of a Captain Cook, who was only the most recent of men to command the *Mary and Elizabeth* in what had been a long string of voyages between North America and the Caribbean.[2] Among the members of this small boarding party was Volunbrun, the daughter and wife of planters from Saint-Domingue's western region of Croix-de-Bouquets. The widow Volunbrun had spent the past decade managing the property—in land and people—of her late father and late husband. Her male companion was Marie Alphonse Cléry, also the offspring of a western planter. Cléry had been born in Paris in 1760, migrating to Saint-Domingue with his father, while his mother and sister remained in Paris with many other colonial planter families.[3] Finally, there was the widow's elderly mother, Laurence Bigot.

At the center of this essay are not, however, these white passengers. The focus instead is those individuals termed slaves who were also in the Volunbrun party. They numbered at best count twenty. We know some of them by name: Gentas, Jean Joseph, Tranquille, Sanite, Louis, Jean Nago,

Prudence, Françoise, Solinette, Jean François, Papote, and Jean Baptiste (whose freedom suit many years later in Baltimore is the focus of this essay). During their Atlantic World journey through slavery and law, we come to know them through transactions by which they were variously bought, sold, mortgaged, bequeathed, rented out, transported, and manumitted between the 1780s and the 1840s.

This scene, unremarkable in Revolutionary-era Saint-Domingue, was framed by extraordinary events. The centuries-long rise of European merchant capitalism and the development of the transatlantic slave trade had transformed the western third of the island of Hispaniola into the most profitable sugar-producing colony in the Americas. By 1796, Saint-Domingue had been shaken to its core by the Age of Revolutions.[4] Enlightenment ideas, civil war, and popular unrest all challenged the colony's order, while the imperial forces of France, Spain, and Great Britain wrestled for control. A critical uncertainty attended the journeys of Saint-Domingue's slaveholding households: Who was a slave and who was a free person? The disorder of the revolution extended into the realm of law. Imperial decrees clashed with everyday practice, and it would be left to the courts of Atlantic World port cities to unravel the puzzle.[5]

This essay is set in Baltimore City, where in 1818, more than twenty years after leaving Port-au-Prince, three men in the Volunbrun household—Jean Baptiste, Jean Joseph, and Jean Augustine—asked Maryland's courts to answer what had been an ever present question: Were they slaves or free men? More than fifteen years after the end of the Haitian Revolution, that conflict still shaped the law of slavery in the U.S. South. We are reminded that while Baltimore was certainly the most northern of southern cities, it was also the northernmost port of the Caribbean.[6] Still, at this moment, a new dynamic, that of the South's domestic slave trade, began to shape the household. The widow, like numerous other Upper South slaveholders, sought to profit by selling slaves in the burgeoning markets of New Orleans. Historian Steven Deyle explains how nearly two million slaves, like Jean Baptiste, faced a new form of forced migration in the decades before the Civil War.[7] Baltimore's connection to the slave South was hence reaffirmed.

The story of the widow Volunbrun and her slaves might be told through differing analytic frames: empire, constitution making, antislavery movements, political economy, high court pronouncements, and biography.[8]

In this essay the answers lie in the intimate dynamics of a household and the lived experience of the enslaved people in it. Can we understand what the problem of slavery and freedom looked like for those enslaved people whose life itineraries were shaped by the meta-forces of commercial, political, and military conflict and exchange? Being enslaved in 1796 Port-au-Prince differed from being enslaved in 1801 New York City or 1818 Baltimore. Along this Atlantic itinerary, the Volunbrun slaves confronted new rules, rituals, and structures of power. Straining to adopt their perspective, we see the lived dimensions of slavery and law. We learn how enslaved people quietly navigated a complex matrix of courts, attorneys, and reformers. We will also see how the claims of Saint-Domingue's slaves in Maryland, making their lives at the intersection of the Haitian Revolution and an emerging domestic slave trade, shaped the parameters of southern legal culture.

Slavery and the Saint-Domingue Diaspora

The Haitian Revolution wrought the independence of what had been the most profitable slave colony in the world. The success of Saint-Domingue's revolutionary leaders reverberated throughout the world, a beacon of hope for millions of enslaved Africans and a specter of disaster for those who continued to enslave them.[9] Most of Saint-Domingue's white inhabitants fled the revolution, seeking refuge in Europe and the Americas. Most people of African descent, former slaves and free people of color, remained to forge a new, independent nation out of a slave society. Still, violence and the uncertainty of war caused many thousands of slaves to abandon Saint-Domingue. Some were forced to leave at an owner's insistence. Others, particularly women and children, fled under a complex form of duress, choosing between the hazards of wartime and the dangers of ports unknown. All those once-enslaved people faced the same question: Would they be slaves or free people at their journey's end?

In the early years of the Volunbrun household, before the revolution, this question could be answered through conventional, though ultimately no less oppressive terms. Those whom the widow termed slaves had been purchased or born into her expansive colonial holdings, including plantations in the sugar-producing region of Croix-des-Bouquets and an urban *maison* in Port-au-Prince. French colonial law sanctioned and sustained slavery in Saint-Domingue.[10] However, revolution transformed slavery on the ground. Many men and some women once deemed slaves took leave of slave-owning households, joining one of the island's military factions. Some joined maroon communities. Others leveraged sustained instability into new terms of labor on rural plantations. The years 1793 and 1794 were transformative in a formal sense. Colonial Commissioner Etienne Polverel abolished slavery in Saint-Domingue's Departments of the South and West (including Croix-des-Bouquets and Port-au-Prince) in October 1793.[11] The following year, a decree of the French National Convention proclaimed slavery abolished in all the French colonies, including Saint-Domingue.

Still, there was little consensus about the meaning of France's abolition. Some slaveholders continued to operate as if possessed of absolute authority. Many people, including some held by the widow Volunbrun, were treated as property in Port-au-Prince, bought, sold, mortgaged, bequeathed, rented out, inventoried, and manumitted in private transactions recorded in the folios of the colony's notaries public. Little in the substance of these transactions reflected a sense that the dominion of slaveholders had been undone.[12] At the same time, the tides of imperial decrees shifted. Occupation of much of Saint-Domingue's south and west by British forces brought the declaration that all slaves "freed" by French authorities were, once again, slaves.[13] Thus, neither by the terms of local practice nor those of imperial law-making were questions of slavery and freedom settled. To follow the migrations of Saint-Domingue's refugees is to search for the answer to this puzzle. As refugees settled in U.S. port cities they presented this question and asked local judges to decide.[14]

After leaving Port-au-Prince in 1796, the Volunbrun household lived briefly in the Bahamas and New York City before finally settling in Baltimore. Arriving there in 1802, they set up a house and factory on the east side's Harrison Street. Many of the enslaved people in the household spent their days manufacturing cigars and snuff. Others were hired out, as was the case for Tranquille and Jean Nago, who worked at a local Catholic seminary, St. Mary's, performing domestic chores. In these years, children were born, some died, and the widow took control of another group of enslaved people left in her charge by a fellow refugee who returned to France.[15] By 1803 a city directory identified the widow Volunbrun as a tobacconist, while the 1810 census noted her as head of a household that included fourteen slaves. Slaveholding was apparently typical among tobacco processors in Baltimore, according to historian Stephen Whitman, who deems the widow the city's "richest businesswoman."[16]

Baltimore had long been shaped by Atlantic World encounters. Mid-eighteenth-century ocean vessels had made regular voyages from Fells Point to the Caribbean, carrying tobacco and foodstuffs and returning laden with sugar, coffee, and cotton. In 1793 the Haitian Revolution sent an early wave of some fifteen hundred refugees from Saint-Domingue. Most settled in Fells Point, establishing an enclave of French culture and commerce; opening schools; teaching French, drawing, music, fencing, and a type of shorthand; and operating tobacco factories, a wig shop, and a French library. The refugees generated a great deal of notice as they landed in Charleston, Norfolk, and Baltimore in the South and in New York, Philadelphia, and Boston in the North. White refugees were the objects of special consideration. Their plight was characterized as dire. They had endured, it was said, a siege by armed black people that caused the loss of property and status. Benevolent societies established special funds for their relief, while state legislatures enacted exceptional laws that permitted slaveholders to import their property in persons despite general strictures against such practices.[17] Some of Saint-Domingue's displaced whites migrated to rural locales, reestablishing themselves as plantation owners. Most remained in cities. Slaves were included among them and deemed essential economic components of these new households. Slaveholding refugees used their slaves in their homes or businesses or hired them out to shipyards and the various maritime industries.[18] Yet, very quickly they generated a new set of problems, both for their refugee owners and U.S. authorities. Through freedom suits, but also through riots and running away, the slaves of Saint-Domingue confronted their status anew. State and local courts soon became embroiled in determining the status of these onetime French colonial subjects.[19]

In 1818, Jean Baptiste filed suit in the Baltimore City Court after securing the representation of a local manumission society attorney, Daniel Raymond.[20] Through a trial court record and proceedings in Maryland's high court, the Court of Appeals, we learn something of what precipitated this turn of events.[21] The widow explained that Jean Baptiste and the others had attempted to run away. Their intended destination was Saint-Domingue. In response, the widow intended to send them "to New Orleans as her . . . property[,] subject to her future orders."[22] There never was a full trial of the matter. Instead, the lawyers "stipulated" to a set of facts and submitted the question to the trial court. Then, with little explication, a three-judge panel concluded that nothing in law supported Jean Baptiste's freedom claim. The petition was dismissed.

Raymond immediately sought relief from the Court of Appeals. That court offered a more thorough consideration of two questions of law. The first turned on a state statute. Had the widow violated a general prohibition against bringing slaves into the state for the purposes of future sale or hire? If so, the sanction was the manumission of the slaves in question. Or, was she excused from this general prohibition by an exception in the statute that permitted those merely "traveling or sojourning" to transport slaves through Maryland? The second question turned on the laws governing slavery in Revolutionary-era Saint-Domingue. Were the slaves in question slaves at all, or were they free people when they arrived in New York in 1797? Hadn't they been manumitted pursuant to France's 1794 abolition decree?

Maryland's jurists were not alone in facing these questions. As historian Sue Peabody explains, courts in Maryland, Louisiana, and Tennessee confronted the puzzle of France's abolition. This was not an exclusively southern question, however, as such claims also surfaced in Pennsylvania, also home to a sizable community of refugees.[23] Maryland did, however, craft its own logic in addressing the question. Volunbrun was, the court reasoned, "an alien, without a fixed home," who had never become a citizen of the United States or of Maryland, having consistently indicated her plan to return to Saint-Domingue. Thus, she fell within an exception to the state's general prohibition against bringing slaves into the state. On the second question the court explained that the lawyer for Jean Baptiste had failed to prove France's abolition of slavery. What had been the evidence proffered? Only a history text, Edward Baines's 1817 *History of the Wars of the French Revolution*. Baines's text did report on France's first abolition of slavery, in 1794. However, the court concluded that a history text was not admissible as evidence of an act by a foreign legislature, including the abolition of slavery. The widow's right to "remove" Jean Baptiste and the others to New Orleans, as her slaves, was thereby affirmed.[24]

What might this case tell us about our original questions? Under what circumstances had Jean Baptiste left Saint-Domingue with the widow Volunbrun, and how did he remain a member of her household for more than twenty years? A closer examination from three perspectives—those of judges, historians, and lawyers—reveals something about the forces that shaped this suit and its outcome. Intersecting narratives of slavery, law, and the Haitian Revolution were deployed to explain the lived experience that had generated Jean Baptiste's case. In Maryland, where the push of the Atlantic World collided with the pull of the domestic slave trade, legal culture strained to assert its supremacy over slavery.

Narrating the Haitian Revolution in Baltimore City

The *Baptiste* case was not the first time the Court of Appeals had encountered people said to be slaves from Saint-Domingue, and through their stories it had developed a stock narrative of the Haitian Revolution. The "history" of the Volunbrun household, as set out by the court, was highly abridged and without any particularized sense of its lived history. Rather than demanding evidence of the household and how it came to be in Baltimore, the court substituted its own story, one that explained the Haitian Revolution in simplistic and partisan terms. Horrors had been visited upon white planters by black slaves, causing individuals such as the widow Volunbrun to flee their homes and fortunes to become sojourners in the United States. By 1820 the court had heard many stories of the Haitian Revolution that it slowly molded to its own reasoning. Saint-Domingue's white refugees were depicted always as merely "traveling through, or sojourning in the state," having been "driven from St. Domingo by the enemies of that country" and flying to Maryland "for protection." They were unfortunate Frenchman, unhappy people who had been obliged to abandon their fortunes.[25]

The earliest story of white victimhood was told in a 1799 case in which Pierre Lewis challenged his enslavement by Pierre Boisneuf. Boisneuf emphasized the circumstances under which he was "compelled" to flee Saint-Domingue and take refuge in the United States. The court recounted his tale: In 1793, at the conclusion of a visit to France, Boisneuf judged that travel back to Saint-Domingue was unsafe and headed instead to the United States. Having arrived in Maryland, Boisneuf had remained in the state "ever since." He settled in Georgetown, Montgomery County, where in 1795 he established what became a 748-acre plantation that relied upon the labor of slaves. Pierre Lewis, along with two children, Lambert and Fillette, had been brought to Maryland from Saint-Domingue, at Boisneuf's direction, just a few months later. The court recognized that the state legislature had granted special status to slaveholders from the "French islands," including permitting a single man to import up to three "domestic" slaves. Lewis's claim was that he and the others had never been employed as "domestic or house" slaves and were thus entitled to their freedom. Notably, the court agreed. But it did little to explain who Lewis in fact was if not a marauding Negro.

Alongside narratives of displacement, like Volunbrun other white Saint-Domingue émigrés were said to have maintained their intent to return to the colony. Such was the case of John Levant, who left Saint-Domingue in 1793, bringing with him three slaves, including John Lewis. Twenty-plus years later Lewis filed a freedom petition in 1815. We learn that Levant had sold Lewis to the defendant, David Fulton, just one year after arriving in Maryland. The court found for Lewis, ruling that he was free pursuant to the terms of a state law that prohibited Levant from re-selling him in the state of Maryland. But while holding for John Lewis, the court countenanced Levant's telling of the Haitian Revolution saga, which included "flying from disturbances" on Saint-Domingue only to return to the West Indies three years later.[26]

After having been "driven from their estate . . . by an insurrection of the negroes," the De Fontaine household arrived before the Court of Appeals. During the revolution, Marine, the husband and father, went to Cuba, carrying with him two slaves, while mother and son departed for Baltimore. In 1805, with "the persecution of the French inhabitants in the island of Cuba," Marine returned to Saint-Domingue "in hopes of recovering his former possessions by arms," but before doing so he "shipped the petitioners," his two slaves, to Baltimore. Marine subsequently joined the "French" army and was killed. Learning of her husband's fate, Mrs. De Fontaine departed Baltimore for Saint-Domingue to recover the family's property, where she also perished. Their fates, though subsequent to the years of the revolution, only reinforced the court's view that Saint-Domingue, now Haiti, was a place necessarily to be avoided by whites. With the assistance of Daniel Raymond, in 1818 the slaves in the De Fontaine household filed a freedom suit. Their claim failed, and they were deemed the property of Faustin De Fontaine, his parents' sole heir, who remained in Baltimore.[27]

These cases shaped the court's interpretation. Jurists selected narrative elements it found relevant for understanding the circumstances of Saint-Domingue's refugees, and a distinct story gained traction. It was a view of the Haitian Revolution as a contest between "marauding slaves" and "defenseless whites," a view that elided the complexities of Revolutionary-era factions that were defined variously by status, color, and geography, not to mention the many moments in which alliances shifted. Nor did Maryland's court recognize any part played by Europe's imperial forces. If the court's explication of the Volunbrun household story lacked much that was particular, it was because it began the case with a stock narrative that posited the widow as yet another French unfortunate. Indeed, there is no evidence that the widow ever set out details of the horrors to which she allegedly was subjected. First and foremost, Volunbrun had fled the British forces that occupied Port-au-Prince in 1796, not rebellious slaves. Her claim of forced migration coupled with an enduring intent to return to Saint-Domingue resonated with the court's stock characterization of Maryland's white refugee slaveholders. Like others before her, it was said that the widow fled "servile insurrections" but always maintained her intent to return.

But if whites were victims and Negroes marauders, who were Jean Baptiste and the others who had accompanied the widow out of Port-au-Prince in 1796? On this the court was silent. Even as the claims of enslaved black refugees generated successive cases, never did the court offer an explanation for how the slaves standing before them, if only figuratively, had come to accompany their owners to the United States. Were they also refugees? Perhaps. Jean Baptiste and the others had indicated that they too sought return to Saint-Domingue. But a fuller counternarrative never surfaced, and the stories of men, women, and children like Jean Baptiste were, in large part, erased from the court's stories of Atlantic World slavery and freedom.

Maryland's jurists had some sense that their view of the Haitian Revolution, as it came to them through the stories of white refugees, was limited. They turned to historical accounts of Saint-Domingue to supplement their understandings. Such perspectives were invited into the courthouse as both judges and lawyers referenced the work of historians in their reasoning.[28] But, this use of historical texts was highly selective. To the extent that such texts provided evidence for the "marauding Negroes" view of the revolution, they were appropriated. But historians had more to say, especially about the status of individuals such as Jean Baptiste. The earliest English-language historians all agreed that France had abolished slavery in Saint-Domingue in 1794. By implication, those once held as slaves had become free people. Why then had they left Saint-Domingue in the company of slaveholders?

What were these histories? Written primarily from firsthand accounts of British planters and military officials, they represented one side in a debate between British and French commentators about the capacity of one or the other empire to grapple with the slave trade and slavery itself. British writers appeared to speak in one voice as they used history to demonstrate British superiority. The argument was that slavery had been better managed by England's rational debate than by France's revolutionary upheavals. In the hands of U.S. judges and lawyers, these texts were used quite literally to frame understandings of what happened in Saint-Domingue and the consequences for slaves now residing in the United States. Historical accounts variously made their way into courtroom deliberations. Sometimes, courts could not avoid confronting history texts. Such was the *Baptiste* case; Daniel Raymond unsuccessfully offered a historical text as evidence of slavery's abolition in Saint-Domingue. Other courts welcomed such "evidence," as in a dispute over a promissory note related to the purchase of slaves in Saint-Domingue. In *Conframp v. Bunel*, the U.S. Circuit Court for Pennsylvania took notice of a history text to show that slavery had been in fact abolished in 1794.[29] In Virginia, the state supreme court in 1809 modified its rules of evidence reasoning that circumstances in Saint-Domingue did not permit the proffering of authenticated copies. With respect to its reliance on a history text for insight into the state of legal culture in Saint-Domingue, the court remarked: "the history . . . cannot be doubted."[30] And, as in the *Baptiste* case, some courts refused to consider history texts as anything more than storytelling that could not bear the weight of legal conclusions. Whatever a given court's view, however, what emerges from these cases is a portrait of jurists engrossed in the work of historians.

Two texts were cited most frequently: Bryan Edwards's *An Historical Survey of the French Colony in the Island of St. Domingo*, published in 1797, and Edward Baines's *History of the Wars of the French Revolution*.[31] Baines's *History* was originally published in London in 1817. Baines was a journalist, owner and editor of the *Leeds Mercury*, and an ally to Britain's anti-slave-trade advocates. While principally a history of the French Revolution, Baines's book went to some lengths to foreground legislative considerations of slavery and the slave trade. Here he was sure to provide details of the British case, as if to bring the ineptness of the French into relief. The end of the trade and indeed slavery itself in France was, in Baines's view, the product of political tumult and violent confrontation. England had, in contrast, ended its role in the international trade after a long but highly rational campaign confined in large part to Parliament. Edwards first published *An Historical Survey* in 1797.[32] His text provided graphic depictions of the revolution as a story of massacred whites and marauding Negroes. Edwards was a Jamaican planter and politician who was among the first British contingents to arrive in Cap-Français on Saint-Domingue's northern coast after early uprisings. His text was intended, in part, to support the continuation of the international slave trade. It was also a cautionary tale, to "serve as an impressive lesson to other nations!"[33]

Both texts were widely available in the United States, while their circulation appears to have loosely paralleled the settlement of Saint-Domingue's refugees in port cities. By 1818, Baines's text was advertised in major U.S. cities, including New York, Philadelphia, New Orleans, and Baltimore.[34] Newspaper editors relied upon Baines for their reportage on subjects related to the French Revolution.[35] Like that of Baines, Edwards's text was widely available in U.S. cities and was relied upon by newspaper editors as a source on the Haitian Revolution.[36] However, in tone the two texts could not have been more distinct. Baines did not endorse an interpretation of the Haitian Revolution that included "massacred" whites and "marauding" Negroes. Instead, he suggested that the colony's revolutionary upheavals were a reasoned outgrowth of unreasonable injustice, with all the massacre and marauding of the Revolutionary era perpetrated by the French, who victimized the colony's black inhabitants. In Edwards's history, jurists found ample support for the massacre and marauding view of Saint-Domingue. The revolution had descended upon the colony's "peaceful and unsuspicious planters" who were met with the "fierce and unbridled passions of savage man . . . uncontrolled." Edwards did not spare his reader any details as he described arson, torture, beheadings, and the rape and murder of women and children. Saint-Domingue's "enslaved negroes" had been subjected to rule by white planters that was "lenient and indulgent as was consistent with their own safety." It was the colony's "mulattoes" who had long meted out harsh treatment to slaves, a circumstance that resulted from their resentment of the maltreatment to which they were subjected by whites. The ineptitude of French republican leaders coupled with the ambition and cunning of free men of color was what had led to the downfall of France's most valuable colonial enterprise.

Baines and Edwards agreed on this one point of fact: France had abolished slavery in 1794. Baines examined this moment in some detail, explaining how the French national convention had acted in February 1794 to decree "the entire abolition of slavery within the dominions of France." His depiction of this scene was replete with details of legislative maneuverings and popular reactions, including that of "a female negro, who attended the sitting, [and] fainted with joy at the passing of the decree."[37] The French had, indeed, abolished slavery in 1794, according to Edwards, but the result was to invite further mayhem and wholly undermine colonial order. Courts may have disagreed about whether or not to deem such texts evidence, but they unanimously embraced Edwards's characterization of events in Saint-Domingue and then incorporated that highly selective view into their own decision making. Law and history worked in tandem to construct a narrative of the Haitian Revolution that had powerful consequences for the freedom suits heard in U.S. courts.

Both Baines and Edwards provided important contexts for understanding the puzzle that confronted the *Baptiste* court. There was indeed something to the claim that Jean Baptiste and the others held in the Volunbrun household had been free people, rather than slaves, when they left Saint-Domingue. But beyond this fact, they offered little additional insights into Jean Baptiste or slaves like him. If he had been by virtue of French law free since 1794, what had led Jean Baptiste to accompany the widow to New York and then Baltimore as a slave? Why would he wait until 1818 to ask a court to affirm his liberty? On this point the historians too were silent.

In the *Baptiste* case it was lawyer Daniel Raymond who attempted to put historical evidence before the court. Perhaps no one was better situated to speak to the matter of Jean Baptiste's story than his own lawyer. An agent for the Protection Society of Maryland, a local manumission society, Raymond remained counsel to the slaves in this case for more than two years, from the filing of the petition through the deliberations at the Court of Appeals.[38] He, more so than the judges and certainly the historians, had an opportunity to hear the stories of Jean Baptiste and his fellow slaves. Indeed, he had heard many such stories. The Protection Society had at least three manumission suits pending before the Court of Appeals in 1820, the product of two years' work challenging the illegal slave trade in Baltimore.[39] The society's most sought-after targets were those it deemed kidnappers—individuals who were seizing both free black people and slaves for the purpose of selling them into lucrative markets elsewhere in the South. Early on, the society had encountered some local criticism prompting its leaders to clarify that their aim was not to abolish slavery. In this spirit, the society advertised its services, so to speak, to free black people, slaves, and slaveholders alike, assuring the latter that the society was committed to securing their property in persons from pliers of the extralegal trade.[40]

Raymond's arguments reflected one foremost objective, the punishment of the widow Volunbrun. He decried her as a "West India planter" who came to Baltimore, not out of necessity, but out of an interest in avoiding the laws of New York, which threatened to work against her. Over sixteen years she had become a resident of Baltimore, with only "some distant and uncertain hope of leaving the state at some future period." The objective from the start of her travels, Raymond argued, had been, not to secure her person (from marauding Negroes) or her health (from New York's climate), but to secure her property and maximize its profitability. This explained, for Raymond, how it was that the widow decided to "remove" Jean Baptiste and the others from Baltimore. Raymond's crowning bit of evidence for this view was a twist that arose between the case's two court rulings. The widow Volunbrun refused to defer to the court's jurisdiction. Instead, she followed through with her plan to send the young men in question to New Orleans. The widow had evidenced "high-handed contempt" for the "justice of the state," Raymond urged.[41] But Jean Baptiste and the other young men in question had already disappeared. Raymond went to great lengths to explain the character and motives of the widow, but he never explained his own client's. About them, Raymond had little else to say. If he had been a free person in 1794, as Raymond argued, why had Jean Baptiste traveled with the widow and delayed in bringing his suit? On this question Raymond was silent like the judges and historians.

Judges and lawyers engaged one another over questions of law, history, and the meanings of the Haitian Revolution. They drew historians into their deliberations, reading some of the earliest accounts of events in Saint-Domingue and in France to help clarify their understandings of slavery and law in the Atlantic World. Their points of view contextualize the difficult-to-discern story of Jean Baptiste and his freedom suit. A few insights emerge. The first is about the juridical climate that greeted slaves in U.S. courts. Saint-Domingue's slaves encountered jurists who believed they knew events in Saint-Domingue all too well to require a deeply particularized inquiry.[42] We see how U.S. legal culture was also part of an Atlantic World circuit. The nature of Jean Baptiste's journeys required judges and lawyers to frame their deliberations in terms that extended in time, space, and jurisdiction to colonial Saint-Domingue. These same deliberations drew U.S. legal culture into the Atlantic World's intellectual currents. As they resolved this freedom suit and others like it, jurists and lawyers synthesized the English-language histories of the Haitian Revolution. Those histories had themselves been shaped by broad debates over the future of the slave trade and slavery itself. Through the selective incorporation of such texts, jurists and attorneys alike extended such histories through their own narratives.

Looking for Jean Baptiste

One other context, the life experience of Jean Baptiste, offers a final way to approach this freedom suit. Setting this critical moment in 1818 in a life history opens a new window on an enslaved petitioner's point of view. We can understand how he learned to use law as a tool by which to negotiate daily life. We also learn how the power of family ties, the risks of challenging a slaveholder, and the balancing of law against other strategies for autonomy may all have shaped the freedom suits of enslaved people. Ultimately we understand something about how it was that young Jean Baptiste boarded the *Mary and Elizabeth* in 1796, in a sense reenslaving himself, and then why he waited some twenty years to bring his freedom suit. To understand what happened to Jean Baptiste in Baltimore, it is necessary to begin again in Port-au-Prince.

Examining that scene at the Port-au-Prince waterfront that opens this essay suggests how family may explain Jean Baptiste's choices. Formally he appeared to be a member of a slaveholding household. Such ties, constructed of blood, bondage, coercion, and compassion, stitched together Volunbrun and her party by threads of law, custom, kinship, and dependence.[43] There was also duress. Many enslaved people, particularly women and children, stood in the colony's ports choosing between the upheaval of revolution, the clashing of empires, and the uncertainty of the sea and foreign ports. For Jean Baptiste, there was also family. Boarding the *Mary and Elizabeth* kept Jean Baptiste close to his family. Alongside him on the dock were four siblings: sisters Françoise, Solinette, and Papote and brother Jean François, all the children of Felicité, also a slave of the widow (who did not, it appears, leave with the household from Saint-Domingue). These kinship ties help us see how Jean Baptiste may have "chosen" this journey rather than the freedom he might have claimed in Saint-Domingue. And these same ties suggest how he came to remain in the widow's household as long as he did. Until he was wrenched away in 1819 when the widow sent him to New Orleans, Jean Baptiste continued to make his home with his sisters Solinette and Papote and their children (though the whereabouts of Françoise and Jean François by that time we do not know).[44]

As a boy Jean Baptiste had also learned potent lessons about freedom suits, lessons that read much like a cautionary tale. Seventeen years earlier, in 1801, the widow's slaves brought a first legal challenge to their captivity. Volunbrun had decided to "remove" all of them, including young Jean Baptiste, from their home in New York City to Norfolk, Virginia. The rumor was that Volunbrun intended to sell them there. The local manumission society instituted a freedom suit based in state laws against such "slave trading" through New York and in France's 1794 abolition of slavery. The local free black community manifested its skepticism about both the widow's intentions and the capacity of the manumission society and the courts to thwart her. On an August morning approximately twenty "French Negroes" with clubs gathered near Volunbrun's home, threatening "to burn the house, murder all the white people in it and take away a number of black slaves." That night hundreds of others, who appeared "ready to commit the worst of crimes," joined them.[45] As the crowd closed in on the house, they managed to destroy only a little of Volunbrun's property, and when they resisted a fight with the night watch ensued. Many escaped during the battle, but officials arrested twenty-three black men, who were then tried, convicted of riot, and sentenced to sixty days in jail.[46] Whites, even those active in the manumission society, were distressed. Its leadership denounced the riot, and one member confessed that, although he believed that all men, black or white, had to be protected by the law, he feared that the release of these slaves would contribute to the city's disorder. Perhaps for this reason, the manumission society dropped the case, and Volunbrun once again took custody of her slaves.[47]

The lessons for Jean Baptiste were indeed potent. Freedom suits were risky propositions. They might lead to liberation. Or, they might lead to violence. This early freedom suit had generated unrest just outside his home on the city streets. It had also provoked violence in the household. As told in ledgers of the manumission society, the widow retaliated against her slaves by way of physical abuse in the days surrounding the freedom suit. Finally, white allies appeared less than reliable. Manumission society activists might go to great lengths to rescue slaves and bring freedom suits, but such support could be suddenly withdrawn, leaving slaves all the more vulnerable to an owner's retribution. Living in Baltimore and still a slave, Jean Baptiste knew both the potential and the dangers of freedom suits. He avoided the risk until it was necessary and, as it turned out, too late.

In the intervening sixteen years, Jean Baptiste learned the meaning of what historians have termed quasi-freedom. For many enslaved people in Upper South cities, autonomy meant hiring out one's labor, earning wages, marrying, learning a trade, joining religious communities, and perhaps owning modest property. We know little more about Jean Baptiste's years in Baltimore beyond the fact of his work as a cigar and snuff producer for the widow. But the glimpses we have of other slaves in the household suggest that Jean Baptiste may have lived pursuant to an awkward equation in which enslavement was not very far from freedom. His examples included Tranquille and Jean Nago, who were hired out to a local Catholic seminary, St. Mary's.[48] There was Basil, a barber who had married and purchased his own home.[49] There were the many among the widow's slaves who were active members of Catholic confraternities. For years they stood alongside one another at baptismal fonts and cemetery plots, charting out life's meanings all beyond the scrutiny of the widow Volunbrun.[50] Their collective demeanor was so remarkable that the widow, in 1815, placed an ad in a local paper:

As to my servants, that I have brought with me to this country, and those entrusted to my care, assume the appearance and conduct of free people, although they are slaves—that they make civil and religious contracts without my knowledge and authority—that they rent houses in spite of the laws and without my knowledge—Now therefore the public are cautioned against all deception from said slaves calling themselves free, and acting as such. I declare I will not be responsible for their contracts, but that I will prosecute with the utmost rigor of the law, any person who shall enter into any agreement with them contrary to the laws of my interests.[51]

The lessons for Jean Baptiste were surely multi-fold. In part, life in Baltimore allowed for qualified autonomy over the rhythms and associations of daily life. Weighed against the uncertainties that a freedom suit might generate, he remained with two of his siblings, their children, and the others with whom he had journeyed from Saint-Domingue—that is, until he and others were threatened with wholesale separation from the household. Then he took up the tool that was law.

Slavery, Law, and the Atlantic World

This chapter of Jean Baptiste's story ends with cruel abruptness. He and three others of Volunbrun's slaves were kidnapped from Baltimore, snatched from their loved ones, their community, and the jurisdiction of a court that ultimately sanctioned such lawless violence. Months later they surfaced in the slave markets of New Orleans in the charge of the widow's agent. In the months that followed, Jean Baptiste confronted the brutal commodification that characterized a world governed by the chattel principle. Here, finally, is evidence of slavery's ever present and cruelest logic. Even those like Jean Baptiste who had sustained lives of family ties and quasi freedom across decades were in a sense slated to be drawn into slavery's darkest and most dire circumstances because their bodies carried a price. By virtue of his own threat to run away, the widow's financial needs, and certainly by the appetites of the domestic slave trade, Jean Baptiste lost his past for slavery's future.[52]

In New Orleans, Jean Baptiste was sold three times in the span of just eight months. Through these transactions we catch sight of his transformation from an individual enslaved man to a person with a price. Clues lie in the words used to describe him. Consider the long phrase employed in the context of his first sale in June 1819. From the widow Volunbrun to Pierre Paul Rossignol Grammont: "a slave with the name of Jean Baptiste black, aged approximately forty eight years, Creole from St. Domingue, who belongs to the said lady Widow Volunbrun who was in possession of him in St. Domingue, as the dependent of one of her plantations in St. Domingue, and whom she sent from Baltimore into this state."[53] Here, Jean Baptiste is a person, with a color, an age, an origin, and a narrative history, albeit a brief one. His description in the note of the second sale, between Rossignol and Clément Moreau in September 1819: "a Negro named Jean Baptiste, aged approximately forty-eight years, Creole from St. Domingue, slave for life, who belongs to the Sir Seller for having acquired him from M. William Papillon, who was charged with the powers of Mme. Veuve de Volunbrun, of Baltimore."[54] Here, just months later, the historical narrative that explained Jean Baptiste's Atlantic migrations had been dropped. Finally, yet a third sale, between Moreau and the widow Caterine Marie Lebeau Guerin in February 1820: "a Negro named Jean Baptiste."[55] He has become a color and a double Christian name, but no more. Gone are signs of origins or identity such as "Creole" or "of Saint-Domingue." Also gone are references to a life history. This Jean Baptiste has no ties to place or to people, not even to his former owners.

No study of this type offers sweeping insights into slavery and law in the Atlantic World. It is instead an intimate exploration of the dynamics of slavery and law with the perspectives of enslaved people as its center. Broad historical forces such as the Atlantic World slavery, the Haitian Revolution, and the domestic slave trade, while they frame the life of Jean Baptiste, cannot fully explain it. Tracing his itinerary, we begin to see slavery and law from the perspective of the enslaved. Jean Baptiste and others like him rarely produced the sorts of artifacts we encounter in archives. Most often they are analyzed as part of a whole, as a demographic, and through composites that cannot grapple with the vagaries of life history. To construct the lives of slaves is to work with the small shards left to us in documents that were most often intended to deny their very personhood. It is to assemble signs of experience and action with the aim of bringing subjectivity to light. In Saint-Domingue's diaspora, only white refugees exercised the privilege of recording their experiences and actions, along with their insights and feeling.

The title of this essay is borrowed from that of an early-nineteenth-century memoir, *My Odyssey: Experiences of a Young Refugee from Two Revolutions, by a Creole of Saint Domingue.*[56] The author was a white Frenchman whose name is lost to us. This young man penned the details of his own Atlantic World journeys from Paris to Saint-Domingue,

Philadelphia, and Baltimore. He wrote in the first person of matters both mundane and grave, using a tone that is both intimate and epic. Most often it is this sort of artifact that we necessarily read against the grain to then tell the story of men and women like Jean Baptiste. This essay is, in part, a counternarrative, one that claims that same sort of particularity for the slaves in the Volunbrun household, a particularity that heretofore has been reserved to Saint-Domingue's white refugees. It is a story of Jean Baptiste, his matters mundane and grave, intimate and epic, and through his story we learn the lived dimension of slavery and law in the Atlantic World.

Notes

1. J[ean]ne Mathurine Drouillard [veuve de Volunbrun], "Declaration de Jne Mathurine Drouillard et de Le Bigot," Archives Coloniales/St. Domingue/Refugees/Actes, Declarations & Depots divers/Consulats New York An II-An III/Norfolk 1792–94, Consulat de France a New York Declarations de differens habitants de St. Domingue Siles en cette Chancellerie, 5MI/1437, 22–25, Centre d'accueil et de recherche des Archives nationales, Archives de France, Paris, France.

2. *American Minerva*, May 3, 1794 (*Mary and Elizabeth* arrives from Jamaica); *Daily Advertiser*, May 5, 1795 (*Mary and Elizabeth* arrives from Curaçao); *Pennsylvania Gazette*, October 21, 1795 (*Mary and Elizabeth* arrives in Philadelphia from Curaçao); *Norwich Packet*, November 5, 1795 (*Mary and Elizabeth* arrives from Curaçao); *Federal Gazette*, February 2, 1796 (*Mary and Elizabeth* arrived in St. Kitts from Philadelphia); *Philadelphia Gazette*, March 8, 1796 (*Mary and Elizabeth* arrives in Philadelphia from Curaçao); *Finlay's American Naval and Commercial Register*, April 8, 1796 (*Mary and Elizabeth*, from St. Domingo cleared in Philadelphia); *Philadelphia Gazette and Universal Daily Advertiser*, June 18, 1796 (*Mary and Elizabeth* arrives in Philadelphia from Jeremie [Saint-Domingue]); *Federal Gazette and Baltimore Daily Advertiser*, September 9 and September 23, 1796 (*Mary and Elizabeth* arrived at Cap Nichola Mole [Saint-Domingue]); *Philadelphia Gazette and Universal Daily Advertiser*, November 18, 1796 (*Mary and Elizabeth*, traveling from Port-au-Prince, Saint-Domingue, reported "lost" off the Bahamas) (also reported in *Gazette of the United States*, November 18, 1796).

3. Marie Alphonse Cléry, "Testament," December 12, 1830, *Glenn v. Belt*, Court of Appeals, Maryland State Archives, Annapolis, Maryland [hereafter MSA].

4. For a view of the U.S., French, and Haitian revolutions as an Atlantic revolution, see Laurent Dubois, "An Atlantic Revolution," *French Historical Studies* 32, no. 4 (2009): 655–62.

5. Note that throughout this essay I often use the term "slave," though such use is always qualified. It is precisely the problem of who was a slave in law and in practice and how those definitions shifted in the Atlantic World that lies at the center of my inquiry.

6. *Baptiste, et al. v. de Volunbrun*, 5 H. & J. 86 (Court of Appeals of Maryland, 1820). I would like to thank my colleague Julius Scott for the apt characterization of Baltimore in the late eighteenth and early nineteenth centuries.

7. Steven Deyle, *Carry Me Back: The Domestic Slave Trade in American Life* (New York: Oxford University Press, 2006).

8. The force of Atlantic World revolutions has been explained through various registers of inquiry. See, for example, John H. Elliott, *Empires of the Atlantic World: Britain and Spain in America, 1492–1830* (New Haven: Yale University Press, 2007); Mary Sarah Bilder, *The Transatlantic Constitution: Colonial Legal Culture and the Empire* (Cambridge: Harvard University Press, 2004); Daniel J. Hulsebosch, *Constituting Empire: New York and the Transformation of Constitutionalism in the Atlantic World, 1664–1830* (Chapel Hill: University of North Carolina Press, 2005); Christopher L. Brown, *Moral Capital: Foundations of British Abolitionism* (Chapel Hill: University of North Carolina Press, 2006); Ira Berlin, *Generations of Captivity: A History of African-American Slaves* (Cambridge: Harvard University Press, 2003); and Arthur Jones, *Pierre Toussaint: A Biography* (New York: Doubleday, 2003).

9. Laurent Dubois, *Avengers of the New World: The Story of the Haitian Revolution* (Cambridge: Harvard University Press, 2004); Carolyn E. Frick, *The Making of Haiti: The Saint Domingue Revolution from Below* (Knoxville: University of Tennessee Press, 1990).

10. The French *Code Noir* of 1685 regulated slavery in the colonial empire. Alan Watson, "The Origins of the Code Noir Revisited," *Tulane Law Review* 71 (March 1997): 1041–57; Carolyn Fick, "Dilemmas of Emancipation: From Saint-Domingue Insurrection of 1791 to the Emerging Haitian State," *History Workshop Journal* 46 (1998): 1–15 and Carolyn E. Fick, "The Haitian Revolution and the Limits of Freedom: Defining Citizenship in the Revolutionary Era," *Social History* 32, no. 4 (2007): 394–414.

11. Robert L. Stein, *Léger Félicité Sonthonax: The Lost Sentinel of the Republic* (London: Associated University Press, 1985), 78–95; Dubois, *Avengers of the New World*, 154–68. Slaves in the colony's North had been freed the previous spring by the proclamation of Commissioner Léger Félicité Sonthonax.

12. Based upon a review of the folios and notarial acts contained therein of French colonial notaries public Monnerons, Cottin, Molliet, Hacquet, Fissoux, Vausselin, Thomin, Barrault in Port-au-Prince and Croix-des-Bouquets for the years 1793 to 1797. Le Centre des Archives d'Outre-Mer, Archives Nationales de France, Aix-en-Provence, France.

13. Dubois, *Avengers of the New World*, 168–70.

14. Sue Peabody, "'Free Upon Higher Ground': Saint-Domingue Slaves' Suits for Freedom in U.S. Courts, 1792–1830," in *The World of the Haitian Revolution*, ed. David P. Geggus and Norman Fiering (Bloomington: Indiana University Press, 2009), 261–83.

15. Volunbrun explains this arrangement with "a certain Mr. Bourget" to the City Court in "Negro Basil, Vs. Mad. Jeane De Volunbrun," *Baltimore Patriot*, June 20, 1822.

16. United States Census, City of Baltimore, State of Maryland, 1810; T. Stephen Whitman, *The Price of Freedom: Slavery and Freedom in Baltimore and Early National Maryland* (New York: Routledge, 1999), 23. Whitman further notes that 80 percent of Volunbrun's assessed wealth lay in the ten men, nine women, and three children she owned.

Her city tax assessment for 1813 listed twenty-two slaves with a value of $2,172. Her only other assets were listed as furniture valued at $10 and plate valued at $42. These figures for 1813 estimate those she held as slaves to be nearly 97 percent of Volunbrun's taxable assets. Assessment Record, Commissioners of the Tax, Baltimore City Wards 5–6, Baltimore County, Maryland, MSA.

17. In Maryland such an exception was enacted in 1792 by way of "An ACT respecting the slaves of certain French subjects," which provided in pertinent part "that slaves imported, or to be imported, by French subjects, who have removed, or might remove, from any of the French islands into this state, since the derangements in the French government, should remain the property of their masters; but not so as to affect any right such slaves might have acquired to freedom." *Baptiste v. de Volunbrun*, 7–8, citing Laws of Maryland, Act 1792, chapter 56 (enacted December 23, 1792). This legislation was repealed in late 1797 by way of "An ACT to repeal an act, entitled, An act respecting the slaves of certain French subjects." Act 1797, chapter 75. William Kitty, *The Laws of Maryland* (Annapolis: Frederick Green, 1799–1800). On the reception of Saint-Domingue's refugees in the United States, see Ashli White, *Encountering Revolution: Haiti and the Making of the Early Republic* (Baltimore: Johns Hopkins University Press, 2010).

18. Christopher Phillips, *Freedom's Port: The African American Community of Baltimore, 1790–1860* (Urbana: University of Illinois Press, 1997), 11; Paul G. E. Clemens, *The Atlantic Economy and Colonial Maryland's Eastern Shore: From Tobacco to Grain* (Ithaca, N.Y.: Cornell University Press, 1980); Glenn O. Phillips, "Maryland and the Caribbean, 1634–1984: Some Highlights," *Maryland Historical Magazine* 83 (1988): 199–214; Walter C. Hartridge, "The Refugees from the Island of St. Domingo in Maryland," *Maryland Historical Magazine* 96 (2001): 475–89; Phillips, *Freedom's Port*, 32–33. Julius S. Scott reminds us that not all such encounters, even for black Baltimoreans, took place in North America as illustrated by the case of Newport Bowers, who left Maryland for Saint-Domingue in 1793. Scott, "Afro-American Sailors and the International Communication Network: The Case of Newport Bowers," in *Jack Tar in History: Essays in the History of Maritime Life and Labour*, ed. Colin Howell and Richard Twomey (Fredericton: Acadiensis Press, 1991), 37–52.

19. On enslaved refugees in the United States, see Alfred N. Hunt, *Haiti's Influence on Antebellum America: Slumbering Volcano in the Caribbean* (Baton Rouge: Louisiana State University Press, 1988); White, *Encountering Revolution*; Gary B. Nash, "Reverberations of Haiti in the American North: Black Saint Dominguans in Philadelphia," *Pennsylvania History* 65 (Supplement) (1998): 44–73; Nathalie Dessens, *From Saint-Domingue to New Orleans: Migration and Influences* (Gainesville: University Press of Florida, 2007); and John Davies, "Saint-Dominguan Refugees of African Descent and the Forging of Ethnic Identity in Early National Philadelphia," *Pennsylvania Magazine of History and Biography* 134, no. 2 (2010): 109–26.

20. Raymond was president of the Maryland Abolition Society and would later run a strong campaign in 1825 for election to city council on a platform based solely on antislavery. Phillips, *Freedom's Port*, 188. He is best remembered as an early American political economist. Donald E. Frey, "The Puritan Roots of Daniel Raymond's Economics,"

History of Political Economy 32, no. 3 (2000): 607–29. Raymond's pamphlet "against slavery" was advertised for sale in Baltimore in these years. *Baltimore Patriot*, December 13, 1819.

21. *Baptiste, et al. v. de Volunbrun*, 5 H. & J. 86 (Court of Appeals of Maryland, 1820).

22. The record is unclear as to how many of her slaves Volunbrun proposed to "remove" to Louisiana. The Court of Appeals decision indicates the number was five, but the power of attorney that authorized the sale of Volunbrun's sales notes only four, while the case records note only three named plaintiffs. "Transcript," *John Baptiste, et al. v. J. M. de Volunbrun*, Baltimore City Court, filed December 5, 1818, MSA.

23. Peabody, "'Free Upon Higher Ground,'" 261–83.

24. Subsequent courts as well as treatises cited the *Baptiste* case as authoritative on questions related establishing a party's domicile. *Bowling v. Turner*, 78 Md. 595, 28 A. 1100 (1894); *Ringgold v. Barley*, 5 Md. 186 (1853); *Houston v. Texas Central Railway*, 70 Tex 51; *State ex rel. Phelps v. Jackson*, 64 A. 657; *Haney v. Marshall*, 9 Md. 194 (1856); *Siemer's Adm'r v. Siemer*, 2 G. & J. 100 (1829); *Londerry v. Andover*, 28 Vt. 416 (1856). See also Melville M. Bigelow, *Commentaries on the Conflict of Law, Foreign and Domestic: In Regard to Contracts, Rights, and Remedies*, 8th ed. (Boston: Little, Brown, 1883). The case is also associated with considerations of the standard of evidence for the admission of the acts of foreign legislatures. *Cappeau's Bail v. Middleton & Baker*, 1 H. & G. 154 (1827).

25. *Ringgold v. Barley*, 5 Md. 186 (Court of Appeals of Maryland, 1853), and *De Kerlegand v. Hector*, 3H. and McH. 185 (Court of Appeals of Maryland, 1794).

26. *Fulton v. Lewis*, 3 H. & J. 564 (Court of Appeals of Maryland, 1815. The court holds for John Lewis, who was sold as a slave when his owner, John Levant, decided to return permanently to Saint-Domingue.

27. The De Fontaine case was never published, but its details were reported by the court in the *Baptiste* case decision. *Baptiste, et al. v. de Volunbrun*, 5 H. & J. 86 (Court of Appeals of Maryland, 1820).

28. *Conframp v. Bunel*, 6 F.Cas. 275 (Civ. Pa. 1806); *Hadfield v. Jameson*, 16 Va. 53 (1809).

29. *Conframp v. Bunel*, 5 F.Cas. 275 (Pennsylvania 1806).

30. *Hadfield v. Jameson*, 16 Va. 53 (1809).

31. Bryan Edwards, *An Historical Survey of the French Colony in the Island of St. Domingo: Comprehending a Short Account of Its Ancient Government, Political State, Population, Productions, and Exports; a Narrative of the Calamities Which Have Desolated the Country Ever Since the Year 1780 . . . and a Detail of the Military Transactions of the British Army in That Island to the End of 1794* (London: J. Stockdale, 1797); Edward Baines, *History of the Wars of the French Revolution from The Breaking Out of the War in 1792, to the Restoration of a General Peace in 1815; Comprehending the Civil History of Great Britain and France, During That Period* (London: Printed for Longman, Hurst, Rees, Orme, and Brown Paternoster-Row; and James Harper, 46, Fleet-Street, by Edward Baines, Leeds, 1818). U.S. jurists also relied frequently upon Moreau de Saint-Mery's history of Saint-Domingue. Moreau's history does not extend into the colony's revolutionary era, however. M. L. E. Moreau de Saint-Mery, *Description Topographique, Physique, Civile,*

Politique et Historique de la Partie Française de L'isle Saint-Domingue. Avec Des Observations Générales sur Sa Population, sur le Caractère & les Mœurs de Ses Divers Habitants; sur Son Climat, Sa Culture, Ses Production, Son Administration, &c. (Philadelphia: Chez l'auteur; Paris, Chez Dupont, 1797–98). See *De Armas v. Mayor, etc. of New-Orleans,* 5 La. 132 (1833); *Seville v. Chretien,* 5 Mart (o.s.) 275 (1817); and, *Marguerite v. Chouteau,* 3 Mo. 540 (1834).

32. Edwards's text was published in an expanded edition in 1801.

33. Edwards, *An Historical Survey,* 81. For an extended examination of Edwards see Edward Rugemer, *The Problem of Emancipation: The Caribbean Roots of the American Civil War* (Baton Rouge: Louisiana State University Press, 2008).

34. *Franklin Gazette* (Philadelphia), August 15, 1818; *Mercantile Advertiser* (New York), May 27, 1819; *Baltimore Patriot,* September 13, 1819; *Louisiana Advertiser* (New Orleans), April 25, 1820.

35. *City of Washington Gazette,* January 22, 1818; "LaFayette," from Baines's *History of the Wars of the French Revolution.* See also *New-York Columbian,* August 26, 1820; *Berkshire Star,* September 17, 1820.

36. *Salem Gazette,* July 8, 1800; *National Intelligencer and Washington Advertiser,* August 23, 1805; *Political Observatory* (Walpole, N.H.), March 28, 1808; *National Standard,* July 30, 1817; *New York Gazette,* April 29, 1802; *Commercial Advertiser* (New York), May 14, 1802; *Poulsons American Daily Advertiser* (Philadelphia), February 20, 1805.

37. Baines, *History of the Wars of the French Revolution,* 133.

38. Whitman, *The Price of Freedom,* 80–81.

39. Along with the *Baptiste* case, Raymond had two additional freedom suits before the Court of Appeals for the June 1820 term, *Davis v. Jacquin & Pomerait,* 5 H. & J. 100 (1820) and *Negro Clara v. Meagher,* 5 H. & J. 111 (1820). The following year the court would decide a fourth of Raymond's cases, *Hughes v. Negro Milly, et al.,* 5 H. & J. 310 (1821).

40. "Protection Society of Maryland," *Baltimore Patriot and Mercantile Advertiser,* July 20, 1818.

41. *Baptiste, et al. v. de Volunbrun,* 5 H. & J. 86 (Court of Appeals of Maryland, 1820).

42. *Hadfield v. Jameson,* citing Edwards's *"History of the West Indies." An historical survey of the island of Saint Domingo, together with an account of the Maroon Negroes in the island of Jamaica; and a history of the war in the West Indies, in 1793 and 1794; by Bryan Edwards, esq. Also a tour through the several islands of Barbadoes, St. Vincent, Antigua, Tobago, and Grenada, in the years 1791 and 1792. By Sir William Young, bart. Illustrated with copper plates* (London: Stockdale, 1801).

43. For a discussion of the idea of a slaveholding "household," see Elizabeth Fox-Genovese, *Within the Plantation Household: Black and White Women of the Old South* (Chapel Hill: University of North Carolina Press, 1988).

44. Historian Gary Nash, in his study of Philadelphia's enslaved refugees from Saint-Domingue, explains that such individuals were disproportionately women and young children, with young, able-bodied men notably unrepresented among refugees settling in that U.S. port city. Nash, "Reverberations of Haiti in the American North."

45. Deposition of John Marie Garvaise, August 11, 1801, *The People v. Marcelle, Sam, Benjamin Bandey and 20 others*, New York County District Attorney Indictment Records, August 8, 1801–February 8/9, 1802, Reel 6, New York City Municipal Archives [hereafter NYCMA]; A Friend to Order, "Citizens of New-York," *New-York Gazette*, September 1, 1801.

46. *The People v. Marcelle, Sam, Benjamin Bandey and 20 others*, NYCMA.

47. For an extended analysis of this New York City freedom suit see Martha S. Jones, "Time, Space, and Jurisdiction in Atlantic World Slavery: The Volunbrun Household in Gradual Emancipation New York," *Law and History Review* 29, no. 4 (2011): 1031–60. The city government vigorously pursued prosecution of the arrested rioters, meting out unusually harsh penalties. Most rioters before 1810 were either acquitted or given light fines. Few had to serve as long as two months in jail. *The People v. Marcelle, Sam, Benjamin Bandey and 20 others*, NYCMA. See also Shane White, *Somewhat More Independent: The End of Slavery in New York City, 1770–1810* (Athens: University of Georgia Press, 1991); Paul A. Gilje, *The Road to Mobocracy: Popular Disorder in New York City, 1763–1834* (Chapel Hill: University of North Carolina Press, 1987).

48. Numerous receipts for the monies paid to Volunbrun for the work of Tranquille as a gardener and Jean Nago as a cook at St. Mary's College are among the college's financial records. FR 125, FR 127, FR 129s, FR 130, FR 132, Saint Mary's Seminary and University, The Associated Archives, Baltimore, Maryland.

49. In 1822, in yet another freedom suit against Volunbrun, a gentleman named Basil would prevail against her after establishing that he had lived for more than a decade as a free man, owing a barbershop, having a wife and children, and owning his own home. "Negro Basil, Vs. Mad. Jeane De Volunbrun," *Baltimore Patriot*, June 20, 1822.

50. Registre, Confraire de Notre Dame du Rosaire, Registre, Confrerie de Notre Dame Auxiliatrice, and Registre, Confrerie de Notre Dame du Mont Carmel. St. Mary's Seminary PS Chapel, Parish Records, Confraternity Records, c. 1796–1851, St. Mary's Seminary and University, The Associated Archives, Baltimore, Maryland.

51. Volunbrun published this notice twice, first in French and then three weeks later in English. Veuve De Volunbrun, "Avis," *Mechanics' Gazette, and Merchants' Daily Advertiser*, August 19, 1815; and Veuve De Volunbrun, "Notice," *Mechanics' Gazette, and Merchants' Daily Advertiser*, September 7, 1815.

52. This idea of the chattel principle comes from fugitive slave James W. C. Pennington and is further explained by Walter Johnson in "Introduction: The Future Store," in *The Chattel Principle: Internal Slave Trades in the Americas*, ed. Johnson (New Haven: Yale University Press, 2005), 1–31.

53. "Jeanne Mathurine Drouillard venue de Volunbrun to Pierre Paul Rossignol Grammont" [sale of slave, Jean Baptiste], Act no. 298, June 2, 1819, Notary Marc Lafitte, New Orleans Notarial Archives, New Orleans, Louisiana.

54. "Pierre Paul Rossignol Grammont to Clément Moreau" [sale of slave, Jean Baptiste], Act no. 342, September 22, 1819, Notary Marc Lafitte, New Orleans Notarial Archives, New Orleans, Louisiana.

55. "Clément Moreau to Catrine Marie Lebeau Guerin" [sale of slave Jean Baptiste],

Act 57, February 21, 1820, Notary Marc Lafitte, New Orleans Notarial Archives, New Orleans, Louisiana.

56. Creole of Saint Domingue, *My Odyssey: Experiences of a Young Refugee from Two Revolutions*, ed. Althea de Puech Parham (Baton Rouge: Louisiana State University Press, 1959). For a thoughtful reflection upon *My Odyssey*, see Jeremy D. Popkin, "Chapter 4: A Poet in the Midst of Insurrection: 'Mon Odyssee,'" in his *Facing Racial Revolution: Eyewitness Accounts of the Haitian Insurrection* (Chicago: University of Chicago Press, 2007), 59–92.

6

....

Ending with a Whimper, Not a Bang

The Relationship between Atlantic History
and the Study of the Nineteenth-Century South

TREVOR BURNARD

There were manifold Atlantic connections that linked the antebellum South in the nineteenth century with the British Atlantic World of the eighteenth century. Yet Atlantic history as a field within our profession is very much a concept and a practice that is popular mostly within the confines of colonial America.[1] Southern historians have shied away from the term, in part because historians of the Atlantic have tended to insist that Atlantic history stopped sometime around the end of the great Age of Revolutions, in the 1820s.[2]

Indeed, the reason Atlantic history has been taken up so enthusiastically by colonial British American historians is that it is a useful term that can be employed as a shorthand both to describe and more importantly to reorient the field of early American history in the light of a new concern about the field's spatial reach. Atlantic history has a number of different points of genesis, but one important reason why it has become so important within early American history in the last two decades is that it allowed for a shared focus and common set of issues around which the field could be redefined. That reorientation has been remarkably successful, meaning that the study of Atlantic history and the study of early America have become almost synonymous, with the important exception that the large group of early American historians who concern themselves with the allied field of continental North American history see their area of interest as counterposed to Atlantic history.[3]

This essay will explore how the move toward an Atlantic perspective for students of the seventeenth- and eighteenth-century British American world has changed early American history and what this means for understanding the connections between the study of colonial British America and the study of the antebellum southern United States. I believe that for all its successes as a means of invigorating the study of early America, and especially in connecting what early Americanists do to the fascinating work being done by historians in a wide variety of other geographical areas—in particular, the North American borderlands, Latin America, and Africa—the practice of Atlantic history has a decided drawback. It has led to an unfortunate distancing between the historiographies and historical practice of colonial America and antebellum American history.

In short, while the study of Atlantic topics in colonial British America has greatly increased the geographical reach of early American history, it has significantly decreased the chronological and temporal connections within separate areas of American history. But while it seems from one angle that the scholarship on early America has diverged from the scholarship on the antebellum South to such an extent that dialogue between scholars of the two periods in American history is difficult, from another angle a much more positive picture emerges. The themes and concerns of colonial British American historians taking an Atlantic perspective supplement the themes and concerns that scholars of the antebellum South should find valuable. Indeed, scholars of the antebellum South are beginning to see that the principal themes of Atlantic history—the movement of goods, peoples, and things within an always changing and dynamic Atlantic World of competing empires and nations—are relevant to their own area of specialization.

Atlantic history has had relatively little purchase in antebellum southern history. More importantly, practitioners of Atlantic history, most of them scholars of the colonial Americas, tend not to see Atlantic history as extending far into the nineteenth century. In large part, this reluctance to explore links between the Atlantic World of the seventeenth and eighteenth centuries and its manifestations in the nineteenth century is connected strongly to a persistent ambivalence about the nation-state (an institution inescapable in understanding the nineteenth century) as a unit of historical analysis.

There are, of course, some honorable exceptions to this pattern, mostly in the field of literature, where scholars on the global South freely include topics from the seventeenth to the twentieth centuries in their analyses. Donna Gabbaccia, for example, in the first issue of a relatively new journal devoted to Atlantic studies, extended the concept of Atlantic studies to what she considers the long nineteenth century. Daniel T. Rodgers also has written an important and influential study of turn-of-the-century America within an Atlantic context. Toyin Falola and Kevin D. Roberts have edited a set of essays that extends Atlantic history up to the late twentieth century and into issues of contemporary globalization. The first two specifically Atlantic textbooks so far published, one written by a group of writers headed alphabetically by Douglas Egerton and one a single-authored account by Thomas Benjamin, also make a valiant attempt to show how nineteenth-century American history has an Atlantic context.[4]

But in general Atlantic historians lose interest in tracing Atlantic connections as the nineteenth century proceeds. Atlantic history, at least in its North American variety, tends to be a discourse for colonialists, not for historians of the United States. Such a dwindling of interest in Atlantic themes as the nineteenth century proceeds is a particular problem for historians of the American South. It is a problem first because the continuities between the antebellum South and the colonial southern and island colonies are so marked (mainly due to the pervasive influence of a colonial institution—slavery—on every aspect of southern culture and society), especially compared to the sharp discontinuities between past and present that occurred as a result of the southern-wide trauma of the Civil War. Second, one of the main virtues of Atlantic history that should appeal to historians of the U.S. South is that Atlantic history has led to a pronounced southward and westward drift in the spatial horizons of colonial British American historians. This move in spatial perspective is not surprising as practitioners of Atlantic history pay particular attention to the interactions between black and white, interactions that were mostly played out in the southern and island colonies.

The American South has a centrality in the historiographies of Atlantic historians that is not the same for a historiography crafted around the nation-state of the United States. Southern historians should want very much to connect their work to the motifs of Atlantic history, if only because it heightens the significance of their subject as an object of historical inquiry and also reduces the tendency among historians of the U.S. South to see their region as exceptional and "peculiar" within the context of a northern-oriented United States.

Atlantic history is meant to be an ecumenical discipline, but as commentators have sometimes noted, Atlantic history more often than it should be is a discussion that scholars of colonial British America hold among themselves.[5] It is an entrée into what colonial historians fancy themselves to be—early modernists—rather than what they are—the medieval branch of U.S. history. We can see how instinctively Atlantic historians confine themselves to the sixteenth to the eighteenth centuries in a 2008 book edited by Jack P. Greene and Philip D. Morgan titled *Atlantic History: A Critical Reappraisal*.[6] The authors are renowned scholars of early America, and the contributors, to a man and woman, are scholars who are prominent for their studies of the Americas before 1800. My own contribution focused on the British Atlantic. Following in the footsteps of Bernard Bailyn and David Armitage of Harvard in their accounts of the evolution of Atlantic history, my chronological survey finished in the early nineteenth century. Indeed, like Philip Morgan, whose treatment of Africa and the Atlantic ends in 1825, and Joyce Chaplin and Anthony Russell-Wood, who end their chapters on the Atlantic as an ocean and on Portuguese America, respectively, in 1808, my account peters out in the early nineteenth century.

I concluded that "the most difficult period to treat within the rubric of British Atlantic history is the . . . the late eighteenth and early nineteenth centuries." This period is difficult to categorize because "these were years of epochal change and crisis that heralded both the completion of an integrated British Atlantic World and its partial destruction." The American Revolution and its aftermath showed how Britain and its colonies were "enmeshed in a common Atlantic world with a common political vocabulary." Nevertheless, the formation of an independent United States "made the British Atlantic a reduced place." The United States remained heavily involved in Atlantic commerce, but the purchase of the Louisiana Territory in 1803 allowed the United States to turn inward, toward continental expansion. In addition, "the advent of the industrial revolution in Britain and in the north-eastern United States, the transition from a world of empires to a world of nation-states, and, within the United States, the increasing urgency of internal disputes between southern and northern states all helped to diminish the importance of Atlantic concerns in the nineteenth century."[7]

This kind of argument in intended to delineate Atlantic history as a topic for colonialists and for historians of the early modern world while recognizing that Atlantic history did not just stop after either the end of the great Atlantic revolutions or after the abolition of slavery in the British

Caribbean in 1834. It is a strategy similar to that employed by Sir John Elliott in his masterpiece, *Empires of the Atlantic World*, where he stops Atlantic history in 1830. It is also a strategy adopted in the 2011 *Oxford Handbook of Atlantic History*, in which none of the thirty-seven essays extends past the mid-nineteenth century and the vast majority of contributors stop their story by 1820.[8]

Of course, this is all pretense. Atlantic history did not stop in the 1820s or even in the 1830s. The expulsion of the United States from the imperial family in 1787 did not mean an end to the British Atlantic. Indeed, from the perspective of historical geography (which is what Atlantic history tends to be a subset of), the British Atlantic became much bigger after 1787 than it had ever been. The expansion of British rule across the upper half of the North American continent in the nineteenth century painted more of that continent pink in the nineteenth century than was painted pink in the eighteenth century. Indeed, one weakness in the historiography of antebellum America is that historians do not pay enough attention to the emergence of Canada as a physical barrier to American expansion to the north. Much of the history of the first half of the nineteenth century is about "Manifest Destiny," which, with the exception of the Oregon Territory, where Britain and the United States came to a mostly amicable agreement as to boundaries in 1846 around the forty-ninth parallel, concerns American and mostly southern ambitions to expand into the perpetually weak Spanish Empire and its successors, such as Mexico. These were regions that always had a soft underbelly that Americans could exploit.

There was no such underbelly in the American North. The 1813 invasion of Canada was not followed up by American invasion but by American defeat. How different would American history—southern, northern, western, and national—have been if Massachusetts's ambition to expand into Upper and Lower Canada had been satisfied?[9] An Atlantic approach takes a wider perspective than is customarily historians' wont. By including Canada in the mix, historians become more aware of how different boundaries were in the antebellum South from those in the North and how this allowed southern historians the luxury of looking southward in order to connect with the Caribbean and Latin America.

The Atlantic dimension was significant in all sorts of ways in the first half of the nineteenth century, for both the American North and even more so for the American South. In an interesting Atlantic-inflected account of British-American interactions up until the end of the Civil War, Duncan Campbell makes it clear just how frequent and complicated Anglo-American relations were in the early nineteenth century. He reminds us again that the primary reference point for most Americans was Britain and that at least a portion of Britons always felt that America was a model against which Britain could measure itself.[10] Of course, for Britons, then and now, America and its "Americanisms" (usually said with a supercilious sneer) tended to be an example to be avoided. The new settlements of Australia and New Zealand, as advanced in the systematic colonization efforts of Edward Gibbon Wakefield, were conceived of as being colonies uncontaminated by the dire influence of the past two centuries of American development, especially its malign reliance on chattel slavery.[11]

That America was an Atlantic nation in the first half of the nineteenth century is powerfully argued in an important essay by José C. Moya. Moya argues that the customary application of the concept of Atlantic history to the period between 1500 and 1800 reflects a formalist perspective temporally bound by the formal political ties of European colonialism in the Americas but that in fact the concept of Atlantic history is more applicable to the late nineteenth century and the early twentieth century than to earlier times. The transatlantic circulation of goods, technologies, capital, ideas, and people reached a magnitude then that dwarfed pre-1800 connections.[12]

Moya sees a major shift in the nineteenth century from what can be seen as a South Atlantic World, dominated by the ramifications of the African slave trade, to a North Atlantic World that was the prefiguration of modernity. The modern world of the late nineteenth century was circumscribed by North Atlantic flows of people, capital, and technologies. Europe and America became more important demographically in this period (their percentage of world population increased from 24 percent to 35 percent in the nineteenth century). They also became more important economically: Britain, France, and the United States increased their share of the world's manufacturing from one-tenth to one-half between 1800 and 1900. Atlantic connections therefore increased rather than decreased in this period. As Moya concludes, "almost all the markers of nineteenth century modernity, from capitalism, to cubism, from railroads to radicalism, emerged within, and before World War One, and were circumscribed mainly by the Atlantic world. The circulation of humans and all sorts of materials and cultural goods linked this world closer than ever and imported it with social meaning." It might be that in the nineteenth century there was a major shift from the centers of modernity being in Indo/mestizo and Afro-American America to being in the great port cities of the American Northeast, the growing metropolises around the Great Lakes, and to cities in the more southerly areas of South America (from tropical to temperate areas), but there was no move away from Atlantic orientations but instead was a geographical reorientation leading to an intensification of Atlantic ties. In other words, the center of modernity shifted from Mexico City, Lima, Salvador, Havana, Kingston, and New Orleans to New York, Chicago, Buenos Aires, and São Paulo.[13]

The American South plays a curious, ambivalent place in this schema, as befits a region midway between these two areas. It continued to grow, develop, and remain culturally confident during the nineteenth century, and even if growth rates were less impressive than in the American North, the American South never suffered the decline in wealth and social and political importance that the first-mentioned places in Moya's analysis suffered during the nineteenth century. But it too was part of this shift: New Orleans was increasingly overshadowed by New York as the nineteenth century proceeded.

Of course, historians of nineteenth-century America, especially southern historians, do not need to be reminded of this momentous geographical shift. Their understanding of southern history in the nineteenth century is shaped by their awareness that the U.S. South evolved in the context of a changing global environment in which first Britain and then the northern United States became the hegemonic Atlantic power. The shift from south to north, from agriculture to industry, from slavery to wage labor is, of course, the story of nineteenth-century America, even if this was an intensely contested process, particularly when the locus of political and, to an extent, cultural and economic power in the United States remained heavily concentrated in the American South until the Civil War. What Moya reminds us of is that these shifts took place in a historical context that was more intensely and more specifically Atlantic in 1900 than it was in 1800.

These shifts also took place, more to the point, in what Kenneth Pomeranz famously has described as the "Great Divergence." By "Great Divergence," Pomeranz traces how the Western world—western Europe and North America, particularly—overcame premodern growth constraints, especially in the nineteenth century, and displaced Asian civilizations as the leading civilizational area in the world. Pomeranz places a great deal of emphasis on transatlantic trade flows in describing this monumental shift in first economic and then geopolitical power. As he argues, fortuitous global conjunctures made the Americas a greater source of needed primary products than any Asian periphery.[14]

These thoughts lead us into areas of global history. When pushed as to why Atlantic history as practiced by early modern historians stops circa 1830, historians usually come up with one of two somewhat contradictory answers. First, they note, as Nicholas Canny and Philip Morgan do in their introduction to *The Oxford Handbook of Atlantic History*, that what changes around this time was the gradual decline in importance of Africa to both Europe and the Americas. Of course, shipments of Africans through the slave trade to Spanish and Portuguese America continued past Latin American independence and until after 1850. But this slave trade was clearly becoming less important as a contributor to migratory streams going to the Americas. Moreover, West Africa itself receded from the European consciousness during the second half of the nineteenth century.

Central to the idea of Atlantic history is that it is the confluence of the histories of four continents. From the mid-nineteenth century, one of those continents, Africa, largely disappeared or at least significantly declined in importance and in European and American consciousness. Of course, as James Sidbury reminds us, the "idea" of Africa remained extremely important in the development of African American thought, and, obviously, the idea of Africa was always present in the United States indirectly by the reality of the massive presence and enormous cultural and social importance of the descendants of Africans in the Americas, notably in the American South. But Canny and Morgan are correct in seeing that Africa as a continent and as a place of contact between Europe and the Americas diminished remarkably over time in American intellectual thought. This decline in the importance of Africa, and hence of Africans, will be discussed in more depth below.

Second, Atlantic historians counterpose globalization to Atlantic history. They argue that what happened after the mid-nineteenth century (what Kevin O'Rourke and Jeffrey Williamson outline as the first genuinely global period in world history) was qualitatively different from what occurred before during the period of Atlantic history. Even though O'Rourke and Williamson subtitle their important book on nineteenth-century globalization "The Evolution of a Nineteenth-Century Atlantic Economy," the late-nineteenth-century trade revolution was a period that allowed producers and distributors to send their goods all over the world, rather than within regional networks. More importantly, it was a period in which economic institutions, practices, and events were increasingly interlinked. The importance of these twinned developments meant that the particular dynamics of the early modern Atlantic World of the late eighteenth and early nineteenth centuries had by the late nineteenth century been supplanted by a new and more vibrant economic order in which discourses of globalization make more sense than do discourses based on Atlantic perspectives.[15]

What is undeniable, however, is that the Atlantic dimension to U.S. history was not finished in the early nineteenth century. The Atlantic dimension was certainly extremely important, in my view, to the shaping of the American South in the early republic and antebellum periods. The U.S. South was as invested in Atlantic concerns in the nineteenth century as it was in the eighteenth or seventeenth century. Here, very briefly, are just four areas where an Atlantic perspective might be useful for historians of the antebellum U.S. South.

First, Atlantic history is a useful corrective to narratives of American exceptionalism. For a non-American historian like myself who studies early America before it became the United States and who concentrates on that part of America (the British West Indies) that did not become the United States, the perpetual and growing tendency of U.S. historians to assume that the only audience for American history is within the United States—as signified by the constant use of "us" or "we" in historical texts—is a continuing reminder of the power of American exceptionalism. Despite the best efforts of scholars such as Thomas Bender to place the development of the United States as but "one history among histories," and despite his attempt to relocate U.S. history within an interdependent world, U.S. history in the first decades of the twenty-first century is not becoming any less insular.[16]

Most Atlantic historians rebel against what they see as the continuing reiteration of American exceptionalist accounts of American history. Of course, Atlantic historians are not alone in such disquiet with exceptionalist accounts: historians of the American South have a long and complicated relationship with exceptionalist accounts of both southern and American history. Many scholars of the American South, especially in the New Southern Studies, are as concerned as Atlantic historians in breaking down older and seemingly outdated paradigms of American exceptionalism.[17] What remains true, however, is that an aversion to exceptionalist narratives remains at the heart of Atlantic history discourse. It is one means whereby students of early America who adopt an Atlantic approach can connect with historians of the American South, who are similarly interested in breaking away from nationalist narratives. The tension between nationalist histories and transnationalist, global, and anti-exceptionalist narratives is a feature of modern historiography, not just in American history before the mid-nineteenth century but also in other historiographical traditions.[18]

Yet, perhaps paradoxically, what an Atlantic perspective on the nineteenth-century American South does is to illuminate the ways in which the nineteenth-century American South is indeed exceptional. It had, for example, an exceptional slave system, an exceptional understanding of racial difference, and an exceptional powerful planter class. These areas of exceptionalism are clear when one compares these features of the U.S. South to comparable Atlantic slave societies such as nineteenth-century Cuba and Brazil. In the period of what Dale Tomich, a world systems sociologist who studies Martinique, calls "second stage slavery," it is only in the United States that one sees, as Eugene Genovese and Elizabeth Fox-Genovese insisted, a fully developed defense of the planter class and a positive defense of slavery as a viable alternative to free-labor democracy.[19]

Genovese and Fox-Genovese's claims for the distinctiveness of American slavery and the American planter class are worth re-reemphasizing. Slavery had to end in the United States through a cataclysmic Civil War rather than fade away as it did in the Spanish Caribbean and in Brazil. That happened because alone in the Atlantic World the slave system in the American South was expanding at the mid-nineteenth century.

One of the few areas in which the ardent Jacksonian democrat Sean Wilentz and the equally ardent Whig Daniel Walker Howe agree in their massive accounts of America in the second quarter of the nineteenth century is that in these years slavery was entrenched in the American South and that a powerful proslavery interest group—the "slaveocracy"—developed. The peculiarity of the politics around that peculiar institution can best be appreciated by removing it from a purely American context and placing second-stage slavery and slave emancipation in an Atlantic context.[20]

A second area where an Atlantic perspective is instructive concerns the importance of Africa within antebellum American life. In part, Africa is important for its absence. What is significant about the Atlantic World in general after 1800 is how Africa's linkages with the New World gradually weakened until they eventually disappeared by the 1860s and 1870s, as noted above. When H. M. Stanley "discovered" David Livingstone in 1871, Africa was the "dark" and unexplored continent, even though Europeans had been in frequent contact with West Africans for centuries. In the United States, direct links with Africa by these dates were minimal, at least in comparison with the West Indies or Brazil. By the second or third decade of the nineteenth century, virtually all enslaved Americans were people of African descent rather than Africans per se, although as Sylvaine Diouf has recently shown us, a few Africans were illegally shipped into the United States as late as the Civil War.[21] As Africans born in Africa declined in number in America, so too the notion of Africa as a dark, barbaric continent increasingly took hold among both the black and white populations of the United States.

Nevertheless, it would be incorrect to declare that Africa was entirely absent from American life in the antebellum period. The idea of Africa remained very important to many African Americans. As Sidbury has intriguingly explored, the notion of Africa as a mythical place of origin and a real place of return played a crucial role in African American self-identification, from Phillis Wheatley through Richard Allen and from Martin Delany through to Marcus Garvey. Moreover, we are increasingly aware that colonization schemes to Africa were not minor idiosyncrasies in the American pattern but were significant if grandiose and unrealizable schemes of social engineering. They attracted major sponsors, such as James Madison and Henry Clay, and achieved some small success, such as in Liberia. The movement may have been killed off by opposition from both southern masters and African Americans themselves, but return to Africa or exile to Canada always meant that African Americans could conceive (contra Stanley Elkins) a different life from that of being either a slave or a free black in the United States.

The life they conceived in opposition to an American life was an Atlantic life.[22] That Atlantic life might, as indicated in the previous paragraph, be one conceived of as occurring in Africa. But it could just as easily be thought of as happening in the English-speaking world where there was no link, as there was in the American South, to enslavement. A letter to his former master from an escaped slave called Joseph Taper living in Ontario, Canada, in 1839 shows his awareness of an Anglophone Atlantic World: "I now take the opportunity to inform you that I am in a land of liberty, in good health . . . Since I have been in the Queen's dominions I have been well contented [for here] all men are born free and equal. This is a wholesome law, not like the southern laws which puts man in the image of God, on a level with brutes . . . God save Queen Victoria."[23]

Third, one of the most significant consequences of the American Revolution is that it sundered artificially the slaveholding colonies of British America. We can argue about whether the West Indian islands were sufficiently similar to the plantation colonies of the Lower South to have conceivably joined in Revolution against Britain in 1776. It is possible that some West Indian colonies might have joined the Revolution, turning thirteen colonies into, say, twenty. The more interesting counterfactual, however, is not why Jamaica did not join the rebellion but why South Carolina, so similar to West Indian islands and later so unhappy with the Union that it determined to leave it, was prepared to make the break that it made with Britain. An Atlantic perspective might encourage historians of the antebellum South to pose an answer to that counterfactual and thus complicate the standard story of the coming of the American Revolution.[24]

The effect of the split in the great slaveholding societies of British America was dramatic—it meant that when abolitionism became important in the 1780s (in and of itself, partly arising in consequence of the ideological ferment of the American Revolution, as Christopher Brown tells us), the forces defending slavery in the British Atlantic were much weaker than they might otherwise have been. If South Carolina in particular had added its voice to Jamaica and Barbados in the proslavery camp in the British Empire, abolition would have been difficult.[25]

We know just how effective South Carolina planters were in dictating early U.S. policy over slavery. Conversely, one suspects that a few South Carolina planters, as controversy led to Civil War and then defeat, might have begun to regret their ancestors' decision to join northern Americans in rebellion rather than stay connected to their West Indian cousins in a confederation devoted to the preservation of slavery. Just as the natural outlook for the people of New Orleans was the Gulf of Mexico and the Caribbean Sea, one can run the tape of history differently and see a British tropical empire of the West Indies and the most southern states—Florida,

Georgia, South Carolina. In such an empire, slavery would have been especially entrenched. Expansion might have led to the annexation of places like Cuba and possibly Saint-Domingue or Haiti, rather than to Texas and the American Southwest.[26]

It was not just the American Revolution, of course, that was important to the antebellum South. The particular configuration of the Louisiana Purchase is hard to imagine without the conflagration in Haiti, and the Mexican War cannot be disentangled from the aftermath of the Latin American revolutions.[27]

Fourth, the history of the nineteenth-century South is to a large extent the history of the expropriation of Native American lands and the successful imposition of ideas of white supremacy over territory increasingly made bereft of Native Americans. Here, the experience of the nineteenth century is similar to the continental history of the eighteenth century, as a number of historians have recognized. For some colonial Americans, the continuities between colonial and antebellum imperial expansion across the American continent are so great as to encourage colonialists to see their expertise as important for describing antebellum history.

The most forceful exposition of this argument was put forward in an article in the *William and Mary Quarterly* by one of the great figures in early American historiography, Jack Greene. Greene makes a powerful case for the imperial takeover by colonialists of at least nineteenth-century American history by colonial historians. It is a clever argument, because Greene marries what he sees as the applicability of postcolonial and postmodern theory to the practice of colonial, and by implication antebellum, history to the demonstrable fact that antebellum America and colonial America are linked through the shared experiences of American expansion. For Greene, the nineteenth century was the culmination and fulfillment of the twin quests for white supremacy and territorial expansion across the North American continent that dominated the last half century of colonial British American history.

What is especially noteworthy, and unnoticed in the several replies, mostly unfavorable, that were made by invited commentators to Greene's deliberately provocative argument, is that Greene makes an explicit claim that it is in the study of early America that the most theoretically sophisticated work in American history is being done—implicitly harking back to the time of the "new social history" of the 1970s, when New England town studies and Chesapeake parish histories were at the advance edge of American historiography. He lays down a challenge that might be good for nineteenth-century historians of the American South to ponder. Greene makes a powerful case that the ubiquity of Atlantic perspectives and "continental" histories (a shorthand term for the mélange of Middle Ground, borderland, and anthropologically influenced Native American histories that have been profoundly remaking the texture of early American studies) combined with a greater predisposition toward postcolonial and postmodernist approaches that is evident in colonial as opposed to antebellum history has led to startlingly new and evidently successful interpretative paradigms.[28]

Greene's argument takes the assumptions behind both Atlantic history and continental history and links them to two bodies of theoretical literature—postcolonial theory and the new literature on state formation. These are two bodies of work not often invoked by colonial historians but of more concerted interest to antebellum historians. Greene argues that we should treat post-1776 states less as creatures of the United States than as "settler" colonies not dissimilar to the colonies that became the original thirteen states. He believes that by doing so we will be led to consider American politics from the viewpoint of states rather than from the position of the American nation.

His argument foreshadows a larger argument, made in a 2010 book he edited, that connects colonial British American history to "new" imperial history and to the developing subfield of British World history. In this book Greene and his contributors posit British expansion into first Ireland and then the wider world between 1500 and the mid-twentieth century as distinctive (a less powerful word than "exceptional" but clearly related to it) insofar as British settlers developed an ideological orientation that stressed egalitarianism for themselves but for themselves only, with a harsh and exclusionary, often racist, attitude to other people whom they felt should be barred from political participation.[29]

Revealingly, Greene's argument in the *William and Mary Quarterly* was met by disfavor from many antebellum historians, who sniffed about the explicit imperialism in the claims Greene was putting forward. Robin Einhorn, for example, wrote in her response a somewhat tedious listing of important nineteenth-century works in order to show that antebellum historians are as much at the cutting edge as are colonial British American historians. She concluded that "if colonial historians approach national historians with peaceful intentions, the traditionally fruitful scholarly conversations will continue. If they enlist in Greene's mission to conquer the national period, however, they will encounter a dense and well-organised native population as wary of imperialistic designs as the Indians who met settlers on the colonial frontiers."[30]

The overly extended metaphor is cute but trite. What Einhorn misses is that behind the seeming imperialist design of Greene and others in respect to colonial insights into nineteenth-century history, and by extension about the applicability to nineteenth-century historiography of the insights of Atlantic history, is the insecurity that colonial American historians feel about their subject. Seemingly arrogant assumptions about what nineteenth-century historians can learn from colonialists masks a not-too-secret fear about the possibility of colonial British American history being made marginal if it persists with its fascination with Atlantic history. Of course, not all colonial British Americanists share this fear. Scholars who study the part of colonial British America that intersects with Spanish America or with French America are a lot less concerned than scholars studying the traditional eastern seaboard where British colonists dominated with maintaining the links between eighteenth- and nineteenth-century history, in part because they want to break down conventional boundaries within colonial history and want more recognition of Native American history, borderlands history, and the importance of other European empires besides the British in shaping U.S. history. Colonial British Americanists are in the curious position of feeling marginal within U.S. historiography while being made to feel imperialistic and insensitive to wider boundaries by historians of the colonial period who argue for a continental approach to early American history.[31]

There are considerable and potentially serious pedagogical implications to Atlantic World orientations that are unwelcome for colonialists. What Atlantic history's takeover of a large portion of early American history portends is a bigger break developing than is apparent even now between the imperatives of colonial British American history and the concerns of antebellum American history. Colonial historians are turning into historical geographers, oriented geographically rather than temporally. One advantage of this reorientation for nineteenth-century historians of the American South is that the increased sensitivity that colonial historians show in respect to how regions connect with larger units coincides with similar reorientations among antebellum southern historians—distinguishing both groups of historians from historians of the twentieth-century United States, where questions of place are of much less urgency.

The problem with Atlantic history is that it can be seen as a marvelous discourse that Atlantic historians are having with themselves. It takes them away from colleagues in nineteenth-century American history who are less and less interested in what colonial history and colonial historians have to say. As Michael Zuckerman astutely points out in his reply to Greene's imperialistic article in the *William and Mary Quarterly*, even if colonial insights would help antebellum historians, there is little evidence that antebellum historians are availing themselves of this grand offer of help. There is no significant rapprochement between colonial and nineteenth-century American historians. Indeed, as Zuckerman notes, given that Americans for the conceivable future will "need an account of American origins that legitimates their national endeavors," there will continue to be "a gaping discontinuity between colonial and national narratives: the one invariably decentered, the other incorrigibly committed to the primacy of the center."[32]

Zuckerman overstates the case. A number of southern historians try to connect early republic and antebellum history to colonial precedents.[33] But it is probably true that until recently there has been a growing gap between early American historiography and nineteenth-century American historiography. That there is such a gap seems undeniable, although one can see encouraging signs of a tentative rapprochement in recent works such as the Pulitzer Prize–winning Oxford history by Daniel Walker Howe on the "Middle Period" of American history that Atlantic history might be one way of closing the gap between the earliest and then the next earliest periods of American history.

Yet even Howe reverts to type, essentially deciding that the Atlantic phase of American history is over by the time of the Monroe Doctrine, with his big themes after that period being continental expansion and looking forward to the Civil War. It is certainly possible that early Americanists' embrace of Atlantic history and the relative indifference of nineteenth-century historians to Atlantic history will exacerbate the growing distances between American historians of the first half of American history for a little while longer yet.

Nevertheless, I see signs of hope that the development of Atlantic history as a new field of historical inquiry can help to bring together rather than separate further scholars of the seventeenth- and eighteenth-century

American South and historians of the nineteenth-century American South. The themes of Atlantic history can be appealing to historians of the American South as well as to colonial British Americanists, especially as southern historians become more interested in placing their subject within a comparative and a transnational context. It helps weaken narratives of American exceptionalism that are increasingly outmoded in a globalizing world; it provides ways in which the longer history of the enslavement of Africans and the exploitation of Native Americans can be understood; and it provides a useful interpretative framework through which nineteenth-century American historians of the American South can create new historical narratives that escape the Whiggish assumptions that twentieth-century historians of the American South, in reading civil rights backward over time and in following a millennialist view of African American redemption that arises out of such Whiggish history, attempt to impose on the earlier, and especially interesting, history of the American South.[34]

Notes

1. Important surveys of Atlantic history by early Americanists include David Armitage and Michael J. Braddick, eds., *The British Atlantic World, 1500–1800*, 2nd ed. (New York: Palgrave, 2009); Bernard Bailyn, *Atlantic History: Concept and Contours* (Cambridge: Harvard University Press, 2005); Bernard Bailyn and Patricia Denault, eds., *Soundings in Atlantic History: Latent Structures and Intellectual Currents, 1500–1830* (Cambridge: Harvard University Press, 2009); D. W. Meinig, *The Shaping of America: A Geographical Perspective on 500 Years of History*, vol. 1, *Atlantic America, 1492–1800* (New Haven: Yale University Press, 1986); Alison F. Games, "Beyond the Atlantic: English Globetrotters and Transoceanic Connections," *William and Mary Quarterly*, 3rd ser., 63 (2006): 675–92; Nicholas Canny, "Atlantic History: What and Why?" *European Review* 9 (2001): 399–411; Alison Games, "Atlantic History: Definitions, Challenges, and Opportunities," *American Historical Review* 111 (2006): 741–56.

2. Games, "Atlantic History," 747, 751–52.

3. The large body of literature on the Atlantic world and on its association with other areas of early American historiography can be traced in "Oxford Online Bibliographies: The Atlantic World," gen. ed. Trevor Burnard, http://aboutobo.com/atlantic-history. Important recent works in Atlantic history that include significant perspectives include Jack P. Greene and Philip D. Morgan, eds., *Atlantic History: A Critical Appraisal* (New York: Oxford University Press, 2008); and Nicholas Canny and Philip D. Morgan, eds., *The Oxford Handbook of Atlantic History* (New York: Oxford University Press, 2011).

4. Donna Gabaccia, "A Long Atlantic in a Wider World," *Atlantic Studies* 1 (2004): 1–27; Toyin Falola and Kevin D. Roberts, eds., *The Atlantic World, 1450–2000* (Bloomington:

Indiana University Press, 2008); Daniel T. Rodgers, *Atlantic Crossings: Social Politics in a Progressive Age* (Cambridge: Harvard University Press, 1998); Thomas Benjamin, *The Atlantic World: Europeans, Africans, Indians, and Their Shared History, 1400–1900* (Cambridge: Cambridge University Press, 2009); Douglas R. Egerton, Alison Games, Jane G. Landers, Kris Lane, and Donald R. Wright, *The Atlantic World: A History, 1400–1888* (Wheeling, Ill.: Harlan Davidson, 2007).

5. Cécile Vidal, "The Reluctance of French Historians to Address Atlantic History," *Southern Quarterly* (2006): 153–89; Silvia Marzagalli, "Sur les origines de l'*Atlantic History*: Paradigme interprétatif de l'histoire des espaces atlantiques à l'époque modern," *Dix-huitième siècle* 33 (2001): 17–31; Jorge Cañizares-Esguerra, "Some Caveats about the 'Atlantic' Paradigm," *History Compass*, www.history-compass.com.

6. Greene and Morgan, *Atlantic History*.

7. Trevor Burnard, "The British Atlantic World," in Greene and Morgan, *Atlantic History*, 120–21.

8. J. H. Elliott, *Empires of the Atlantic World: Britain and Spain in America, 1492–1830* (New Haven: Yale University Press, 2006).

9. Elizabeth Mancke, *The Fault Lines of Empire: Political Differentiation in Massachusetts and Nova Scotia, ca. 1760–1830* (New York: Routledge, 2005).

10. Duncan Andrew Campbell, *Unlikely Allies: Britain, America and the Victorian Origins of the Special Relationship* (London: Hambledon, 2007).

11. James Belich, *Replenishing the Earth: The Settler Revolution and the Rise of the Anglo-World, 1783–1939* (Oxford: Oxford University Press, 2009).

12. José C. Moya, "Modernization, Modernity, and the Transformation of the Atlantic World in the Nineteenth Century," in *The Atlantic in Global History, 1500–2000*, ed. Jorge Cañizares-Esguerra and Erik R. Seeman (Upple Saddle River, N.J.: Pearson Prentice Hall, 2007).

13. Ibid.

14. Kenneth Pomeranz, *The Great Divergence: Europe, China and the making of the modern World Economy* (Princeton: Princeton University Press, 2000).

15. James Sidbury, *Becoming African in America: Race and Nation in the Early Black Atlantic* (New York: Oxford University Press, 2007); Canny and Morgan, Introduction, in Canny and Morgan, *Oxford Handbook*; and Kevin O'Rourke and Jeffrey Williamson, *Globalization and History: The Evolution of a Nineteenth-Century Atlantic Economy* (Cambridge: MIT Press, 1999).

16. Thomas A. Bender, *A Nation among Nations: America's Place in World History* (New York: Hill and Wang, 2006).

17. See, for example, Walter Johnson, *River of Dark Dreams: Slavery, Capitalism, and Imperialism in the Mississipp Valley* (Cambridge: Harvard University Press, forthcoming).

18. Ann Curthoys, "We've Just Started Making National Histories and You Want Us to Stop Already?" in *After the Imperial Turn: Thinking with and through the Nation*, ed. Antoinette Burton (Durham: Duke University Press, 2003), 70–89.

19. Dale Tomich, *Slavery in the Circuit of Sugar: Martinique and the World Economy, 1830–1848* (Baltimore: Johns Hopkins University Press, 1990); Eugene Genovese and

Elizabeth Fox-Genovese, *The Mind of the Master Class: History and Faith in the Southern Slaveholders' Worldview* (Cambridge: Cambridge University Press, 2005).

20. Daniel Walker Howe, *What Hath God Wrought: The Transformation of America, 1815–1848* (New York: Oxford University Press, 2007); Sean Wilentz, *The Rise of American Democracy: Jefferson to Lincoln* (New York: Norton, 2005).

21. Sylvaine Diouf, *Dreams of Africa in Alabama: The Slave Ship "Clotilda" and the Story of the Last Africans Brought to America* (New York: Oxford University Press, 2007), 15–20.

22. Sidbury, *Becoming African in America.*

23. Joseph Taper quoted in John Hope Franklin and Loren Schweninger, *Runaway Slaves: Rebels on the Plantation* (New York: Oxford University Press, 1999), 294–95.

24. Trevor Burnard, "Freedom, Migration and the Negative Example of the American Revolution: The Changing Status of Unfree Labor in the Second British Empire and the New American Republic," in *Empire and Nation: The American Revolution in the Atlantic World*, ed. Eliga H. Gould and Peter S. Onuf (Baltimore: Johns Hopkins University Press, 2004), 295–314. For a persuasive, Atlantic-inflected account of how the factors that encouraged Jamaica to stay loyal in 1776 helped persuade South Carolinians to join in the American rebellion, see Robert Olwell, "'Domestick Enemies': Slavery and Political Independence in South Carolina, May 1775–March 1776," *Journal of Southern History* 55 (1989): 21–48.

25. Christopher Leslie Brown, *Moral Capital: Foundations of British Abolitionism* (Chapel Hill: University of North Carolina Press, 2006). For the American Revolution in the Gulf Coast, see Kathleen Duval, *Revolution without Rebels: The Battle of Pensacola and the American Revolution* (forthcoming). For the subsequent nineteenth-century history of South Carolina that stresses the continuing resemblances between South Carolina and the West Indies in respect to planter outlooks see William W. Freehling, *The Road to Disunion*, vol. 1, *Secessionists at Bay, 1776–1854* (New York: Oxford University Press, 1990), and *The Road to Disunion*, vol. 2, *Secessionsist Triumphant, 1854–1861* (New York: Oxford University Press, 2007).

26. Adam Rothman, *Slave Country: American Expansion and the Origins of the Deep South* (Cambridge: Harvard University Press, 2005).

27. Wim Klooster, *Revolutions in the Atlantic World: A Comparative History* (New York: New York University Press, 2009).

28. Jack P. Greene, "Colonial History and National History," *William and Mary Quarterly*, 3rd ser., 64 (2007): 235–50. See also Ann Laura Stoler, "Tense and Tender Ties: The Politics of Comparison in North American Studies and (Post) Colonial Studies," *Journal of American History* 88 (2001): 829–65.

29. Jack P. Greene, ed., *Exclusionary Empire: English Liberty Overseas, 1600–1900* (New York: Cambridge University Press, 2010). For "new" imperial history see Kathleen Wilson, ed., *A New Imperial History: Culture, Identity and Modernity in Britain and the Empire, 1660–1840* (Cambridge: Cambridge University Press, 2010). For British World history see Belich, *Replenishing the Earth*, and Carl Bridge and Kent Fedorovich, eds., *The British World: Diaspora, Culture and Identity* (London: Frank Cass, 2003). For an

appreciation of both the British World and new imperial history, see Tony Ballantyne, "The Changing Shape of the British Empire and Its Historiography," *Historical Journal* 53 (2010): 429–52.

30. Robin Einhorn, "The Nation Is Already There," *William and Mary Quarterly*, 3rd ser., 64 (2007): 280.

31. For a case in point see the admonitions against the dominance of east-coast United States early Americanists in Claudio Saunt, "Go West: Mapping Early American Historiography," *William and Mary Quarterly*, 3rd ser., 65 (2008): 745–78. For a more balanced but equally critical look at Atlantic history from the perspective of continental history, see Peter H. Wood, "From Atlantic History to Continental History," in Greene and Morgan, *Atlantic History*, 279–98.

32. Michael Zuckerman, "Exceptionalism After All; Or, the Perils of Postcolonialism," *William and Mary Quarterly*, 3rd ser., 64 (2007): 262.

33. For examples see Rothman, *Slave Country*, and Emily Clark *Masterless Mistresses: The New Orleans Ursulines and the Development of a New World Society: 1727–1834* (Chapel Hill: University of North Carolina Press, 2010).

34. See Robin D. G. Kelley, "How the West Was One: The African Diaspora and the Re-Mapping of American History," in *Rethinking American History in a Global Age*, ed. Thomas Bender (Berkeley: University of California Press, 2002), 123–47.

7

Was U.S. Emancipation Exceptional in the Atlantic, or Other Worlds?

JEFFREY R. KERR-RITCHIE

On July 4, 1876, hundreds of thousands of Americans gathered through-out thirty-nine states to commemorate the centennial of the founding of the Republic. They listened to orations, speeches, songs, and poems. These public presentations covered numerous themes: the current eco-nomic crisis facing the nation, America's providential roots, the inevita-bility of national progress, and the importance of reunion after a fractious civil war. The recent abolition of slavery in 1865 was also mentioned and widely praised. In Philadelphia, prominent New York State lawyer Wil-liam M. Evarts proclaimed that the centennial "crowns with new glory the immortal truths of the Declaration of Independence by the emancipa-tion of a race." "Thanks be to God, who overrules everything for good," former Massachusetts senator Robert C. Winthrop told a large gathering in Boston, "that great event, the greatest of our American age . . . has been accomplished; and by his blessing, we present our country to the world this day without a slave, white or black, upon its soil." According to the Baptist Rev. Thomas Armitage, abolition was not only the greatest American event but was also unique compared to the practices of other nations. Unlike the abolition of slavery by Great Britain, explained Armit-age, emancipation in the United States had been a principled act: "She [Britain] adopted it merely as a policy and paid for it as a bargain, failing largely to bring down the doctrine of freedom to the question of man's rights as the root of his humanity." In case his audience in New York City missed the point, he reminded them that "the American Republic has done more for liberty and against bondage than all other people have done before."[1]

These ideas of God's Republic, national progress, and exceptional emancipation—together with an evocation of the unique frontier spirit of the American people—meshed during the era of the professionalization of U.S. history in the late nineteenth century. The subsequent emergence of a historiography of American exceptionalism has been well explained and critiqued by Ian Tyrell, Robert Gregg, and others and requires little elaboration here.[2] What is important to note is that it was in response to the chauvinistic, parochial, and unique aspects of this historiography that there emerged the first generation of comparative emancipation scholars in the United States during the 1970s and 1980s. At Yale University, Comer Vann Woodward, one of the pioneers of modern southern historical studies, sought to compare the role of the American Civil War in ending slavery with other abolition processes in the nineteenth-century Americas.[3] At Columbia University, Eric Foner, one of the major historians of nineteenth-century American political history, compared the extension of political rights to former slaves in the United States with ex-slaves in other post-emancipation societies.[4] At Stanford University, George Fredrickson, an influential scholar of comparative history, compared race relations in the postbellum American South, post-abolition Jamaica, and fin de siècle South Africa.[5] As we will see, although their comparative approaches have broadened our understanding of nineteenth-century U.S. history, they have also resulted not only in privileging American emancipation but in further buttressing the argument for the uniqueness of America's past compared to other national experiences. A geospatial framework, expanded to situate the U.S. South in the Atlantic World, ended up generating its own kind of exceptionalist narrative.

Besides general problems with an exceptionalist U.S. historiography, there were several specific reasons why these scholars thought it important to pursue comparative work. There was a belief that such work would prove as efficacious as the comparative study of slave systems. The publication of Frank Tannenbaum's *Slave and Citizen: The Negro in the Americas* in 1946 had heralded a generation of rich historical scholarship comparing and contrasting slave systems in both the New and the Old World.[6] Woodward explained that one reason for his comparative study was that since there were as many abolitions as slave systems, "it might be presumed that as much light could be shed upon the American experience by the comparative study of the one as the comparative study of the other."[7] Moreover, this comparative work set out to slay the behemoth of America's exceptional past epitomized by the remarks of Winthrop and Armitage at the 1876 centennial commemoration. Woodward's description of the problem of the triumphant narrative of historical progress in U.S. history remains compelling: "One habit of mind that has complicated American ways of dealing with the problem of failure," he argued, "has been the isolation of American experience from comparative reference."[8] Foner points out that "comparative analysis permits us to move beyond 'American exceptionalism' to develop a more sophisticated understanding of the problem of emancipation and its aftermath."[9] It should be added that Foner's *Nothing but Freedom* was published while he was preparing his massive synthesis *Reconstruction: America's Unfinished Revolution*, with both works insisting on major historical change in the postbellum United States in opposition to numerous studies that focused on its continuity.[10] According to Fredrickson, a comparative approach to racial attitudes after the abolition of slavery might further our knowledge of post-emancipation race relations as well as enlarge our geographical knowledge. New cases for comparison, he adds, "might significantly aid our understanding of the processes involved in racial classification."[11] In other words, comparison with racial attitudes in other carefully selected environments might help us learn more about the nature of American racial attitudes.

These prominent historians at major U.S. research universities have shaped the ways in which generations of scholars, students, and general readers comprehend nineteenth-century American history both in the United States and globally. They have been particularly successful in situating U.S. emancipation within the broader contours of hemispheric and Atlantic history. Collectively, three comparative arguments stand out in this historical literature. First, the American Civil War represented a unique abolition process in the Americas. Woodward argued that its "unique magnitude," together with its "association with a terrible war," made it a historical experience unlike any other.[12] Second, the postbellum United States represented an exceptional moment in the expansion of national democracy, especially during Reconstruction. Woodward writes: "For nowhere in Plantation-America during the nineteenth century did the white man share with black freedmen the range of political power and office that the Southern whites were forced to share for a brief time with their freedmen."[13] Fredrickson agrees: "Such an extension of full citizenship to a mass of propertyless and largely illiterate former slaves was, by

nineteenth-century standards, an extraordinarily bold and radical inno-
vation."[14] The most insistent statement on this remarkable expansion of
democracy was provided by Foner, for whom "Reconstruction, in a comparative context, stands as a unique and dramatic experiment in interracial democracy in the aftermath of slavery."[15] Black workers' struggles in
the rice fields of post-abolition South Carolina, he tells us, "reveal how the
existence of sympathetic local and state governments during Reconstruction afforded American freedmen a form of political and economic leverage unmatched by their counterparts in other societies."[16] Indeed, this
insistence on the remarkable enfranchisement of former slaves into the
American polity compared to other post-emancipation societies would
not have sounded alien to celebrants at the 1876 centennial.

The third argument claims that there was a post-Reconstruction nadir
in race relations unique to the American South compared to other post-
emancipation societies. Fredrickson's comparison of local white responses
to the freeing of slaves and the abolition of legal and political distinctions
based on race or color in three areas—the southern United States, the
Cape Colony of South Africa, and Jamaica—concludes that the "reaction
of southern whites to the new racial order seems on the whole to have
been less affected by purely economic concerns [i.e., labor relations] than
that of the white Jamaicans or the majority of the Cape colonists. Emancipation presented itself to most southern whites pre-eminently as a racial
or social challenge—a threat to the elaborate structure of caste privilege
that had developed before the Civil War."[17] Although both Woodward
and Foner eschewed comparing race relations in post-abolition societies,
their findings imply that they would not have disagreed with Fredrickson's
argument.[18]

In sum, then, what did these early comparative U.S. emancipation
studies add up to? The abolition of slavery in the United States was unique
because of its magnitude and origins in a bloody and terrible war. The
postbellum political terrain was transformed primarily because former
slaves gained unique access to political power. It was because of all these
factors—bloody war, the abolition of slavery, and congressional Reconstruction—that race relations were to become so bad in the post-Reconstruction South.

Let us proceed with a critical examination of these comparative arguments. First, was the American Civil War of greater magnitude in ending U.S. slavery compared to the abolition of slavery elsewhere? This is

unpersuasive given the central role that military conflict played in bringing about immediate abolition in French Saint-Domingue (Haiti) during the 1790s, in Peru in the 1850s, and in Spanish Cuba in the 1870s–80s, as well as gradual abolition in Spanish South America in the generation between the 1820s and 1850s. Recent scholarship suggests that revolution, colonial invasions, and national independence struggles played an indispensable role in slavery abolition struggles throughout the nineteenth-century Americas.[19] To be precise, the role of military conflict in the abolition of slavery was part of a familiar pattern in the nineteenth-century Americas rather than being unique to the United States. Rather than being the exception to all other emancipation experiences, as implied by Woodward and others, revolutionary emancipation in Haiti should be seen as entailing similar carnage to the American Civil War and Cuban national independence, albeit the most bloody variant. Indeed, if there was a major exception to this linkage between war and emancipation it occurred in Brazil, where the abolition of slavery in 1888 was preceded by a decade of social unrest rather than emanating from military conflict.[20]

Moreover, if the loss of human life is the measuring stick of abolition, then the American Civil War was not of the greatest magnitude. Around 620,000 Americans died during the Civil War, including 36,000 African Americans. This amounted to about one-sixtieth of the white population and one-thirteenth of the black population. Most white Americans fought either to preserve the Union or for southern independence. (More southerners than northerners lost their lives.) Most black Americans fought for their own freedom, the destruction of U.S. slavery, and preservation of the Union. Compare this loss of life with the devastating decline of Cuba's population from 1.4 million to 1.2 million between 1862 and 1877. This devastating drop in Cuba's population was largely due to the First War of Cuban Independence between 1868 and 1878, which hastened Cuban abolition in 1886.[21] Haitian emancipation was even bloodier, with 100,000 to 200,000 people forfeiting their lives between 1791 and 1804.[22] The loss of 20 to 40 percent of Haiti's population resembled a demographic disaster on par with France's loss of 1.6 million soldiers, or almost 20 percent of military-age men, in World War I between 1914 and 1918.[23] Thus, the American Civil War exemplified rather than deviated from the link between war and emancipation: the price of liberty was of enormous magnitude across the nineteenth-century Americas, especially for those who fought for their own liberty.

An additional interpretive challenge concerns how to reconcile the view of the American Civil War with its terrible loss of life as a national tragedy with the final overthrow of a system of brutal slavery stretching back to the seventeenth-century Chesapeake region. Woodward never fully extricated himself from the belief that the Civil War was a national tragedy. This point remains deeply embedded within the American psyche as continually demonstrated at contemporary history conferences as well as in battlefield reenactments and on personal websites. But many abolitionists viewed the war and its outcome as a necessary path toward liberty and national redemption. And Americans of African descent who fought for the Union in an epic battle to destroy U.S. slavery did not see the Civil War as an unfolding tragedy. Listen to seventy-four members of Company D of the Fifty-fifth Massachusetts Volunteers explain why they enlisted: "we came to fight for Liberty justice & Equality. These are gifts we Prize more Highly than Gold For these We left our Homes our Famileys Friends & Relatives most Dear to take as it ware our Lives in our Hands To Do Battle for God & Liberty."[24]

Black veterans of these wars of liberation remained proud of their military contribution. For them, the tragedy was postwar America's refusal of racial equality to those who had risked their lives on behalf of the Union. Triumph trumped tragedy in the recollections of other veterans of wars of emancipation. After the legal abolition of slavery in 1886, former slave soldiers in Spanish Cuba claimed they won their freedom through fighting for it rather than receiving it as a governmental boon.[25] There is little doubt that Haitian veterans who battled and defeated British, Spanish, and French troops for individual liberty and national independence during the Haitian Revolution felt the same way. In short, who could disagree with Woodward's evocation of Robert E. Lee's famous quip that war is a terrible thing, except for former slaves across the nineteenth-century Americas for whom the horrors of war were usually the only realistic way to destroy the terrors of slavery?

Second, was American Reconstruction exceptional? Foner successfully inverts an older racist historiography depicting the "Africanization" of the postwar South with U.S. Reconstruction representing an important moment not only for the "Americanization" of former slaves but also for the realization of the American ideal of freedom first passionately expressed by W. E. B. Du Bois in his monumental *Black Reconstruction*, published in 1935.[26] It is important, however, not to forget the essential limitations of ex-slaves' political power during U.S. Reconstruction. Republican Reconstruction of the southern states always depended upon the approval of Congress, which provided for state constitutions and voter registration and ensured the presence of the Union army. Furthermore, Reconstruction legislatures between 1867 and 1877 mainly consisted of coalitions between northern Republicans, southern Unionists, and African Americans (former slaves and formerly free blacks), with the latter often serving in a minor role. About one thousand delegates participated in the rewriting of southern state constitutions, of which around one-fourth were African Americans.[27] Black American delegates were a demographic majority in Louisiana and South Carolina, about 40 percent in Florida, 20 percent in Alabama, Georgia, Mississippi, Virginia, and around 10 percent in Arkansas, North Carolina, and Texas.[28] It is useful to recall an important generalization made by Kenneth Stampp in his revisionist study of American Reconstruction published in 1965, the same year as the passage of the U.S. Voting Rights Act: blacks "did not control any of them [state legislatures]" during Reconstruction.[29] The irony of overemphasizing freedmen's politics during Reconstruction is that it echoes an older white South's criticism of dominant black political power due to federal intrusion into the region.

Moreover, while it is clear that ex-slaves in the American South enjoyed more political power than, say, ex-slaves in Jamaica or in Brazil, this was not the case in post-emancipation Haiti. In 1804 a black elite comprising former slaves and *ancien libres* (long-term free blacks) controlled the government after overthrowing the French colonial state and its administrative apparatus. It is true that Haitians did not exercise the constitutional right to vote, but this was primarily due to the revolutionary nature of the transition to power. In the same way, there was not an expansion of democratic rights in post-revolutionary England (1640s), France (1790s), Russia (1920s), China (1950s), and Iran (1980s). This contrasts with the American Civil War, in which one political party (the Republicans) sought to consolidate its wartime advantage by extending the suffrage to former slave men in the virtually solid (Democrat) South. The key point is to heap qualification upon qualification to the statement that emancipated southern blacks enjoyed more political power than other newly freed peoples. They were enfranchised for the purpose of political expediency. They rarely enjoyed local political domination. They lost influence in federal politics by 1877, and eventually at the state level in North Carolina by 1898 and Virginia by 1902. Most important, their brief political power pales in comparison to that of black elites in post-abolition Haiti. In short, an argument for the uniqueness of American Reconstruction says more about historians' unshakable belief in national democratic ideals than it does about ex-slaves' political power in comparative perspective.

One final point about the uniqueness of American Reconstruction concerns the skewing of its key conceptual source. Du Bois's *Black Reconstruction* sought to challenge existing racist depictions of the postwar South by stressing the nation's democratic moment. Foner and others have subsequently pushed this argument further to make a claim for American democracy's exceptionalism compared to other post-emancipation societies. But this has served to downplay an important argument made by Du Bois concerning certain commonalities among the wretched of the earth during the 1930s. After an eloquent indictment of racist historians of U.S. Reconstruction, he writes: "Immediately in Africa, a black back runs red with the blood of the lash; in India, a brown girl is raped; in China, a coolie starves; in Alabama, seven darkies are more than lynched; while in London, the white limbs of a prostitute are hung with jewels and silk. Flames of jealous murder sweep the earth, while brains of little children smear the hills."[30] This poetic passage connotes the similarities of oppression rather than unique democratic differentiation. It also recalls other worlds beyond the American South, the United States, and the Atlantic.

The argument that the extension of political rights made the post-abolition U.S. South unique among post-emancipation societies has been most strongly contested by *The Political Languages of Emancipation in the British Caribbean and the U.S. South*, published in 2002.[31] Its author, Demetrius L. Eudell, completed his dissertation under Fredrickson at Stanford University. Drawing upon J. G. A. Pocock's dialectical concept of political languages, Eudell examines competing paradigms and ideologies of planters, government officials, and racial scientists to argue for the similarity of racial debasement in post-abolition Jamaica and South Carolina. "In both postslavery situations," argues Eudell, "the dominant society found a way to disempower (Jamaica) or disfranchise (South Carolina) its respective Black majorities and still continue to see itself as being a nation that embodied free and democratic principles."[32] In contrast, former slaves in Jamaica and South Carolina "appropriated and expropriated the dominant languages of liberty and freedom" to provide alternative understandings of what they thought freedom entailed.[33]

Eudell's *Political Languages of Emancipation* is in serious disagreement with the notion of exceptional U.S. emancipation. At the end of his chapter comparing the "civilizing" policies of Freedmen's Bureau officials and special magistrates representing the British Colonial Office, Eudell explains that such an understanding "can provide the basis for an analysis of the postslavery Anglo-America from a new angle," namely the work of Reconstruction.[34] More generally, Eudell offers a more static interpretation of the post-abolition past than does Foner, for whom U.S. emancipation represented a radical break, or Fredrickson (as well as Woodward), for whom, without this radical rupture, there is no satisfactory explanation for the breakout of vehement racism in the late-nineteenth-century American South. Most reviewers of Eudell's book managed to ignore his key comparative points, with the unfortunate consequence that the author's challenge to earlier views of exceptional U.S. emancipation went unrecorded.[35]

These contributions by Eudell are informative and positive, but the problem is what exactly we are learning anew about the limits of freedom and post-abolition societies more generally through the comparison. First, so much work has already been done on post-abolition Jamaica and South Carolina (as implied by the ten pages of secondary sources listed in Eudell's bibliography) that his comparison often reads thinly. Second, the choice of a colony (Jamaica) and a state (South Carolina) for regions (British Caribbean, American South) as being representative is debatable. These places are chosen, we are told, because they were "significant" places in slave and post-slavery politics, they contained black numerical majorities, and limited access to land became a major political bone of contention in both areas.[36] Although most southern states did not have black majorities (except Mississippi and South Carolina), this was not the case for the British colonies, all of which had large black majorities, while it is hard to separate any of these three factors (politics, demography, land) from the post-abolition experience of British colonies and southern states. Also, when Eudell informs us that the southern Black Codes and British colonial acts had "local variations" but "contained some unifying elements," we are left wondering why the analysis of Jamaica and South Carolina is *necessarily* more useful than that of any other post-abolition

British colony and southern state?[37] After all, both Foner's optimism about striking black rice workers and Eudell's pessimism concerning former slaves' limited democracy are simply reverse sides of the same post-abolition South Carolina coin. This recalls one of the problems of the first generation of comparative emancipation scholars, for whom a place often took the proxy of a nation. Indeed, although Eudell's argument for a similar racial subjugation clearly differs from his former doctoral adviser's view that the post-emancipation South was far worse than anywhere else, including Jamaica, both draw upon questionable representative units. Finally, it is unclear how this comparison advances our understanding of post-emancipation developments. Because the two emancipation experiences are conflated, there is a stress on similarities rather than differences. Consequently, we are treated to a fairly familiar account of two emancipation experiences whose comparison (re: similarities) reveals little that is actually innovative.

The argument that the postbellum United States represented a unique moment in the expansion of national democracy has been powerfully stated by Steven Hahn. Currently a professor of history at the University of Pennsylvania, and former member of the Freedmen and Southern Society Project, Hahn completed his doctorate under Woodward at Yale University on the political and social transformation of life among yeoman farmers in postbellum upcountry Georgia. An interesting comparative dimension to this work was its conceptual affinity with the famous transition debate from feudalism to capitalism that was the hallmark of European historiography for generations.[38] In a 1990 essay, Hahn provides a comparative treatment of the links between abolition and nation building among the *fazendeiros* (planters) of Brazil, the Prussian Junker landlords, and planters in the American South, concluding that "what stands out in the course of emancipation and unification is the swift and dramatic decline in the fortunes of the Southern planter class."[39] This was an argument—minus the Brazil/Prussia comparison—many southern opponents of federal Reconstruction made at the time; it was also eloquently expressed in Woodward's magnum opus, *The Origins of the New South.*[40]

It might have been because of Hahn's initial lack of attention to the subject of "race" in the nineteenth-century South that he turned in 2003's *Nation under Our Feet* to rural black southerners and their political mobilization after the abolition of slavery. The result is a deep documentary excavation revealing kinship, work, communication, and mobilization among generations of black southerners culminating in a social politics of rural working people's struggles.[41] At the same time, the author situated these social politics within a comparative post-emancipation framework. The participation of blacks in the local politics of southern courthouse towns was of a "magnitude unprecedented in the region, nation, or hemisphere." "In the history of slavery and freedom in the Atlantic world," Hahn concludes, "there never has been nor ever would be anything quite like it."[42]

Hahn's *Nation under Our Feet* has been praised as a major work in U.S. historiography. Most of the reviews, however, ignored the book's comparative statements. Furthermore, it seems a little odd that a book concerned with revealing the rural roots of southern black nationalism should fail to draw upon a vibrant black nationalist historiography by Sterling Stuckey, Lerone Bennett, John Blassingame, Vincent Harding, and Mary Berry, among others. Most important, the comparative argument for a unique democratic experiment is highly debatable for all the reasons mentioned earlier: limited ex-slave political power in the postbellum South, ex-slaves' winning of state power in Haiti, and so forth. Indeed, Hahn's arguments for *both* ex-slaveholders' decline and ex-slaves' politics are part of the same argument for the exceptional expansion of democracy in the postbellum South. But this argument for the uniqueness of American Reconstruction simply reminds us that an explicit argument is already implicit because of its existing assumption of the revolutionary dimensions of the Civil War.

Our third rebuttal of unique U.S. emancipation concerns the argument for the nadir of race relations in the postbellum South. First, there were obvious regional differences that were more important than national differences. The activities of Ku Klux Klan chapters as well as spectacle lynching appear to have been more marked in states in the Lower South than in those in the Upper South.[43] White supremacist attitudes might well have been more akin between extremists in South Carolina and the Boer Republic and between moderates in Virginia and the Cape Province rather than for the entire post-emancipation South compared with fin de siècle South Africa.

Moreover, if the nadir refers to racial violence during the post-abolition decades, then we have to look beyond the post-abolition American

South for its most extreme expression. In the aftermath of colonial abolition in the British West Indies, there were riots and rebellions in 1856 Guiana (now Guyana), 1876 Barbados, and 1884 Trinidad resulting in considerable death and destruction. The Morant Bay revolt in Jamaica in 1865 claimed the lives of 20 whites and more than 430 blacks.[44] In 1912 the Afro-Cuban political organization Partido Independiente de Color pursued armed struggle for the "relegalization of their party" twenty-six years after the abolition of Cuban slavery. The Cuban state's response was a race war against the militants resulting in the deaths of between 2,000 and 6,000 rebels. One contemporary reported: "the roads are strewn with dead bodies."[45] It was Haiti, however, that witnessed some of the worst racial violence. During the war of national liberation in 1802–3, the French military invading forces under General Charles Leclerc tried to reassert their control through a systematic campaign of terror and torture to intimidate the local populace. General Jean Jacques Dessalines responded by massacring white men, women, and children, leaving "stacks of corpses rotting in the sun to strike terror into the French detachments."[46] In April 1804, President Dessalines ordered the systematic extermination of all remaining French citizens in the new nation-state. This act was designed both to mobilize national sentiment and to warn French citizens to stay away from Haiti.[47] In other words, struggles over power between freedom's new generations and older custodians of colonial control and white domination were an inevitable part of post-abolition racial disorder. From this comparative perspective, the emergence of white supremacy in the American South was less unique than it was part of a broader racist reaction to post-emancipation developments throughout the nineteenth-century Atlantic World.

In short, there are two major problems with the argument for exceptional U.S. emancipation. First, it seems that an explicit argument is already implicit because of the assumption that the American Civil War constituted a social revolution. This notion of sweeping revolutionary change is shared by all of these comparative emancipation scholars, in which case we are either reading a more sophisticated version of an existing argument or are reading about American history in more cosmopolitan ways. These are welcome challenges to the parochialism of U.S. history, but what exactly are we learning that is new through the comparison? Second, the nation-based approach toward comparative analysis ends up supporting rather than challenging American difference. The result is that studies motivated by a genuine desire to demonstrate the difference of the American experience through comparison with other national case studies end up providing a more sophisticated version of America's unique historical trajectory.

One possible objection to these rebuttals of comparative U.S. emancipation studies is that they rely on subsequent publications unavailable to earlier scholars. This criticism, however, is unpersuasive for two reasons. First, it ignores the tremendous influence that this first generation of U.S. emancipation scholars has had on reshaping our understanding of post-abolition societies *despite* the emergence of new scholarship. Second, it overlooks the easy assimilation of the original approach and findings into many more recent studies of comparative U.S. emancipation. Thus, Woodward's view of the revolutionary nature of the American Civil War remains uncontested in Hahn's comparison of U.S. emancipation, while the limitations of representative units for comparative analysis remain unchallenged in the work of Fredrickson's mentee Eudell.

This brings us to the influential work of economic historian Stanley L. Engerman. A teacher at the University of Rochester since 1963, Engerman has spent a long career examining the economics of U.S. slavery and emancipation, especially family structure, demographic patterns, and the treatment of slaves. He has also published extensively on various aspects of slavery and emancipation in the British Caribbean, including black fertility, contract labor, land and labor ratios, and regional demographics. It was this expertise that helps explain his selection to deliver the prestigious Walter L. Fleming Lectures at Louisiana State University on April 13–14, 2005.[48] These were subsequently revised and published as *Slavery, Emancipation, and Freedom: Comparative Perspectives* in 2007.[49]

The book provides a comparative examination of slavery, emancipation, and freedom in global perspective divided into two chapters and a postscript. The first chapter concludes that "by world standards, slavery in the American South was not an unusual institution."[50] What was unusual about American slavery, however, was its demographic differences from other slave societies, in particular its higher fertility rates, more equal sex ratios, and more stable family units. This was to be explained by "some combination of better nutrition, lesser work demands, and a more favorable disease environment," with consequences for understanding "differences in slave culture, the nature of slave revolts and resistance, and the question of African survivals."[51]

The second chapter turns to emancipation and focuses on certain commonalities. Thus, most slave emancipation was accomplished with some form of compensation for former slaveholders; the abolition of slavery, with its "combination of increased leisure time, a lessened intensity of labor, and lowered labor force participation rates," had similar positive effects for ex-slaves.[52] The heart of the chapter, however, compares U.S. emancipation with emancipation elsewhere and argues for the former's exceptional nature in two familiar ways. Former slaves' enfranchisement "compared favorably" with that of other ex-slaves as well as citizenship struggles of European immigrants.[53] And the "level of violence" in the postbellum South compared to other post-emancipation societies was unprecedented.[54] The postscript expands the temporal lens by comparing past slavery with contemporary forms of unfree labor, concluding (correctly I think) that many existing evils have little in common with the "permanent purchase and sale of individuals for lifetime labor and with inherited status."[55]

Professor Engerman's 2007 book provides a succinct statement on the global dimensions of slavery and emancipation. Indeed, its publication met with fulsome praise, as suggested by glowing endorsements on the dust jacket by fellow scholars of slavery and abolition studies such as David Brion Davis, Seymour Drescher, and Herbert Klein. But its contribution to comparative U.S. emancipation studies seems less evident for several reasons. First, the unique reproductive rate of slaves in the antebellum South is a very familiar argument in comparative slave studies. Second, the comparative generalization that abolition was often accompanied by compensation is misleading. Slaveholders were compensated in the British West Indies, the Dutch West Indies, and Spanish Puerto Rico, while Haiti was forced to indemnify France twenty-two years after the revolution in exchange for diplomatic recognition. But abolition was not accompanied by compensation in Mexico, the French West Indies, and the Danish West Indies, and particularly in Brazil, Cuba, and the United States, where the majority of slaves in the nineteenth-century Americas were emancipated. The distinction is an important one because emancipation was rarely an orderly legal process, as implied by the previous comparative analysis.

Third, the comparative framework is outdated. In 1959, Stanley Elkins's *Slavery* argued that slaves in the American South had been infantilized by unimpeded capitalism compared to slaves elsewhere in the hemisphere. Students of slavery (and abolition) all owe an inestimable debt to Professor Elkins for provoking many scholars to prove him wrong, resulting in slave studies periodically becoming one of the most vibrant fields in U.S. historiography. Yet Engerman's 2007 preface still refers to "two critical questions" about slavery's legacy and master/slave psychology first raised by Elkins![56]

Fourth, much of the exciting historical literature exploring the local, regional, national, and comparative dimensions of slave and emancipation studies is simply ignored. Many pre-2007 publications listed in this chapter's endnotes do not show up in Engerman's bibliography. Furthermore, the author fails to engage exciting new historical literature on topics like the imperialist and gendered dimensions of Asian indentured servitude since the 1990s by Verene Shepherd, Bridget Brereton, Barbara Bailey, Madhavi Kale, Rosemarijn Hoefte, Patricia Mohammed, and Andrew Wilson.[57] As one reviewer reminds us, what is missing "is a full explication of race and the issues of cultural survival and regeneration," issues germane to most current studies of slavery and emancipation.[58]

Most important for our purposes, Engerman fails to move the comparison of U.S. emancipation beyond its original moorings. In other words, U.S. abolition was exceptional in its enfranchising of ex-slaves, while racial violence in the post-emancipation American South was unprecedented in its ferocity. Moreover, the author's insistence on the demographic uniqueness of U.S. slavery is not pursued into the post-emancipation era. Engerman's reiteration of the familiar argument of higher fertility rates, a more balanced gender ratio, and greater familial stability among southern U.S. slaves compared to slaves elsewhere should have made American emancipation exceptional compared to other post-emancipation societies with presumably less fertility, more males than females, and less stable family units. Instead, Engerman concludes that ex-slaves' desires to "become family farmers on small units" in the American South was also common in the post-abolition British Caribbean. How, we might reasonably inquire, could such profoundly different social conditions of slavery result in strikingly similar post-emancipation outcomes?[59] The author's conclusion begs questions concerning the significance of slave/ex-slave demographic differences in the British Caribbean and the American South as well as their intra-regional comparison.

This brief essay is less concerned with providing a comprehensive review of U.S. emancipation studies and other comparative treatments of abolition than in seeking to show the significance of the choice and interpretation of comparisons and their legacy.[60] One of the major problems of comparative U.S. emancipation scholarship is its national and nationalist focus. The consequence is that studies motivated by a genuine desire to demonstrate the difference of the American experience through comparison with other national case studies end up providing a more sophisticated version of America's unique historical trajectory. Thus, U.S. comparative emancipation has become a new secular version of an older narrative of God's Republic. Moreover, this comparative approach transcends its particular historical moment of the 1970s and 1980s stretching back into the past (1870s) as well as into subsequent comparative studies (post-1990s). In short, although U.S. emancipation was far from exceptional, the view that it was unique and special continues to exert a major influence in the field of emancipation studies.

What is the significance of comparative U.S. emancipation for this volume's exploration of various "geospatial frameworks" for understanding the modern American South? There are several key points. First, the expansion of the spatial framework makes little difference if there is a nationalist bent to comparative emancipation studies. When the spatial framework is expanded to situate the U.S. South in the Atlantic World, it remains exceptional. Race relations in the post-abolition American South were unique in their violent breakdown compared to Jamaica and South Africa. The extension of political rights to former slaves in the American South was unique compared to other post-emancipation societies in the Atlantic World. Second, the claim for exceptional U.S. emancipation downplays the significance of emancipation in other regions of the hemisphere. For instance, the argument for the revolutionary nature of slavery abolition in the United States implies a greater degree of continuity elsewhere in post-abolition societies. Yet some slave societies experienced total revolutions (Haiti), others went through political transformations associated with the establishment of national independence (Cuba), and others were transformed from monarchies into republics (Brazil).

Third, comparative U.S. emancipation studies ignore *connections* between the United States and emancipation elsewhere in the Americas.

The overthrow of slavery in Haiti had a major impact on slaveholders, abolitionists, free blacks, and slaves especially in the United States and Cuba throughout the nineteenth century.[61] The passage of British colonial abolition during the 1830s was to play a significant role in the mobilization of antislavery protest movements throughout the English-speaking Atlantic World.[62] The legal abolition of slavery in the United States in 1865 contributed to the ending of the Cuban slave trade in 1867. It also left Cuba, Puerto Rico, and Brazil as the sole surviving slave regimes in the Americas, a disjuncture yet to be fully explored by historians.[63]

Finally, if the subjects are slavery and emancipation, then the nineteenth-century Atlantic and the Western Hemisphere must be privileged geospatial frameworks over the Pacific Rim and continental territories because this was the place and time for slavery and emancipation. As this essay has demonstrated, however, there are limitations to a comparative method with expanded spatial dimensions, especially if the premise is the national unit of organization or if the expanded framework serves to confirm a preexisting argument of magnitude.

Let us return to 1876. It is evident that even though too many comparative U.S. emancipation studies smack of a new version of uniqueness, these are beyond the sort of celebratory nationalist rhetoric of the first centennial. It would be foolish and dishonest to reduce the critical deliberations of important liberal and leftist scholars to the ebullient shouts of nationalist cheerleaders. At the same time, one is struck by the compatibility of U.S. history in comparative perspective. We live in a particular historical conjuncture during which the United States has been busy spreading "liberty" globally over the past two decades. This was exemplified in rhetorical triumphs like the fall of the Berlin Wall and the end of history in democratic free-market systems, together with American military enforcement in Kuwait and the Balkans during the 1990s. After the attacks of September 11, 2001, the United States has more aggressively sought to oust tyrannical regimes, especially in the Arab-speaking world. Only future historians will be able to reveal not only the contours of this historical moment but also its impact on a subsequent generation of comparative U.S. scholarship. What is disturbing is the lack of discontinuity between existing U.S. policies of spreading freedom globally, arguments for exceptional U.S. emancipation compared to other abolitions, and the boisterous claim by British-born Thomas Armitage that America has done more for liberty and against bondage than all other nations.

Notes

My thanks to Ashraf Rushdy, Rob Gregg, Ana Araujo, Edna Medford, and Elizabeth Lindquist for critical feedback, and to Brian Ward, Dave Brown, and Bill Link for editorial improvements.

1. Frederick Saunders, ed., *Our National Centennial Jubilee* (New York: E. B. Treat, 1877), 52, 191, 215, 352. The bargain referred to by Armitage was 20 million pounds sterling in compensation to slaveholders as one of the key terms of the 1833 British Abolition of Slavery Act.

2. Ian Tyrell, "American Exceptionalism in an Age of International History," *American Historical Review* 96 (October 1991): 1031–55; Ian Tyrell, "Making Nations/Making States: American Historians in the Context of Empire," *Journal of American History* 86, no. 3 (1999): 1015–44; Robert Gregg, *Inside Out, Outside In: Essays in Comparative History* (New York: St. Martin's Press, 2000).

3. C. V. Woodward, "Emancipations and Reconstructions: A Comparative Study," International Congress of Historical Sciences (Moscow: NAUKA Publishing House, 1970), subsequently republished as "The Price of Freedom" in *What Was Freedom's Price?* ed. David G. Sansing (Jackson: University of Mississippi Press, 1978), 93–113. All references are to the 1970 edition.

4. Eric Foner, *Nothing but Freedom: Emancipation and Its Legacy* (Baton Rouge: Louisiana State University Press, 1983).

5. George Fredrickson, "After Emancipation: A Comparative Study of The White Responses to the New Order of Race Relations in the American South, Jamaica, and the Cape Colony of South Africa," in Sansing, *What was Freedom's Price?* 71–92. This was subsequently republished as "White Responses to Emancipation: The American South, Jamaica, and the Cape of Good Hope" in George Fredrickson, *The Arrogance of Race: Historical Perspectives on Slavery, Racism, and Social Inequality* (Middletown, Conn.: Wesleyan University Press, 1988), 236–53. All references are to the 1988 republication.

6. Frank Tannenbaum, *Slave and Citizen: The Negro in the Americas* (New York: Vintage, 1946); Stanley Elkins, *Slavery: A Problem in American Institutional and Intellectual Life* (Chicago: University of Chicago Pres, 1959); Eugene D. Genovese, ed., *The Slave Economies: Historical and Theoretical Perspectives*, vol. 1 (New York: John Wiley, 1973). For a good recent comparative slave study that is less useful for U.S. events, see Laird W. Bergad, *The Comparative Histories of Slavery in Brazil, Cuba, and the United States* (New York: Cambridge University Press, 2007).

7. Woodward, "Emancipations and Reconstructions," 155–56.

8. Ibid.

9. Foner, *Nothing but Freedom*, 2.

10. Eric Foner, *Reconstruction: America's Unfinished Revolution* (New York: Harper and Row, 1988).

11. Fredrickson, "White Reponses to Emancipation," 236–37.

12. Woodward, "Emancipations and Reconstructions," 159.

13. Ibid., 172.

14. Fredrickson, "White Reponses to Emancipation," 251.

15. Foner, *Nothing but Freedom*, 6.

16. Ibid., 3.

17. Fredrickson, "White Reponses to Emancipation," 247.

18. Woodward, "Emancipations and Reconstructions," 172; Foner, *Nothing but Freedom*, 3.

19. George Reid Andrews, *Afro-Latin America, 1800–2000* (New York: Oxford University Press, 2004); Peter Blanchard, *Under the Flags of Freedom: Slave Soldiers and the Wars of Independence in Spanish South America* (Pittsburgh: University of Pittsburgh Press, 2008); Ada Ferrer, *Insurgent Cuba: Race, Nation, and Revolution, 1868–1898* (Chapel Hill: University of North Carolina Press, 1999).

20. Andrews, *Afro-Latin America*, 80–83.

21. Bergad, *Comparative Histories*, 21.

22. Alex Dupuy, *Haiti in the World Economy: Class, Race, and Underdevelopment Since 1700* (Boulder, Col.: Westview Press, 1989), 54; Laurent Dubois, *Avengers of the New World: The Story of the Haitian Revolution* (Cambridge: Harvard University Press, 2004), 302. Patrick Manning, *The African Diaspora: A History through Culture* (New York: Columbia University Press, 2009), 149, suggests that battlefield losses and massacres in Saint-Domingue make "the revolutions in the United States, France, and the Latin American nations appear as gentlemanly disagreements in comparison." This exaggeration still makes the point.

23. Eric Hobsbawn, *The Age of Extremes: A History of the World, 1914–1991* (New York: Pantheon Books, 1994), 26.

24. Ira Berlin et al., *Freedom's Soldiers* (Cambridge: Cambridge University Press, 1998), 125.

25. Ferrer, *Insurgent Cuba*, 68.

26. W. E. B. Du Bois, *Black Reconstruction in America, 1860–1880* (New York: Atheneum, 1935).

27. Foner, *Reconstruction*, 317.

28. Ibid., 318.

29. Kenneth M. Stampp, *The Era of Reconstruction, 1865–1877* (New York: Vintage, 1965), 167.

30. Du Bois, *Black Reconstruction*, 728.

31. Demetrius L. Eudell, *The Political Languages of Emancipation in the British Caribbean and the U.S. South* (Chapel Hill: University of North Carolina Press, 2002).

32. Ibid., 180.

33. Ibid., 12.

34. Ibid., 100.

35. *International History Review* 25, no. 2 (2003): 422–23; *American Historical Review* 108, no. 1 (2003): 160–61; *South Carolina Historical Magazine* 104, no. 2 (2003): 126–27; *Journal of American History* 90, no. 1 (2003): 239–40.

36. Eudell, *Political Languages of Emancipation*, 14–15.

37. Ibid., 53.

38. Steven Hahn, *The Roots of Southern Populism: Yeoman Framers and the Transformation of the Georgia Upcountry, 1850–1890* (New York: Oxford University Press, 1983).

Hahn's concluding essay on sources acknowledges the influence of British Marxist historians Eric Hobsbawn and Edward Thompson.

39. Steven Hahn, "Class and State in Postemancipation Societies: Southern Planters in Comparative Perspective," *American Historical Review* 95 (February 1990): 98.

40. C. Vann Woodward, *The Origins of the New South, 1877–1913* (Baton Rouge: Louisiana State University Press, 1951).

41. Steven Hahn, *Nation under Our Feet: Black Political Struggles in the Rural South from Slavery to the Great Migration* (Cambridge: Harvard University Press, 2003); Jeffrey R. Kerr-Ritchie, review of *Nation under Our Feet* by Hahn, in *Virginia Magazine of History and Biography* 113, no. 4 (2005): 429–31.

42. Hahn, *Nation under Our Feet*, 218, 115.

43. W. Fitzhugh Brundage, *Lynching in the New South: Georgia and Virginia, 1880–1930* (Urbana: University of Illinois Press, 1993).

44. Michael Craton, *Testing the Chains: Resistance to Slavery in the British West Indies* (Ithaca: Cornell University Press, 1982), 323–34.

45. Aline Helg, *Our Rightful Share: The Afro-Cuban Struggle for Equality, 1886–1912* (Chapel Hill: University of North Carolina Press, 1997), 222–26.

46. C. L. R. James, *The Black Jacobins: Toussaint L'Ouverture and the San Domingo Revolution* (New York: Vintage, 1963), 310.

47. James, *Black Jacobins*, 370–75; Dupuy, *Haiti in the World Economy*, 75–76.

48. Foner's *Nothing but Freedom* drew upon Engerman's 1982 Fleming lectures.

49. Stanley L. Engerman, *Slavery, Emancipation, and Freedom: Comparative Perspectives* (Baton Rouge: Louisiana State University Press, 2007).

50. Ibid., 16.

51. Ibid., 33–36.

52. Ibid., 51.

53. Ibid., 62.

54. Ibid., 65.

55. Ibid., 91.

56. Ibid., x.

57. Verene Shepherd, Bridget Brereton, Barbara Bailey, eds., *Engendering History: Caribbean Women in Historical Perspective* (New York: St. Martin's Press, 1995); Madhavi Kale, *Fragments of Empire: Capital, Slavery, and Indian Indentured Labor in the British Caribbean* (Philadelphia: University of Pennsylvania Press, 1998); Rosemarijn Hoefte, *In Place of Slavery: A Social History of British Indian and Javanese Laborers in Suriname* (Gainesville: University Press of Florida 1998); Verene Shepherd, *Maharani's Misery: Narratives of a Passage of from India* (Mona, Jamaica: University of West Indies Press, 2002); Patricia Mohammed, *Gender Negotiations among Indians in Trinidad, 1917–1947* (Basingstoke, U.K.: Palgrave, 2002); Andrew Wilson, ed., *The Chinese in the Caribbean* (Princeton: Marcus Wiener, 2004).

58. Paul Lovejoy's review in the *Journal of Interdisciplinary History* 39, no. 2 (2008): 283. Engerman's sole reference to racism concerns the importation of sugar plantation indentured workers to late nineteenth century Australia on page 58.

59. Engerman, *Slavery, Emancipation, and Freedom*, 55. Even more remarkable is the failure to pursue this important demographic difference in Pamela Scully and Diana Paton, eds., *Gender and Slave Emancipation in the Atlantic World* (Durham: Duke University Press, 2005), a collection that insists that "gender was central to slave emancipation and to the making of the nineteenth-century Atlantic world" (1).

60. For instance, we have not examined the Freedmen and Southern Society Project's influential work on emancipation because it is primarily concerned with the United States. Although the FSSP seeks to place U.S. emancipation within a global framework of capitalist social relations, new property rights, and slavery abolition, it is not explicitly comparative. Similarly, important comparative emancipation studies by Thomas Holt on Jamaica and Ireland, Rebecca Scott on Cuba and Louisiana, Fredrick Cooper on Africa, and Kim Butler on Brazil are not included because these are not U.S. comparative emancipation studies.

61. Jeffrey R. Kerr-Ritchie, *Freedom's Seekers: Essays in Comparative Emancipation* (forthcoming). This eight-chapter manuscript offers an alternative comparative emancipation methodology.

62. Jeffrey R. Kerr-Ritchie, *Rites of August First: Emancipation Day in the Black Atlantic World* (Baton Rouge: Louisiana State University Press, 2007).

63. Bergad, *Comparative Histories*, 278.

8

The Textual Atlantic

Race, Time, and Representation in the Writings of AME Bishop Levi Jenkins Coppin

LEIGH ANNE DUCK

Born on December 24, 1848, to a free family in Frederick Town, Maryland—which he proudly identifies as the birthplace of Frederick Douglass—Levi Jenkins Coppin was elected bishop of the African Methodist Episcopal Church in 1900, at a time when it was solidifying its connection with the South African Ethiopian Church.[1] As historian James T. Campbell explains in *Songs of Zion: The African Methodist Episcopal Church in the United States and South Africa*, these two denominations had a great deal in common: each was created through separation from a white-controlled Methodist or Wesleyan Church in societies largely governed through white supremacist policies, and the leadership of each—recognizing the societal obstacles they would face in establishing autonomous black denominations—immediately set to work to clarify institutional theology and structure.[2] The AME Church was formed in 1816 in Pennsylvania—which was largely, but not completely, free at the time—by former slaves, but the Ethiopian Church, founded in 1892, faced even greater organizational difficulties, as it sought to establish itself across two Afrikaner republics and two colonies of the British Empire while also evangelizing persons with diverse religions and languages.[3] Aware of these challenges, Coppin nonetheless reports in his autobiography, *Unwritten History* (1919), that he was eager to see and learn about a bit of the African continent as the AME's first bishop of Cape Town.

Coppin's mission in South Africa was acutely ambivalent: although it shared much with the philosophy and procedures of colonialism, his motivations and experiences led him to question and critique that project.

His primary tropes for exploring this ambivalence were temporal, as he negotiated the prevailing rhetorics—as well as his own ideas—concerning "modernity" and "backwardness." Jennifer Rae Greeson argues that, after the Civil War, many U.S. writers compared the nation's role in its southern region to the European imperial powers' simultaneous interest in Africa: both region and continent were seen as constituting a "site unequivocally destined for imperial administration from without" and a "challenge to the 'Civilizing Mission.'"[4] This analogy is implicit in Coppin's writing on both areas, as he believed his role—and that of the AME—was to uplift the previously enslaved and the currently colonized. He credited racist and capitalist exploitation with the "moral and intellectual darkness" that he projected onto enslaved persons, and he believed that through providing the "uplifting influences" that would inculcate bourgeois norms, the AME would defy such exploitation.[5] But this temporal tension is irreducible: critical of the modernity with which he identified, he was also often critical of those he considered backward. The contradiction was no less acute in South Africa. Even as he worried about the "millions . . . yet in darkness" without the "advantages of civilization," he also noted that "modern civilization" was producing discrimination and exploitation, or, in his words, "exceeding sinfulness."[6]

Coppin's work provides not only a substantial record of how one AME pastor explored a vexing question in that church's mission but also profound consideration of how transnational archives can facilitate or inhibit understanding. The phrase "textual Atlantic" revises Paul Gilroy's famous concept of "Black Atlantic" in a way that is crucial for Coppin's case, because Gilroy's model, in Sandra Gunning's words, risks "romanticizing" "diaspora identification," displacing differences across African and diasporic spaces in order to emphasize "revolutionary and subversive power" amid the latter.[7] For some such analyses, creating a coherent diasporic identity involves imagining West Africa chiefly as the home of a racial past and occluding other regions of the continent.[8] In contrast, Coppin is not only interested in the modernity of his new dwelling but also duly circumspect regarding whether he shares a common ancestry with his new parishioners. In preparing for his mission, however, he becomes acutely aware that African Americans and South African peoples of color share a history of insidious misrepresentation. In his case, awareness of a shared struggle against racist print culture produces a sense of commonality with his new parishioners; an ardent bibliophile—in his autobiography, he notes, "The Angel said to John, 'What thou seest, write in a book'"—he sets out to correct the record.[9] His efforts in this regard illustrate the argument of Bill Ashcroft, Gareth Griffiths, and Helen Tiffin that in "early post-colonial texts . . . the potential for subversion . . . cannot be fully realized. . . . Both the available discourse and the material conditions of production for literature in these early post-colonial societies restrain this possibility."[10] Coppin's difficulties are compounded by the geographical and conceptual limitations of his beliefs, including his identification—however questioning and ambivalent—with Western modernity. Nonetheless, his efforts to explore this tension illustrate the difficulty, as well as the dynamism, in what Brent Hayes Edwards describes as the risky intellectual labor of diaspora.[11]

Race, Time, and Representation

From his very first description of Cape Town in *Observations of Persons and Things in South Africa* (1905), Coppin challenges the trope of a monolithically backward continent: describing the "beautiful modern city," he observes, "many people, in thinking about Africa, 'Darkest Africa!' do not always stop to consider that civilization has been in this portion of the Continent for a long time."[12] Coppin's understanding of "civilization" directly associates that term with capitalist development, especially industrial and corporate advancement. Accordingly, he exults, "The sanitary improvements are up to date. Electric cars are plentiful. . . . Telephone, telegraph and cable facilities are the same as in London or New York."[13] Like many other African Americans of his era, Coppin was fascinated by Henry Morton Stanley's travelogues concerning Africa, which did so much to promote the image of "Darkest Africa" in the United Kingdom and the United States. Passages in Coppin's *Observations*, as Campbell points out, resemble "any of a hundred other late nineteenth-century 'Dark Continent' travel accounts," and Coppin openly identifies with "the explorers, the Livingstons and the Stanleys."[14] Coppin, however, believes that these travelers are more aware of the continent's diversity than other visitors, and he inscribes himself into a similar position of expertise in order to contest the imperial tropes that aligned the continent's people with an earlier, childlike or savage stage of development.[15] Although he retains the idea that some people are more advanced than others—a form of temporal distancing—he insists on complicating the map.[16]

Coppin's autobiography reveals that he had long been interested in—albeit ambivalent about—ideas of national and racial progress, in which the projects of sociopolitical and technological improvement unfold continuously through linear time. Reproducing a column he wrote in 1893 as editor of the *AME Review*, this volume records his impressions of the Columbian Exposition in Chicago, which he describes as demonstrating "the march of civilization."[17] Coppin unsettles this concept, however, by obliquely referring to the fair's exclusion of any specifically African American exhibit and of African Americans themselves from the managing commission. Wilberforce University's exhibit, as well as the Haitian Building, represent, in his account, "a people, the genius, industry, and capability of whom, but for them, would have been without representation, or, as is frequently the case . . . misrepresented."[18]

Like Ida B. Wells, the driving force behind the pamphlet *The Reason Why the Colored American Is Not in the World's Columbian Exposition* (1893), Coppin argues that "the genius of the Negro is interwoven with the civilization of America, and indeed of the world, but in such a way as to leave him without credit."[19] Because this "civilization" has progressed through largely oppressive and stolen labor—and because elites still refuse to recognize the efforts of black people in the Americas—Coppin implies that such advancement may impose spiritual and moral costs. Observing that most industrialized nations represented "are Christian," he imagines a future moment of assessment: "At the expiration of another century, when all the civilized nations assemble to take account of their achievements, what nation will be first in the sisterhood? May we not give the answer of our Lord, when he was asked who shall be greatest in the kingdom of heaven?"[20] Citing Jesus' response to the disciples' jostling over rank—an answer that emphasized the rewards not of sophistication but of humility—Coppin does not specifically situate this reversal in the afterlife, suggesting that the earthly status of "first" may be fleeting.

This criticism of the "advanced" nations reflects the AME's complicated relationship to capitalist notions of progress. Believing that racial equality could be successfully pursued through economic gain and bourgeois acculturation, the church embraced market values in many respects but also criticized the racial exploitation and discrimination encompassed in much capitalist activity.[21] Coppin promoted both of these messages, perpetually advocating "study, toil, and sacrifice" for those who would take "progressive steps in civilization" and insisting, in his *Observations*, that "To carry civilization and the Gospel to a benighted people is the indispensable duty of the Christian Church," but also decrying the racist policies that denied African Americans the tools—"civil, political and economic rights, privileges and opportunities"—needed to participate fully in U.S. modernity.[22] His complex, even freighted approach to the linear chronology of capitalist "progress" coexists with a very different view of time rooted in his theological beliefs and understanding of racial history. From this perspective he notes that slaves' intellectual and spiritual achievements despite excruciating circumstances testify to "the moral nature and moral power of God"; sadly, however, this view—which transcends linear time—is inaccessible to humans, because that "unique chapter in the world's history . . . is unwritten, unwriteable, and largely unknown."[23]

Coppin's use of the book to imagine a divine perspective on history and progress—in God's eyes, slavery constitutes a *chapter* in world history—reflects a continuing theme in his work, wherein both divine and textual realms introduce chronotopes (representational space-times) through which human activity may be judged in a way that cannot yet be presumed.[24] Such a link well suits a cleric whose attachment to text is in part biographical: in his autobiography he admiringly describes his mother's labors to imbue him with both legally proscribed literacy and a religious faith unsupported by his father.[25] Further, for an adherent to a faith with roots in the Enlightenment, text and scripture constitute a central aspect of spiritual experience; the history of Methodist development created that denomination as a dispersed community of writers and readers.[26] Textuality and rhetoric were arguably even more important in the development of the AME, which sought both spiritual and political influence. A vigorous reader across multiple literary styles and periods, and a vigorous writer in multiple genres and discursive contexts, founder Richard Allen sought to inscribe his new denomination within, in the words of his biographer, "the Republic of Letters."[27] Coppin contributed to such efforts from early in his ministry, serving as editor of the *AME Review* for eight years and penning, as his second book, *The Key to Scriptural Interpretation* (1895).[28] He was also a close friend and supporter of Bishop Daniel Alexander Payne, the AME's first historian and, not incidentally, an influential devotee of uplift and liturgical conservatism. This connection may have prompted Coppin's opening reflection in the *Observations*: "The *first things* in the history of an organization are of special importance. . . . And yet, the historian so often finds when he comes to write, that those first things have been lost."[29]

Coppin's bibliophily may also have offered some resolution to the tensions of uplift, with its simultaneous censure and support. Coppin may have felt these tensions with particular acuteness, as he was highly attuned to differences in "deportment"; further, his autobiography recounts that, when he first stood for election to the bishopric, his candidacy was derailed by the rumor that "he hates Southern men."[30] Coppin contests that charge through both biography—"I, myself, a Southerner by birth. . . . Father and mother sleep in southern soil"—and affiliation, noting that he had traveled throughout the region for the AME and had come to admire the leaders there.[31] But Campbell reports that Coppin had indeed expressed patronizing attitudes toward the familial and religious practices of ex-slaves, and when he later complained, in his letters to AME colleagues in the United States, that South African ministers lacked "maturity and experience" and tended too often to "'polemical indiscretions' and to flouting denominational policies and procedures," he compared them in these ways to early AME ministers in the U.S. South.[32]

Nonetheless, when his books describe the challenges confronting parishioners in each context, he worries less about the pace of their progress than the distorting way in which it would be represented. Although his ministerial comments and practices suggest that he felt an urgent pressure to instruct oppressed peoples in contemporary bourgeois propriety, his reflections on archives are guided less by a sense of linear time—in which one must not fall behind—than by a desire to impart lasting wisdom, such that present and future readers will be able to more fully understand the lives of the oppressed.

Paradoxically, then, Coppin's recourse to a divine temporality fuels his interest in historicity. As Yogita Goyal argues, romantic fictions of the Black Atlantic often mobilize a messianic mode "to imagine diaspora as a utopian horizon" or to "collapse distances of time and space to imagine a simultaneity of experience."[33] In contrast, Coppin's nonfiction figures Atlantic sites as utterly distinct places linked by an incomplete and often insidiously misleading archive. Further, the utopian elements of his work are less diasporic than divine—a heaven in which the faith of people of color is recognized and rewarded and "all will be judged impartially, the oppressed and the oppressor."[34] *Unwritten History* does include monadic figures whose suffering seems both to transcend linear history and to demand human (as opposed to solely divine) response; such images, to cite Walter Benjamin, seem to "flare up" from Coppin's prose as "at a moment of danger," and such a representational strategy corresponds to some critical work on the Black Atlantic, particularly that of Ian Baucom.[35] The most notable of these, in Coppin's autobiography, is the violated slave woman, who "had no one to write of her wisdom and heroism," was required to produce numerous "illegitimate births," was subjected to the "nameless crime," and was forced to choose "between submitting, or undergoing hellish tortures that cannot be named."[36] But Coppin's depiction of this suffering serves less to collapse the difference between past and present than to highlight the ways in which misrepresenting the past (through either falsehood or omission) jeopardizes the present.

In his autobiography, Coppin argues that correction of the archive should contribute directly to the goals of uplift, for while the loss of slaves' biographies is saddening in and of itself, it also threatens to demoralize later generations: "Unless we, as a people, do some writing of a historical nature, we may but expect that much that would be inspiring and educative to our youth, will be buried in the past, while much that is unfavorable, and hence depressing, will be exhibited as true history."[37] He situates this discussion in the context of the virulent racism pervading U.S. popular culture, remarking that Thomas Dixon's *The Clansman* (1905) "has gone ahead with its story of slander and misrepresentation and not altogether without making the impression that was originally intended."[38] Coppin argues that such representations perpetuate and compound the harms of slavery, during which "it was so rooted and grounded in [some slaves'] very nature that they were inferior beings that the belief was literally transmitted to their children."[39] Coppin can only surmise such beliefs, and his motivations for doing so emerge in part from his experience of class tensions; shortly before writing his autobiography, while riding in a "drawing room" car, he heard "a young Negro . . . still of school age" call out in apparent "horr[or] at the presumption? of 'niggers'—mind you—riding in a car that could have only been intended for 'white folks.'"[40] But his desire for his bourgeois status to be recognized and appreciated corresponds with a desire to see aspiration among the young, which he hopes will be inspired by awareness of previous black achievement. Accordingly, he emphasizes the accomplishments of slaves who, "in spite of [their] environment," had "highly developed intellects" and "moral strength to an amazing degree" as a way to both counter misrepresentation and sustain people "not yet out of the wilderness of proscription and prejudice."[41] He also promotes the work of African American authors, creating a section in his personal library titled "Black Boys" (with apparent irony, though he attributes this bit of wit to his friend Bishop Benjamin Arnett) and arguing that "When our authors and editors of marked ability get a hearing before the world, public opinion will undergo a change, because the merits and virtues of the 'brother in black' will be set forth as well as his demerits and so-called backwardness."[42] His *Observations* suggest his belief that such recognition must ultimately be global.

Race and the Global Archive

Observations was also written with an eye to more pragmatic concerns, as the AME bishop of Cape Town sought to address multiple and in some respects incommensurable audiences. Coppin had to persuade the church in the United States that its South African project was both worthy and promising. Campbell notes that, throughout Coppin's tenure in South Africa, he faced criticism from Africans that the AME had failed to fund the college it had promised during its early negotiations with its partner, while the church in the United States wanted South Africans to provide the central church greater financial support.[43] Even the suggestion of shared racial identification could be controversial among some of Coppin's potential readers: though such ideas underpinned AME interest in African missions more generally, white South African elites found such rhetoric threatening.[44] Accordingly, his argument that "the Native man does not readily confide in men of a different race variety. . . . In this the Native man is after all very much like other men"—like his insistence that the AME Church in South Africa has chosen to "make no distinction on account of race or color"—may be strategic, for together such claims suggest that any sense of racial exclusivity emerges from South Africans themselves, and that Coppin's church, while inclusive in orientation, merely fills the need created by preexisting understandings of race.[45]

Still, Coppin's enthusiastic description of South Africa's "cosmopolitan people" seems unrelated to either of those goals; rather, it supports his repeatedly referenced goal of correcting the textual record.[46] Although he argues, in his *Observations*, that black South Africans "generally" greet him as one of the "kinsmen from whom for long years [they] had been separated," he does not claim this sense of shared ancestry, instead explaining in his autobiography, "I wanted to see . . . the land of Ham."[47] Citing the familiar trope mobilized by white supremacists in the United States and elsewhere as they sought biblical authorization for the enslavement and oppression of Africans and their descendants, Coppin emphasizes the discursive production of race and its insidious effects. This is not to say that he forswears the racial discourse that was so influential in his own country. On the contrary, his prose reflects his avid interest in the era's racial pseudo-science, assigning "low" and "superior" assessments to various "types" of ethnicity, and attributing detrimental economic effects to Jews.[48] But in some cases he uses this discourse against reductive representations of race, complaining that the diversity of African ethnicities has been overlooked in "the school geography" presented to Americans and others. Contradicting the "model" of "the true African type with the characteristic thick lips, big feet, and receding fore heads," Coppin insists, "The variations in size, features and even color are as great among Africans, as among other race varieties" and argues that the peoples of Africa and its diaspora, because they are more diverse than Europeans, provide a better field for the "science of Ethnology."[49] Arguing throughout his text that those who have not visited Africa are "deluded" by the representations they have encountered, Coppin "confess[es] that upon seeing the African at his home, I was surprised," but rather than dispensing with the interpretive frameworks that produced his misconception, he seeks, in his *Observations*, to improve the information contained therein.[50]

Although his adherence to certain forms of racial categorization makes his strategy paradoxical, much of his critique nonetheless mocks racial hierarchy and accounts of racial purity. Impressed with the nation's diversity—noting migrants from Europe, Asia, and the Americas, as well as "a mixed multitude, sharing the blood of almost every nation under the heavens"—he criticizes those who "class themselves" above others, attributing such practices to "the policy of the Europeans," by whom "the colored man was taught to feel that he was better than the native."[51] Admiring the work of the "Mohammedans, who unite all races by their religion," he hopes that the AME will contribute to the "spirit of unity," which he argues is already emerging. Arriving in Cape Town during the Anglo-Boer War, he argues that changing political structures as well as the growth of the city, the influx of international capital, and the recent outbreak of plague had intensified conflict between whites and people of color and had thus also begun to mitigate the "gulf between the Natives

and Cape colored people, and between these, and the Indians and Ma-
lays."[52] Insisting that racial division is ethically wrong—an "unchristian
deception"—he also suggests that it misrepresents ancestry; in this way, he
uses racial pseudo-science to argue for the blurring of racial distinctions.
Accordingly, for example, South Africans' use of "the expression 'European extraction' cannot by any interpretation be made to mean persons
of pure Caucasian blood according to the Blumenbach theory."[53]

In criticizing hypocrisy concerning a history of racial mixing, Coppin
is not differentiating South Africa from the United States but rather noting a trait there that he would later remark in his home country. In his
autobiography, he points to the history of rape: having noted "the nameless crime . . . that filled our land with mulattoes," he argues that "the
amalgamations Americana that slave conditions brought about gave us
so many American fathers, that should such offsprings go to Africa, it
certainly would not be going to Father Land."[54] Although his tone here
is wryly matter-of-fact, Coppin approaches a related topic from a more
playful angle. Speculating as to whether his family's "peculiar friendship"
with some white Coppins, whom he believes to be of German ancestry,
indicates that they knew "more about the origin of our father than they
ever told us," he concludes, "This is not the most auspicious time to look it
up, while the Kaiser is in such disfavor."[55] Remembering the family fondly,
and reporting the history of his speculations in the manner of a linguistic
and ancestral mystery, his point seems less to cast blame on a previous
white Coppin than to underscore how the familial histories of black and
white Americans are intertwined. In the process of debunking assumptions of racial coherence and purity, he also notes their potential to yield
intolerance—even against white people.

Similarly, in his writing about South Africa he inscribes less a sense of
racial commonality than of shared confrontation with racist misrepresentation and abuse. I do not want to overstate the significance of Coppin's
geographical path. On one hand, African American writers who travel
to Africa's western coast have often noted the ways in which their understandings or expectations of shared racial identity are disrupted by their
experiences there.[56] On the other hand, Coppin does rather whimsically
argue, based on certain physical features, that a woman from his home-
town must have been a "Hottentot."[57] But his autobiography reports that,
as he undertook his voyage to Cape Town, his understanding of South
African cultures was entirely textual, and his anecdote so starkly renders

the connection between race and representation as to merit extended reproduction:

> I filled some lecture engagements, as means of collecting some funds to assisting the work over there. Of course the subject of my lectures was: "Africa," or "South Africa," or "The Dark Continent." It is amazing, how much one can say upon a subject that he knows absolutely nothing about. But are there not books upon every imaginable subject? Yes, verily: "of making many books, there is no end." I soon collected a small library on various phases of Africa, its peoples etc. Those books contained a great deal of information, but most of them contained also many errors. . . . In the books I read, I saw much about the Kafirs, and so, supposing that they were the principal tribes among whom I would have to work, I informed myself concerning them, and lectured about them before leaving America.
>
> Now imagine my mortification when I found that there was no such tribe. . . . The word originated among the Mohammedans, and meant, something like "infidel": one outside of the faith: no reference to race at all. . . . It finally came to be used opprobriously, just as in America the word "nigger" is used.
>
> Just imagine my chagrin, when, in conversation with a Wesleyan—white—minister on the boat between Southampton and Cape Town I, informed him, with much confidence and zest, that I was on my way to South Africa, to labor among the "Kafirs," and he, with a sarcastic retort, replied: "there are no Kafirs to labor among." It was a "home blow." I could not reply. I had only "read" about them. From what I afterwards learned about the gentleman and his work among the Natives, I think he must have enjoyed the shot that took my breath.[58]

Coppin's predicament parallels historical discussions about translation described by Edwards in *The Practice of Diaspora*—particularly concerning the words "*Négre*," "*négre*," "*noir*," "Negro," "nigger," and "black"—except that before Coppin boards the ship for South Africa, he lacks sufficiently diverse sources of information even to realize that he has encountered a quandary.[59] And the shock is profound: for a bishop preparing to deal with an entirely new and almost thoroughly unknown constituency and a black man traveling across the Atlantic from one white supremacist nation to another, to hear that he has been traveling about the United States applying racist epithets to his new parishioners is, as he notes, "mortifying."

To receive this news from a representative of the very church that his new constituents have abandoned before allying with his church—and to realize that this white man, who has badly offended and restricted these parishioners, actually has more information about their social and political context than does Coppin—produces breathtaking chagrin.

Coppin describes his dismay not only in terms of shame, embarrassment, and anxiety but also even betrayal. He was, after all, a writer, educator, and unapologetic proponent of uplift through education. Elsewhere in his autobiography, he argues, "Books are the records of what men have seen and learned and believed, and proved, since the world began. Books have what we need for instruction, for investigation and enlightenment."[60] Discovering in this instance that the reading he had hoped would prepare him has led him astray, he inscribes a moment of despair: citing Ecclesiastes 12:12, he implies that the "making of many books" is vanity and that "much study is a weariness of the flesh." But daunting as this revelation is, it does highlight a similarity between Coppin and his new parishioners: though he knows now to distrust what he has learned about their culture and society, he also knows that they have been subjected to the practice of racist misrepresentation, with which he is intimately familiar. This similarity creates its own sense of commonality—not biological or cultural, but experiential and strategic—which fuels his attempt to set the record straight. That effort, however, is only ambiguously successful.

Text, Time, and Travel

Observations is permeated by moments in which Coppin "writes back" to the archive he had consulted before his journey and which he suspects may also shape his audience's preconceptions of South Africa. Describing a General Conference of the South African AME, for example, he notes that the session for women featured the wives of both American and South African ministers on the platform, and speculates that, as several of the "ladies were Natives, the reader may wonder what contribution they could make to a meeting of that nature. This leads me to remark that those who have not been on the ground have no true idea of really prevailing conditions."[61] He goes on, as in his description of the "modern" amenities of Cape Town, to explain how many of "Africa's sons and daughters . . . have had the advantages of civilization for years," enabling them to become "prominent factors in the business and work of the world."[62] Continuing his adherence to uplift ideology, he here adds vigilance against ideas of temporal difference: "We are so accustomed to refer to the Native people as children, that we scarcely know ourselves what we really mean by the expression."[63]

Despite this resistance to the idea that black South African cultures are childlike or primitive in their distance from Western modernity, he maintains an ethnographic interest in what Johannes Fabian calls "culture gardens," "fenced off . . . as boundary-maintaining systems based on shared values."[64] "Hence," as Coppin puts it, "the desire to go to the bush, and see the Native at home, free and easy, untouched and uninfluenced by modern civilization."[65] This desire to attain expertise concerning different ways of living—which leads, as Fabian explains, to the textual production of a seemingly fixed and immutable cultural alterity—seems almost directly to contradict uplift's impulse to "civilize," but the two are mediated in Coppin's writing by his relationship to a preexisting archive. Seeking to correct this record by which he is nonetheless deeply informed, he sometimes inscribes epochal difference even as he points to its contingency:

> A very remarkable thing about these wild Native people is, their universal desire for education; or rather to secure educational advantages for their children. . . . The older ones seem to appreciate readily the superiority of the civilization of the newcomer. And while they think it too late for them to make radical changes in their manner of life, they are anxious that their children shall enjoy the benefits of that which has come to them too late. When they are satisfied that the missionary is duly accredited and competent . . . they will readily give up their children.[66]

In this representation, indigenous South Africans are both "wild" and extraordinarily sophisticated judges of cultural difference, not only appreciating Coppin's "civilization" but also able to comprehend its standards and gauge whether its participants meet those criteria. Untenable as this combination seems, the passage can nonetheless be understood as what M. M. Bakhtin calls a "hybrid construction," which "belongs, by its grammatical (syntactic) and compositional markers, to a single speaker, but that actually contains mixed within it two utterances, two speech manners, two styles, two 'languages,' two semantic and axiological belief systems."[67] Where Bakhtin uses this description to analyze intentional irony within fiction, it fits the perhaps inadvert jostling of ideologies in Coppin's work because, as Robert Gregg aptly states, "If the master and servant, colonizer and colonized, oppressor and oppressed had different roles to play in the quest for 'uplift,' then African Methodists played both roles."[68] Coppin here manages to incorporate such duality within a single sentence.

The hybridity of Coppin's prose cannot be read as simple irony, because his interest in the "wild Native" is too persistent. His illustrations, in particular, often suggest a zeal more ethnographic than evangelist: amid fairly extensive description of diet, social structure, and dwelling, he includes photographs of "Native" styles of dress and adornment—as in "A High Class Native Girl," "Native Maidens: Hair Culture," "In Native Costume," and "A Bearded Type of Native"—as well as objects, as in "A Native Piano" which "these children of the forest" are said to "play harmoniously."[69] On the other hand, as suggested by his depiction of the wary elders who test and assess any missionary with designs on their children, Coppin is equally determined to substantiate these South Africans' perspectives on Western culture. Directly before referring to "these wild Natives," after all, he describes the tensions created by their encounters with Europeans, and especially the accompanying saloons. Explaining that the traditional corn-based beer of the region had not been "demoralizing," he argues that the influence of European "whiskey" has changed "Native" tastes and drinking practices; absolutely opposed to "the sale of liquor to Natives," he is also opposed to laws that "undertake . . . to say who shall drink and who shall not," because these intensify black South Africans' perceptions of Western hypocrisy and discrimination.[70] As he explains later, "according to [Native] customs and traditions, a thing that is wrong is prohibited by law, and the prohibition affects all the people alike."[71]

Coppin's stylistic multiplicity reflects, then, his imbrication in the colonialist discourse as well as his recognition that "traditional" and "modern" cultures are in the process of influencing each other, forcing him repeatedly to reassess his own temporal values. This complexity can also be tracked through his illustrations. Although "A Game of Billiards" (fig. 8.1), for example, accompanies his disapproving account of South African saloon culture, nothing in the photograph suggests any discomfort or disappointment on the part of the traditionally dressed black South Africans as they play. Nor are his photographs restricted to persons in "Native" dress, as many appear to be portraits of bourgeois individuals and families. The first illustration of the volume depicts "Rev. M. M. Mokone," the

Figure 8.1. "A Game of Billiards" from Levi Jenkins Coppin, *Observations of Persons and Things in South Africa* (1905), 87.

founder of the Ethiopian Church, who faces the camera as he stands by a podium, and this portrait style (though often sitting, rather than stand-ing) recurs several times, from the representation of Coppin, his wife, and their associates to an unnamed group of black South Africans in suits and dresses, titled "What Education Has Already Accomplished."[72] Amid such representations, the style and pose of those photographs that represent a "Native" or "Type" might be recognized by turn-of-the-century AME readers in the United States as similar portraiture, such that even these images diverge substantially from the exotic details of hairstyle and cos-tume drawn, for instance, in Stanley's *Through the Dark Continent* (1879).

The "Native Girl in Full Dress" (fig. 8.2) provides a representative ex-ample of how the cultural difference suggested by title and apparel is miti-gated somewhat by formal similarity in pose and framing. Like the sitters in conventional Western clothing seen elsewhere in the volume, she is pic-tured against a neutral background and looks toward the camera, though perhaps slightly to the side. Several of the women labeled "Natives" in Coppin's captions appear in this way, presenting, as Shawn Michelle Smith writes of U.S. photography in this period, "the lofty gazes of contempla-tion that signal interiority."[73] This tension between ethnographic caption

Figure 8.2. "Native Girl in Full Dress" from Levi Jenkins Coppin, *Observations of Persons and Things in South Africa* (1905), 131.

and style of portraiture is even starker in Coppin's photograph of the "Cape Colored Type," in which every visual attribute, including clothing, suggests a bourgeois family keepsake.[74] In contrast to the women labeled "Native" in Coppin's volume, "Native" men are more often pictured in natural environments and, when photographed singly, tend to look downward. Still, none of these photographs replicate the sideways poses or overt measurement seen in eugenicist physiognomic photographs—those that sought to measure features and define "types"—still popular in this era. As Smith argues of the photographs of the "Georgia Negro" that W. E. B. Du Bois assembled for the 1900 Paris Exposition, many of Coppin's images "'*signify on*' . . . the scientific, eugenicist, and criminological archives" arrayed to proclaim the "inferiority" of African Americans and "all peoples of African descent"; also like Du Bois, Coppin incorporates the "sentimental and commodified forms of the middle-class portrait"

that could serve "to challenge and undermine dominant institutional archives of racialized photographic meaning."[75] But while some of Coppin's
images suggest cultural simultaneity, through which people of different
geographies and wardrobes share an interest in recording and conveying
their images, some of Coppin's text—which arguably shapes and controls
observers' interpretation of images—is unabashedly patronizing and even
primitivist.[76] The portrait of an older man is titled "A True Child of the
Bush,"[77] for example, and Coppin explains his illustrations of "The Way
Native Women Carry Their Children"[78] by noting that "they seem as prolific as rabbits."[79]

It is characteristically ironic that Coppin should employ some of his
most condescending and eugenically inflected rhetoric on the issue of
"Native home life," concerning which he reports receiving many questions
and which, in any case, was one of his central concerns.[80] His autobiography demonstrates a similar commitment to reforming the familial arrangements of freedpeople in the United States, of whom he claims, "One
of the most prevalent evils of Quarter life was . . . the happy-go-lucky
custom" through which "many just 'took up' with each other."[81] Coppin's
perspective here constitutes one side of a "debate over the nature of slavery's immediate and longterm effects on the marital and familial relations
of African Americans" that has, as Ann duCille argues, "raged throughout
much of the last century," and his is an especially conservative view, for
Coppin was a devout adherent to the AME's emphasis on respectability,
particularly in sexual life.[82] But while some of his remarks in this regard,
as we have seen, can seem flippant or even demeaning, they exist alongside real indignation at how the options of oppressed peoples were limited
by their circumstances. Accordingly, he blames not only slaveholders but
also the continuing "lusts of the [southern U.S.] master class" for institut-
ing a reign of public violence and institutional control, which inhibited
"the Colored Community, dependent, perilous," from fully expressing
their opinions on sexual arrangements or even demanding full freedom
of choice.[83] As with his reflections on ex-slaves, so with his thoughts on
his South African parishioners: in his *Observations*, which begins with
the clergy's quest to be recognized as "Marriage Officers," he protests that
white churches had "neglected" their non-white members, who, though
paying dues, "have been permitted to herd as cattle, and bring up families
without any legal status."[84] Complaining that they have not been "treated

like other human beings," he nonetheless implies that provision of marital services, at some level, defines humanity, as his analogy to cattle replicates, at least rhetorically, the white churches' previous rejection.

These contradictory tendencies to demean and defend may demonstrate, yet again, conflicting temporal positions—not simply between a "backward" and a "modern" culture, but rather between the writer's perceptions of his urgent need to uplift and his lasting need to record thoughtfully. In his autobiography, Coppin describes his impression, in the immediate aftermath of slavery, of reform as a pressing duty—"it was now time to set the house in order morally, and spiritually"—and *Observations* suggests that he felt the exigence of time throughout the composition of that text: "As the facts here given were jotted down at different times and places, there occur occasional repetitions, but this does not make them any the less facts, and they will serve to impress upon the mind of the reader the things that impressed us most."[85] Accordingly, *Observations* includes less overt consideration of the archive against which it will be read, but where that does occur, Coppin tends to compare "Native" practices more positively against those of the West. In one such passage he indicates that his understanding of South African culture may put his text at odds with both the philosophy and the archive that influence its production: "I would not be understood as proclaiming the doctrine that heathenism is, under any circumstance, better for the Native than Christian civilization, but I desire to state some facts, because they are facts."[86] Explaining, for the benefit of "those who are not informed as to the primitive life of the Natives," that "family and tribal relations are highly regulated," he admires their insistence that sex be confined to marital relations:

> We hear much among civilized people about the looseness of the divorce laws. . . . It might be well also to consider how easily under the loose customs of civilized society men and women can come together and go along as companions without any specific form of marriage. It is not enough to say that no such laxness has the sanction of law, the fact that it is tolerated, permitted or overlooked is a thing that heathen people could not be made to understand.

He also chastises facile critiques of polygamy, explaining, "It is altogether a mistake to regard the custom of plural marriage among the heathen people as an evidence of a want of moral restraint."[87]

At such moments he confronts the central tension in his philosophical stance, for while he proclaims "that [Western] civilization betters the condition of a people is not an open question," this closure perpetually asserts its prematurity. He attempts to distinguish the exploitative purposes of colonialism from the evangelizing ones of the church, a task that proves challenging because "it is seldom that the Christian Church goes out into the savage regions on her mission of love and mercy, until the explorer, the gold hunter, or the pleasure seeker has first opened the way."[88] The racism of many denominations compounds his difficulty, as he notes the extraordinary obstacles placed by this "modern civilization" against the efforts of "Native[s]" to marry and worship.[89] Although he uses the term "Christian" and "civilization" with full sincerity in most instances, he occasionally satirizes them, using a question mark to be sure that readers will understand his point: South Africa's white "Christians (?)," for example, "keep the colored races divided" in order to prevent them from "striv[ing] for a common destiny."[90] These instances of racial injustice and manipulation call to mind his experiences and observations in the United States. He notes that indigenous South African cultures "have laws, and they are administered with an impartiality worthy of the admiration of our boasted civilized Governments . . . among the more advanced tribes no one is thrown into a chain gang as the result of prejudice, nor is there among them a system of peonage as a substitute for slavery."[91] His observation of racial injustices leads him to warn readers not to confuse the term "heathen" as bespeaking the "cruelties and irregularities of a barbarous people"; the latter charge, in this volume, remains pending against Western societies.[92]

Conclusion

Coppin's tenure as the bishop of Cape Town was ultimately unsuccessful: by the time his *Observations* were published, he had been ousted over parishioners' complaint that, in his relentless choice of African American over African appointees, he had effectively denied the latter the autonomy for which they had left the Wesleyan Methodists.[93] Misguided and alienating as Coppin's administrative practices were, he was not the AME representative least attuned to his African constituents' concerns; ironically, one of the practices he justly criticizes amid previous white missions in

Africa was hazarded by some of his successors. Observing that the AME is perpetually challenged by "older organizations [that] regard the newcomer as an interloper," he explains that white-run missions "have succeeded in building up a pecuniary heritage which they wish to hand down to posterity."[94] Applying "the charitable declaration that the 'workman is worthy of his hire,'" Coppin nonetheless insists that newly "enlightened" parishioners should be able "to share in the positions and emoluments which they themselves have made possible." Thus, while Coppin condescended to African ministers and cultures, others sought to follow the example of their white peers in terms of commercial activity. As Campbell explains, they "had been taught to see the continent . . . as a field of service and of opportunity" and "argued that African Americans, in uplifting their benighted brethren, would raise their own social and economic standing."[95] Kenneth W. Warren notes that such ideas became increasingly prominent in African American, Afro-Caribbean, and European thought during the early twentieth century, demonstrating that though uplift ideology could provide a transnational strategy for challenging white supremacy, it could also promote circum-Atlantic class divisions.[96]

It is noteworthy that Warren's essay, which elucidates a far more critical perspective on African American approaches to Africa than Gilroy's *The Black Atlantic*, was also published in 1993; though the latter work makes much of its defiance to "volkish popular cultural nationalism" in "African American letters," its less conflict-ridden account of Black Atlantic exchanges was more thoroughly embraced.[97] Coppin's writings, however, demonstrate that, in addition to tensions emerging from the project of uplift, many persons seeking to forge transatlantic relationships also had to negotiate an archive whose dangerous misrepresentations, even when recognized as such, may inform their ways of categorizing and comprehending information. As we pursue scholarly understandings of Atlantic archives, however, this ambivalence is precisely what makes his work interesting. As Xiomara Santamarina argues, study of such contradictory texts "stipulat[es] the historical contingency, specificity, and material constraints under which African-descended and European-descended populations wrote."[98] Writing in periods when racial segregation was hardening and intensifying in two different countries, and at a time when cultural differences were often conceptualized as hierarchical stages of development, Coppin sought to challenge white supremacy and racist misrepresentation by expanding cultural similarity; in the process, he occasionally demeaned the practices of African and diasporic people. This irony, however, highlights another problem in the study of the Atlantic World and the U.S. South, in addition to the long-standing questions of "race," "culture," and "modernity": What are—and have been—effective representational strategies for challenging oppression? As modes and logics for exploitation change, efforts at resistance require endless revision, and tracing their progress uncovers missteps. Still, observing how these dynamics play out across diverse spaces can only help us to understand that question, as well as its potential answers.

Notes

1. Levi Jenkins Coppin, *Unwritten History* (1919; New York: Negro Universities Press, 1968), 15, 7, 302, 310.

2. James T. Campbell, *Songs of Zion: The African Methodist Episcopal Church in the United States and South Africa* (New York: Oxford University Press, 1995), 142.

3. Ibid., 141–42.

4. Jennifer Rae Greeson, *Our South: Geographic Fantasy and the Rise of National Literature* (Cambridge: Harvard University Press, 2010), 237.

5. Coppin, *Unwritten History*, 168, 167.

6. Levi Jenkins Coppin, *Observations of Persons and Things in South Africa, 1900–1904* (Philadelphia: A.M.E. Book Concern, 1905), 43, 55.

7. Sandra Gunning, "Nancy Prince and the Politics of Mobility, Home and Diasporic (Mis)Identification," *American Quarterly* 53, no. 1 (2001): 33. Andrew van der Vlies argues for analysis of the "textual Atlantic" in "Transnational Print Cultures: Books, -scapes, and the Textual Atlantic," *Safundi: The Journal of South African and American Studies* 8, no. 1 (2007): 45–55.

8. To cite three influential scholars in Atlantic studies, after West Africa is configured as one point of origin in the Atlantic slave trade, it recedes, for Paul Gilroy, into "pre-slave history," for Ian Baucom, into a past that writers from Europe and the Americas have struggled to position in relation to the present, and for William Boelhower, behind its "drowned peoples." If the regions involved in the slave trade thus seem to be frozen in time (except, in Gilroy's work, for Sierra Leone and Liberia, to which some members of the diaspora returned), other spaces along Africa's long Atlantic coast are, in these models, effectively omitted from consideration. See Gilroy, *The Black Atlantic: Modernity and Double Consciousness* (Cambridge: Harvard University Press, 1993), 58; Baucom, *Specters of the Atlantic: Finance Capital, Slavery, and the Philosophy of History* (Durham: Duke University Press, 2005); Boelhower, "The Rise of the New Atlantic Studies Matrix," *American Literary History* 20, no. 1 (2008): 95. For more on the geographical and chronological problems raised by Gilroy's work, see Joan Dayan, "Paul Gilroy's Slaves, Ships,

and Routes: The Middle Passage as Metaphor," *Research in African Literatures* 27, no. 4 (1998): 7–15; Ntongela Masilela, "The 'Black Atlantic' and African Modernity in South Africa," *Research in African Literatures* 27, no. 4 (1998): 88–97; Brent Hayes Edwards, "The Uses of *Diaspora*," *Social Text* 19, no. 1 (2001): 45–73; Patrick Manning, "Africa and the African Diaspora: New Directions of Study," *Journal of African History* 44 (2003): 487–506; Paul Tiyambe Zeleza, "Rewriting the African Diaspora: Beyond the Black Atlantic," *African Affairs* 101, no. 414 (2005): 35–68; Ben Vinson III, "Introduction: African (Black) Diaspora History, Latin American History," *The Americas* 63, no. 1 (2006): 1–18.

9. Coppin, *Unwritten History*, 261.

10. Bill Ashcroft, Gareth Griffiths, and Helen Tiffin, *The Empire Writes Back: Theory and Practice in Post-colonial Literatures* (New York: Routledge, 2002), 6.

11. Brent Hayes Edwards, *The Practice of Diaspora: Literature, Translation, and the Rise of Black Internationalism* (Cambridge: Harvard University Press, 2003), 13.

12. Coppin, *Observations*, 21.

13. Ibid., 22.

14. Jeannette Eileen Jones, *In Search of Brightest Africa: Reimagining the Dark Continent in American Culture, 1884–1936* (Athens: University of Georgia Press, 2010), 26–27; Campbell, *Songs of Zion*, 228; Coppin, *Observations*, 73.

15. For an overview of English depictions of Africa and especially South Africa in the period before Coppin's journey, see Jean and John Comaroff, *Of Revelation and Revolution: Christianity, Colonialism, and Consciousness in South Africa*, vol. 1 (Chicago: University of Chicago Press, 1991), 86–125.

16. For a discussion of perceived temporal difference as historically and anthropologically understood in relation to geography, see Johannes Fabian, *Time and the Other: How Anthropology Makes Its Object* (New York: Columbia University Press, 1983), 1–36.

17. Coppin, *Unwritten History*, 274.

18. Ibid., 272.

19. Ibid., 272.

20. Ibid., 276. Robert Gregg indicates that Coppin contemplated this passage often but did not always derive from it social messages. Gregg, *Sparks from the Anvil of Oppression: Philadelphia's African Methodists and Southern Migrants, 1890–1940* (Philadelphia: Temple University Press), 90.

21. Campbell, *Songs of Zion*, 60; Gregg, *Sparks*, 1–6, 69–85.

22. Coppin, *Unwritten History*, 274, 275, 169; Coppin, *Observations*, 130.

23. Coppin, *Unwritten History*, 168, 171.

24. For a discussion of the "chronotope" as a representational conjunction of a space and time with specific qualities, see M. M. Bakhtin, "Forms of Time and of the Chronotope in the Novel," in *The Dialogic Imagination: Four Essays*, ed. Michael Holquist, trans. Caryl Emerson and Michael Holquist, (Austin: University of Texas Press, 1981), 84–85.

25. Coppin, *Unwritten History*, 18–22.

26. David Hempton, *Methodism: Empire of the Spirit* (New Haven: Yale University Press, 2005), 32–85.

27. Richard S. Newman, *Freedom's Prophet: Bishop Richard Allen, the AME Church, and the Black Founding Fathers* (New York: New York University Press, 2008), 120.

28. Gregg, *Sparks*, 88–89.

29. Coppin, *Unwritten History*, 168; Campbell, *Songs of Zion*, 38–41; Coppin, *Observations*, 8.

30. Coppin, *Unwritten History*, 37, 299.

31. Ibid., 299.

32. Campbell, *Songs of Zion*, 61, 235.

33. Yogita Goyal, *Romance, Diaspora, and Black Atlantic Literature* (Cambridge: Cambridge University Press, 2010), 9.

34. Coppin, *Unwritten History*, 107.

35. Walter Benjamin, "Theses on the Philosophy of History" (1950), *Illuminations*, ed. Hannah Arendt, trans. Harry Zohn (New York: Schocken, 1968), 256, 255. Baucom incorporates an array of theoretical influences, but these lead him to differ from Benjamin chiefly in that the historic image does not so much "flare up" as perpetually emit light, such that the "now . . . accumulates within itself the moment of loss, the long after-history of loss, and the moment of confrontation with loss." *Specters of the Atlantic*, 325. Kenneth W. Warren argues that Baucom's approach to time "obliterates history" as a distinct linear sequence; see *What Was African American Literature?* (Cambridge: Harvard University Press, 2011), 82. Coppin's cosmology, which includes the space of acute social struggle, the divine space of rest, and the archival space of simultaneous risk and contemplation, may mitigate this kind of encompassing time.

36. Coppin, *Unwritten History*, 31, 40, 41, 168.

37. Ibid., 169–70.

38. Ibid., 170. Remarkably, he does not even acknowledge the existence of D. W. Griffith's notorious adaptation, *The Birth of a Nation*, released to widespread acclaim and protest only four years before Coppin's autobiography was published. I suspect his disdain for that film may be indicated in his wry understatement concerning the influence of Dixon's novel.

39. Coppin, *Unwritten History*, 74.

40. Ibid., 74–75.

41. Ibid., 168, 169.

42. Ibid., 263, 264, 266.

43. Coppin, *Observations*, 234.

44. Campbell, *Songs of Zion*, 96; Coppin, *Observations*, 50.

45. Coppin, *Observations*, 59, 32.

46. Ibid., 5.

47. Ibid., 91; Coppin, *Unwritten History*, 309.

48. Coppin, *Observations*, 194, 23, 139.

49. Ibid., 194, 147.

50. Ibid., 194.

51. Ibid., 12, 28.

52. Ibid., 23–32, 28.

53. Ibid., 42.

54. Coppin, *Unwritten History*, 41, 309.

55. Ibid., 14.

56. Kenneth Warren, "Appeals for (Mis)Recognition: Theorizing the Diaspora," in *Cultures of United States Imperialism*, ed. Donald Pease and Amy Kaplan (Durham: Duke University Press, 1993), 392–406.

57. Coppin, *Unwritten History*, 26.

58. Ibid., 312–14.

59. Edwards, *Practice of Diaspora*, 23–38.

60. Coppin, *Unwritten History*, 261.

61. Coppin, *Observations*, 42.

62. Ibid., 43.

63. Ibid., 60.

64. Fabian, *Time and the Other*, 47.

65. Coppin, *Observations*, 68.

66. Ibid., 86.

67. Bakhtin, "Discourse in the Novel," *The Dialogic Imagination*, 304.

68. Gregg, *Sparks*, 5.

69. Coppin, *Observations*, 61, 71, 79, 191, 83, 74, 83.

70. Ibid., 85.

71. Ibid., 134–35.

72. Ibid., 9, 51, 45.

73. Shawn Michelle Smith, *Photography on the Color Line: W. E. B. Du Bois, Race, and Visual Culture* (Durham: Duke University Press, 2004), 67.

74. Coppin, *Observations*, 25.

75. Smith, *Photography*, 9, 16, 9, 10.

76. For the relationship between text and image, see Roland Barthes, "Rhetoric of the Image" (1961), in *Image, Music, Text*, trans. Stephen Heath (New York: Hill and Wang, 1977), 40–41.

77. Coppin, *Observations*, 75.

78. Ibid., 93; see also 65.

79. Ibid., 74.

80. Ibid., 125.

81. Coppin, *Unwritten History*, 124.

82. Ann duCille, "Marriage, Family, and Other 'Peculiar Institutions' in African-American Literary History," *American Literary History* 21, no. 3 (2009): 606; Campbell, *Songs of Zion*, 61.

83. Coppin, *Unwritten History*, 130–31.

84. Coppin, *Observations*, 16, 121, 120.

85. Coppin, *Unwritten History*, 124; Coppin, *Observations*, 112.

86. Coppin, *Observations*, 125.

87. Ibid., 114.

88. Ibid., 130.

89. Ibid., 55, 54.

90. Ibid., 28, 102.

91. Ibid., 129.

92. Ibid., 125.

93. Campbell, *Songs of Zion*, 235–40.

94. Coppin, *Observations*, 96.

95. Campbell, *Songs of Zion*, 236.

96. Warren, "Appeals for (Mis)Recognition," 399.

97. Gilroy, *The Black Atlantic*, 15. On the influence of Gilroy's volume, see Jonathan Elmer, "The Black Atlantic Archive" (review essay), *American Literary History* 17, no. 1 (2005): 160–61.

98. Xiomara Santamarina, "'Are We There Yet?': Archives, History, and Specificity in African-American Literary Studies," *American Literary History* 20, nos. 1–2 (2008): 306.

9

....

Whose "Folk" Are They Anyway?

Zora Neale Hurston and Lady Augusta Gregory in the Atlantic World

KATHLEEN M. GOUGH

What the colored poet in the United States needs to do is something like what Synge did for the Irish; he needs to find a form that will express the racial spirit by symbols from within rather than by symbols from without, such as the mere mutilation of English spelling and pronunciation. He needs a form that is freer and larger than dialect, but which will still hold the racial flavor; a form expressing the imagery, the idioms, the peculiar turns of thought, and the distinctive humor and pathos, too, of the Negro, but which will also be capable of voicing the deepest and highest emotions and aspirations, and allow for the widest range of subjects and the widest scope of treatment.

James Weldon Johnson, *The Book of American Negro Poetry*

Theatricality has become central to our imagining of the historical *real*.

Alan Ackerman and Martin Puchner, *Against Theater:*
Creative Destruction on the Modernist Stage

The first epigraph to this essay marks an important moment in Irish and African American relations. It is now seen as a kind of textual "origin story" for how literary critics and cultural historians have developed comparisons between the Irish and Harlem Renaissances in the early twentieth century. The second epigraph, by contrast, allows us to understand the historical weight of Johnson's analogy. In 1922, when Johnson published his anthology, he recognized the efficacy of theatrical representation as a mode of defining and presenting the "New Negro," and drew most of his examples on how to create an authentic Negro poetry from African American spirituals, folk stories, dance, and performance.[1]

In cultural studies across disciplines his analogy is cited, recited, and repeated to help explain and theorize historical relations between the Irish and Harlem Renaissances, and later relations between Irish and African American cultural representations.[2] The language of performance is the evidence on which claims to historical relationships are made. That is, "theatricality has," indeed, "become central to our imagining of the historical *real*."[3]

But what if this historical moment is not initiated by James Weldon Johnson's evocation of Synge? What if this historical moment (where one Renaissance speaks to another) is not initiated through the strong intentionality of aesthetic influence that went on to activate shared strategies of cultural engagement and cultural national struggle? What other relations are obscured when this moment is continually repeated? A different path into the relations between the two movements—a longer and seedier path—follows from theater history and performance studies and suggests ways of understanding how two key figures, Zora Neale Hurston and Lady Augusta Gregory, operated in the movements, how they were intrinsic to the success of these movements and yet often appeared everywhere extrinsic to them. In the late twentieth century, their biographical life returns to the stage and their iconic images return to the landscapes of the U.S. South and the West of Ireland. If "performances carry with them the memory of otherwise forgotten substitutions—those that were rejected and, even more invisibly, those that have succeeded,"[4] I suggest that these returns—as characters to the stage, as names affixed to festivals, museums, summer schools, and hotels—function, using James Clifford's phrase, as "allegories of salvage."[5]

In doing so, they operate as concrete allegories and "forgotten substitutions." Their alleged permanence in the regional landscape means that the historical memory of their own contested place in national and regional narratives is forgotten. Their ambivalent place is now substituted by their contemporary capacity to engender regional authenticity and symbolize the life of the community. In this way, their return tells us less about the relations between the Irish and Harlem Renaissances and far more about the anxious relations between the regional imagination of the nation and the contemporary migratory patterns that keep divesting these regions of their ability to serve as "authentic" touchstones in national origin stories. In fact, their own "salvaging" of the folk in their early-twentieth-century ethnographic work sheds light on how these regions have salvaged Hurston and Gregory at the moment when the South and Ireland are becoming home to new migratory "folk" circulating the Atlantic World (and beyond).

This examination will require a reframing of the rules and signatures of the modernist paradigm that allows these two movements to cohere in historical and critical studies. It will mean attending to the particularities of this historical moment while simultaneously understanding it as carrying along the general (generic) qualities of all other historical "flash-points" in Black and Green Atlantic exchange (the cultural and political relationships between the African and Irish diasporas). Broadly stated, this "generic" quality revolves around the absence of women. From the mid-nineteenth-century political kinship between Frederick Douglass and Daniel O'Connell to the late-twentieth-century stage performances that elucidate and make explicit cultural kinship between the Irish and African diasporas, women are everywhere visible and nowhere relevant to the production of knowledge or the circum-Atlantic exchange of ideas. Instead, women who helped to instantiate the political and cultural movements recorded by historians and literary critics are framed as singular, exceptional, extraordinary, peculiar, and anomalous.

I put pressure on these categories and take seriously the generic quality that casts women in such a way that visibility rarely equals recognition. The paradigm I use to unsettle the particularity of women's visibility at this historical "flashpoint" is articulated by what I call "haptic allegories." The term "haptic" means "able to come into contact with." It is the way bodies orient themselves to the world through touch, through both bodily feelings and muscular sensation. Haptic "is also related to kinesthesis, the ability of our bodies to sense their own movement in space."[6] Allegory, on the other hand, is an incoherent narrative or image that says other than it means and means other than it says. "Within philosophy," however, "allegory has another status as the mode in which not the subject, but the objective world expresses meaning."[7] Yoking these two conceptions of allegory together—one that attributes intentions to subjects (the writer, the social actor, the artist) and one that attributes intentions to objects (the play, the theatrical character, the image)—requires that we take seriously the haptic qualities of the allegory: the tactile and kin(esth)etic gestures that move both subjects and objects across the historiographical stage-surface together. Hurston's and Gregory's reified place in the contemporary regional landscape must be balanced against their own dynamic movements. Tracking the way they continue to jump between the real (reflection) and the ideal (creation), I hope to "make intelligible series of phenomena whose kinship ha[s] eluded or could elude the historian's gaze."[8]

At first glance, this pursuit (one invested in the philosophical foundations of mimesis) seems quite a distance removed from the material conditions that precipitated relations between the Black and Green Atlantics. I will begin by tracing the intersections, the crossroads, where theatricality and colonialism circulate around a feminine still point and are joined via a dialectical, metaphoric relationship. While not denying the efficacy of this relationship, I spend time thinking about the still point, the singular feminine models that resist dialecticism. This allegorical paradigm is one whose "movement goes from singularity to singularity and, without ever leaving singularity, transforms every singular case into an exemplar of a general rule that can never be stated a priori."[9] Gordon Teskey writes, "singularity operates in allegory as does the vanishing point in a linear perspective: it is never visible itself, but everything that is visible directs the eye toward it."[10] I want to spend some time focusing on this vanishing point, to train the eye to see its image, in all of its fraught, fractured, and impossible detail.

Lady Augusta Gregory (1852–1932) and Zora Neale Hurston (1891–1960) do not—on the surface of things—seem to form a likely kinship. This is particularly the case when we take into account that Gregory was a member of the Anglo-Irish gentry who resided at the Roxborough Estate (in County Galway) during her childhood and at her husband's estate in Coole Park (also in County Galway) during her adult life. Hurston grew up in America's first incorporated all-black township, Eatonville, Florida. From there she moved to Washington, D.C., and then to New York City, where she studied anthropology with Franz Boas at Columbia University. Their participation in what have become known as the Irish Renaissance (1890s–1930s) and the Harlem Renaissance (1910s–1930s) is well documented. Gregory is considered the matriarch of the Irish Renaissance, while Hurston is given prominence of place as an artist of the Harlem Renaissance.

Gregory is like Hurston in two significant ways: she not only helped to create the manifesto for an Irish national theater during the Celtic revival (a task that Hurston begins to chart for the Harlem Renaissance in her essay "Characteristics of Negro Expression" [1934] and in her infamous collaboration with Langston Hughes on the play *Mule Bone*), but also contributed to enriching the folk aesthetic of the movement through both ethnographic fieldwork in the West of Ireland, where she collected folklore, and, of course, in her dramatic works. Hurston was also an ethnographer, and her fieldwork—where she collected African American folklore—took her back to Eatonville before going farther South to New Orleans, the Bahamas, Haiti, and Jamaica. This fieldwork would inspire her theories of performance, which she worked out in plays, musical reviews, novels, and short stories and in the creation and writing of the ethnographies themselves. Even more than Hurston, Gregory was in almost all respects at the epicenter of the Irish Renaissance (although she is typically used as a foil to clarify the artistic projects of W. B. Yeats and J. M. Synge).

Indeed, both women worked across artistic genres: folklore collecting, playwriting, theatrical directing, and, in Hurston's case, novel writing while also writing poetry and essays on drama and political culture. It is, perhaps, because of the range of their interests and their place as women who are both constructed as artistic "insiders" and political "outsiders" that they find themselves everywhere mentioned in the history of these movements and nowhere relevant in political and cultural exchange between them. That is, Hurston's conservative views on segregation and Gregory's seemingly ambivalent position in relation to unionism and Irish nationalism are often noted in ways that position them "outside" the progressive politics of their peers and collaborators. Yet, their dramatic output (in a variety of genres) makes them interesting companions when considering how kinships are predicated on their absence.

From Frederick Douglass and Daniel O'Connell in the mid-nineteenth century to Marcus Garvey and Eamon de Valera in the early twentieth, we see antislavery wed to anticolonialism and black nationalism wed to Irish independence.[11] I am interested in the twinned efficacy of political kinship (via anticolonial struggle) and cultural kinship (via the theatrical idiom) that helped to define the "New Negro" and the character of Ireland's "Ancient Idealism."[12] Throughout this essay I unpack these relationships—ones forged through regional and national struggle, Atlantic exchange (though often more rhetorical than literal), and cultural echoes and borrowings. In this way I wish to explore "wounded kinships" that other, more explicit forms of kinship make invisible.[13] I want to take seriously the claim that "theatricality has become central to our imagining of the historical real," and expand the implications to move far beyond the modernist stage and into the historiographical stage-space of the U.S. South and the West of Ireland. In this instance I do not wish to use history to contextualize theater, but to illuminate how theatrical production and performance theory animated historical life and continues to animate historiography.

Kinship, Authenticity, and the Folk

In order to explore this, let us return to James Weldon Johnson, who starts to stake a claim for cultural kinship with the Irish Revival by wanting the African American poet to do "what Synge did for the Irish." To make claims for kinship using the theatrical idiom and theatrical practice (via mimesis; reflection) is often in a dialectical struggle with an Aristotelian model (via poesies; action). To update Aristotle's thoughts here, one must first "make it up" and then "make it *real*." It is this tension between the reflection of an ideal (mimesis) and re-presentation and creation (poesies) that underpins so much of the anxiety regarding authenticity and performance during the Irish and Harlem Renaissances (and beyond). That Johnson could invoke Synge as a model is an irony only tacitly addressed by contemporary critics. Indeed, Synge's *Playboy of the Western World* would have been known to Johnson when the Abbey Theater toured America in 1911 under the management of Lady Gregory and two years after Synge's death. The play spurred transnational controversy among Irish and Irish American audiences, who rioted at theaters because they thought his depictions of the West of Ireland were inauthentic. The line from the play that incited rioting audiences was: "a drift of females standing in their shifts." It was an ostensible outrage to chaste Irish women everywhere in large part because the mention of actual female sexuality—even via an undergarment—was a sacrilege to the nationalist cause, which liked its women mute and mythical. It was Gregory who was left to defend it against censors on the American tour.

Moreover, it was Zora Neale Hurston, in her essay "Characteristics of Negro Expression" and in her plays, prose fiction, and ethnographic work, who manifested and enriched Johnson's call to revise and reimagine the place of Negro folk performance for the movement. When she did so, she was castigated as returning the Negro to a world of blackface minstrelsy. Nevertheless, Johnson's word in the *Book of American Negro Poetry* has never ceased to form the basis of the textual origin story for how relationships between the Irish and Harlem Renaissances are framed. It remains instructive, however, precisely because it conceals so well what is essential to it: the rift between reflection and creation; authenticity and performance; the "illegitimate" kinship between historical materialism and theories of performance (in other words, our haptic and allegorical encounters with the "real").

These are anxieties that Hurston and Gregory emulate. Curiously, they are constantly pushing this struggle to its limits, evoking the "authenticity" of the folk in their ethnographic work, self-consciously inserting themselves into their ethnographies (most significantly in Hurston's *Mules and Men* [1935] and Gregory's *Visions and Beliefs in the West of Ireland* [1920]), writing comedic drama and tactically employing irony and laughter to combat the legacy of blackface minstrelsy and the Irish caricature of English melodrama, and often coming very close to the bone, perhaps too close. In doing so, they themselves become the focus of anxiety where compatriots in the artistic struggles doubt their own "authenticity."

Suspicion about their work and their "misplaced" politics begins in their own lifetimes. In his 1937 review of Hurston's *Their Eyes Were Watching God*, Richard Wright states: "Miss Hurston *voluntarily* continues in her novel the tradition which was *forced* upon the Negro in the theater, that is, the minstrel technique that makes the 'white folks' laugh. Her characters eat and laugh and cry and work and kill; they swing like a pendulum eternally in that safe and narrow orbit in which America likes to see the Negro live: between laughter and tears."[14] In the same article he also reviews Waters Turpin's novel *These Low Grounds*. He uses Turpin's novel as a foil for Hurston's work and states that "Turpin's faults as a writer are those of an honest man trying desperately to say something; but Zora Neale Hurston lacks even that excuse."[15] Hurston's representations are not "honest" (authentic); by extension, neither is she.

In his autobiography, George Moore (Irish novelist, dramatist, and critic who was a part of the Celtic revival) remarks, "Lady Gregory has never been for me a very real person. I imagine her without a mother, or father, or sisters, or brothers, *sans attaché*."[16] Throughout this volume he pulls apart her credibility—not only her personhood but also her credibility as a folklorist and dramatist who, he says, knows nothing of the Irish language. He writes that Gregory is "content to pepper her paper with a few idiomatic turns of speech which she very often does not use

correctly" and that she should have studied "the differences between urban and rural speech" in Ireland.[17] Gregory is imagined without kin; her
work is described as inauthentic.

As these short excerpts suggest, to doubt the legitimacy of representation (aesthetic, social, and political) is also to doubt the legitimacy of the
person. To be cast out as not "honest"' and not "real" is to be cast into the
theatrical imagination where the condition of genealogy and kinship is
illegitimacy. Thinking more philosophically about the anxieties that were
produced by a particular historical moment (or reproduced using a different frame) shows how historical production itself is often riddled with
this anxiety about the relationship between reflection and creation.

Hurston and Gregory both write about the rural folk during times of
great migration (African Americans from the South to the North, the
Irish from the West of Ireland to the American North), while the "folk"
they write about are continually interpreted as spatially isolated and temporally distant from the modern. Their relationship to the "authentic folk"
is negotiated (albeit differently) with their own positioning in the communities they study, where the "folk" are both "not them" and "not *not*
them."[18] There is a significant analogical relationship between these two
women. In *Rethinking Folk Drama*, Steve Tillis, borrowing from biolo-
gist Stephen J. Gould, reminds us that analogies are "similarities formed
within different genetic systems by selective pressures of similar environments." Homologies, on the other hand, are "similarities based on inheritance of the same genes or structures from common ancestors."[19] This
analogical examination of Hurston and Gregory leads toward an understanding of a "common ancestor or inheritance." If this is true, however,
that common ancestor will emerge in the frame of theater (an impossibly
double and dubious ancestor). It is in this frame that several competing
and interrelated narratives are brought to the fore. They concern mimesis,
gender, and how the representational spaces of the Atlantic World's "originary" plantation colonies continue to circulate the waterways.

Colonial Mimesis

Before Gregory and Hurston arrived on the scene to collect folklore in the
West of Ireland and the southern United States, these regions had long
fascinated the Atlantic imaginary. From the mid-nineteenth century to

well into the twentieth, the regions became synonymous with the "Irish question" and the "race problem." In the Atlantic World, this was also how their regional relationship was contiguously understood. The nineteenth-century Land Wars (1870s–90s) that took place in Ireland after the Great Irish Famine (1845–51) and amid the rising tide of anticolonial struggle was historically situated at the moment when the American Civil War (1861–65) had been conceded and the subsequent Reconstruction had failed (1880s). Of course, the "Irish question" and the "race problem" were of national importance to Great Britain and the United States, but the West of Ireland and the South provided the political and cultural stage-space where these questions and problems were made manifest. And, when questions and problems regarding these regions are invoked, the thesis for understanding them is inevitably developed around the figure of woman who allegorizes a politics of threat, that is, a figure who specifically acts as the "ground" upon which threats emerge.

In the English imagination this was most visibly represented in the *Punch* cartoons with their ubiquitous depictions of Fenian "apes" who threatened the feminine and vulnerable Hibernia (Ireland) and needed protection from Britannia. In the southern imagination this took the image of the southern white woman whose chastity and safety were under constant threat from black men, who were also depicted as "apes" and as potential rapists, a sexual threat linked to the fear of miscegenation and a fear of "hybrid" origin. This myth justified the lynching of black men in the South throughout the nineteenth and twentieth centuries and was first revealed as myth in the tireless research of Ida B. Wells in her 1892 publication, *Southern Horrors: Lynch Law in All Its Phases*. Thus, a threat to a way of life, to legal and political control of the land—either for the white southerner or the landed gentry in Ireland—was constituted as a threat to the white female body, which was figured as property. The more invisible threat in this construction was to the black female body, which was considered sexually available, thus keeping women across the color line from seeing their construction as related (as there is a fine line between being imagined as property and as prostitute).

But if the land imagined as woman was *under* threat during this time, this was precariously balanced alongside woman *as* threat: as political conversations circulated around the "race problem" and the "Irish question," the "woman question" held tightly the hand. All of these issues were played out—sometimes separately, sometimes together—on political and theatrical stages in Europe and America. In all respects, the "woman question" fractures the binary realms of the colonial and anticolonial imagination. That is, when cultural nationalism linked to anticolonial struggle denounces the official discourse, it does so without having to displace the imagined place of "woman."

The figure of woman loses its ground, so to speak, when the bodies and voices of real women begin to act on their own behalf and threaten the stable referent on which grounds for political power are waged. If the figure of woman was used to illuminate a threat to "heritage," a way of life and political control, the bodies of women in the public sphere during this time threatened claims to self-sameness, the homogeneous relationship between their bodies and their allegorical images. Though neither Gregory nor Hurston was politically active in the suffragette movement, their work in the cultural sphere and their own independent movements are not unrelated to the "universality" of the "woman question" that emerged during this time period.

Significantly, their own race and class positioning in these narratives means that their movements are not always culturally intelligible within the feminist frame. After all, Hurston was very aware of how southern black women were used as a foil for understanding white femininity and the New (male) Negro. Moreover, as a member of the Anglo-Irish gentry, Lady Gregory would hardly be imagined as the figure of the vulnerable Hibernia. No longer a reflection of a struggle for control, but active agents, they become "the same as what?"[20] The essential and immutable character of woman where, as Plato put it, she "imitates the earth" shows signs of disaggregating and disintegration. If her image allegorizes a politics of threat, her body—particularly in this context the bodies of Hurston and Gregory—literalizes a politics of doubt. In order for the allegory to work, women qua women who act on their own behalf must be jettisoned to a singular category of aberrant: operating outside the normalizing framework that allows ideology to make coherent (allegorical) sense of the "figure" of woman. If Hurston and Gregory are veiled in suspicion as to their own "legitimacy" it is because they make the South and the West of Ireland speak in other voices: voices that say other than what they mean and mean other than what they say.

In the remainder of this essay I explore how Gregory and Hurston produce, and are produced as, allegory. I consider how anachronistic and universalistic depictions of women are made sense of through the historical details of a particular period in such a way that we forget that we have seen them before and we mis-recognize when we see them again. It is precisely because in the allegorical paradigm I discuss here where "there are hybrids of archetype and phenomenon, first-timeness and repetition" that kinship (with its desire to locate itself in single origins, familial and national structures of legitimacy) alludes our gaze.[21] This allegorical frame is both a form of creation and a poetics of interpretation—it is not legible through inductive reasoning (particular to universal) or deductive reasoning (universal to particular), which typically function as the organizing principles in historical studies. Instead, the paradigm "is defined by a third and paradoxical type of movement, which goes from particular to particular."[22]

Figures of Women in Movement

It is in the political and cultural context of the early twentieth century that Gregory and Hurston arrive on the scene with their desire to collect "authentic" folklore in regions whose "authentic character" is already at the epicenter of representational struggle. While this struggle is being waged via the circulation of popular images and bodily reproduced on the stage, these images were not confined to the cultural sphere. They were everywhere being substantiated by "scientific" research on the ground, particularly in the field of anthropology. "Authenticity" and the "folk" animated social life in the early twentieth century as both artistic and scientific communities attempted to understand "art in the age of mechanical reproduction." As Walter Benjamin writes, "the presence of the original is the prerequisite to the concept of authenticity."[23] Mechanical reproduction, Benjamin suggests, defies the search for origins. While it might defy this search, the reflex was (and is) pervasive. The "folk," which falls under the umbrella idiom of the "primitive" (articulated as the search for origins, a return to "authentic" expressive culture), took artists, scholars, and scientists of very different aesthetic and disciplinary dispositions into a past that was figured in both historical and geographic terms.[24]

In this respect, Gregory's and Hurston's ethnographic folklore collecting can be placed in the genealogy of colonial anthropological pursuits of the time. Yet, their "intentions" and their physical presence in the field muddy the waters between art and science, between imitation and authenticity. Strictly speaking, neither Gregory nor Hurston was as committed

to the "scientific rigor" of anthropological methods as she was to recording the idioms and dialect of the folk stories in her community. Of course,
Hurston was trained as an anthropologist under the direction of Franz
Boas at Columbia and draws on the methods of the discipline with much
greater ease and facility than the untutored Gregory. Nevertheless, as
women ethnographers in the early decades of the twentieth century who
were collecting folklore in their own backyards, so to speak, they were
both agents of their studies while aware that their relationship to the communities (and their own subject position) could just as easily make them
objects of inquiry.

Returning to folk expression was a paradigm of modernism's relationship to performance across the arts and sciences. Returning to the "folk"
during the Irish and Harlem Renaissances, which was predicated on a
return to the West of Ireland and the southern United States, was a means
of returning theater to its "roots"—something more "primitive" and "archaic," more emotive and, thus, more "real." Gregory and Hurston headed
out to the fields of the West and South to collect folklore in an attempt
to capture, salvage, and make manifest (through their writing and stage
performances) the formula of pathos that would lead to the origins of
expressive culture for a *nation*. In turn, they become part of the formula.
They are figures of women in movement caught between two representational regimes: the poetic and the mimetic. While they are on a search
for the pathos formula (a search for archetypes of expressive culture) they
are "read" in terms of an "ethos" formula (Plato's pervasive sphere of influence where mimesis is understood as representing the characteristic
spirit, prevalent tone of sentiment, of a people or community).[25]

This is most clearly understood when one explores how their anthropological pursuits were inextricably bound to their theatrical ones. Gregory
alludes to the relationship between the "folk" and theatrical expression
in *Our Irish Theatre* (1914), where she begins to articulate the goals of an
Irish national theater project. This is written in concert with her folklore-
collecting projects in the West of Ireland during this time. She writes:

> We hope to find in Ireland an uncorrupted and imaginative audi-
> ence trained to listen by its passion for oratory, and believe that our
> desire to bring upon the stage the deeper thoughts and emotions of
> Ireland will ensure for us a tolerant welcome, and that freedom to
> experiment which is not found in theaters of England, and without

which no new movement in art or literature can succeed. We will show that Ireland is not the home of buffoonery and of easy sentiment, as it has been represented, but the home of ancient idealism. We are confident of the support of all Irish people, who are weary of misrepresentation, in carrying out a work that is outside all political questions that divide us.[26]

In order for Gregory to be a part of the "ancient idealism" of the people, the theater must be "outside all political questions that divide us"; this is possible (at least rhetorically possible in this instance) because she "brings upon the stage the deeper thoughts and emotions of Ireland" that she collected in the field. That both projects—ethnographic fieldwork and dramaturgical creation—were happening simultaneously (and that Gregory was the linchpin between them) will be important to this discussion.

Hurston's plans for "the new, *real*, Negro theater" are expressed in letters to Langston Hughes that she sends "during the early period of her research in the South, collecting black folklore at Columbia under Franz Boas."[27] In a letter from April 12, 1928, she shares with Hughes her plans to create "a culturally authentic African-American theater, one constructed upon the foundations of black vernacular."[28] In this letter she writes: "Did I tell you before I left about the new, the *real* Negro theater I plan? Well, I shall, or rather we shall act out the folk tales, however short, with the abrupt angularity and naivete of the primitive 'bama Nigger. Quote with native settings. What do you think?"[29]

Hurston reformulates many of the ideas she writes to Hughes in "Characteristics of Negro Expression" (1934). In this essay she makes complex (and some would say contradictory) claims in reference to "originality" and "drama." She states, "it is obvious that to get back to original sources is much too difficult for any group to claim very much as a certainty. What we really mean by originality is modification of ideas."[30] With regard to drama she states, "the Negro's universal mimicry is not so much a thing in itself as evidence of something which permeates his entire self. And that thing is drama."[31]

Hurston's and Gregory's quest for authentic "folk" is not unique. Modernist artists and early-twentieth-century anthropologists all found rich material for artistic creation and scientific theorizing. What is unique was that they found the "folk" in their own backyard and readily identified the "folk" with the theater (and, by extension, cultural national projects) while also inserting themselves into their folklore collections. They created *personae* for themselves that, in turn, allowed the "ethnographic encounter" to become "the subject of the book, a fable of communication, rapport, and, finally, a kind of fictional, but potent, kinship."[32] While other modernist artists and theater practitioners may have found inspiration from "exotic" folk (Bertolt Brecht from Chinese acting; Antonin Artaud from Balinese dance; Pablo Picasso from African masks), there was never any desire or inclination to become an anthropologist, to study the "authentic" culture from the "inside." These "exotic" and "archaic" forms of expression were fashioned as detachable characteristics from cultures displaced both historically and geographically and that served as inspiration for a new Western art and drama.[33] Gregory's and Hurston's structure of address was unique in this regard: they presumed to both "speak for" and be a part of the "exotic" cultures they studied.

While they, too, found forms of expression in the field that could be detached and re-presented onstage, these "detachable" characteristics—idioms and gestures of folk expression—carried with them the gravitas of real Irish folk and southern folk. That is, for them, performance led back to the folk whose self-expression was inextricably tied to the land and their history on that land. For Hurston and Gregory, their folk drama was a part of the formula of pathos that resided—nay, originated—in the South and in the West of Ireland. The multiple images—folkloric and theatrical—were held in a precarious balance insofar as it was not clear what form of expression was imitating the other. Their "intentions" for theatrical representation presuppose that one could "arrang[e], as far as possible, the individual images in chronological order by following the probable generic relation that, binding one to the other, would eventually allow us to go back to the archetype, to the 'formula of pathos' from which they all originate."[34]

This is implied not only in *Our Irish Theatre* and "Characteristics of Negro Expression" but also in the structure of address in the folklore collections that are fashioned as faithful recordings of cultural expression. In the introduction to her first chapter in *Visions and Beliefs in the West of Ireland*, Gregory announces that she "had no theories, no case to prove, I but 'held a clean mirror to tradition.'"[35] Hurston re-inflects the mirror metaphor by announcing in the introduction to *Mules and Men* that she was "glad when somebody told me: you may go and collect Negro folklore." She was able to collect the folklore, she says, because she had the "spy-glass of anthropology to look through."[36]

However, by inserting themselves as personae in the folklore they record, they continually make explicit the poetic regime that they inhabit. That is, Gregory announces, "even when I began to gather these stories, I cared less for evidence given in them than for the beautiful rhythmic sentences in which they were told," because they "provide a clue, a thread, leading through the maze to that mountain top where things visible and invisible meet."[37] When Hurston announces to the Eatonville folks that she has come "to collect some old stories and tales," she is asked by B. Moseley: "What you mean, Zora, them big old lies we tell when we're jus' sittin' around here on the store porch doin' nothin'?"[38] These "lies," Zora reports, "are not as easy to collect as they sound," because people are "reluctant to reveal that which the soul lives by."[39] They go into the field knowing that they are collecting lore that cannot be confirmed and cannot be denied: folklore stories that are "lies" and have no "evidence," and at the same time are the expressive means by which "the soul lives" and "where the visible and invisible meet." But if the stories they record cannot be confirmed and cannot be denied, the veracity of the folklore is considered suspect in relation to the teller, not the tale.

Gregory's critics say that the folklore was made up for her, that her place in the stories (and by proxy in her community) was that of a unionist who was separated from the community by her class and ethnicity (indeed, that there are very few "bad landlord" stories appears as the "proof" that the tales are not "real").[40] Gregory also includes at least one reference to a comedy she has written for the stage (*The Full Moon*) when she introduces a section in the volume on "The Fool of Forth."[41] This last example illuminates what appears to be Gregory's gravest error in having her folklore collection "authenticated": the stories, it is sometimes assumed by her contemporaries, are not collected for their own sake but simply as "material" to be mined for theatrical representation.

Hurston's persona, "Zora," is the guiding principle and our guide through *Mules and Men*, whose narrative structure complicates how we are to read it in terms of genre. By using a narrative conceit more akin to the work of fiction (particularly the novel) than to ethnographic reportage, the veracity of the tales is questioned because the very form makes critics doubt how the "real" can possibly be represented via a medium too artistic to be scientifically authentic, and a writing style where the ethnographer fashions herself as the protagonist. In other words, Gregory's and Hurston's self-conscious structure of address—their own allegorical conceits—allows for commonsensical readings of their work that become displacement exercises that tell us about their person. And their person is all the more dubious because they do not seem to be collecting the folklore for itself, but in order to use it as material for staged performances and fiction.

While it is clear that Hurston and Gregory think of authenticity in terms of a poetic regime (movement, action, creation, self-expression which they articulate in "Characteristics of Negro Expression" and *Our Irish Theatre*), their work is judged by a related but discontinuous regime: the ethical regime where an image is the reflection of an ideal form (origin) that should represent and guide the beliefs of a community, nation, and ideology. Following this line of thinking, Gregory's and Hurston's critics are convinced that their formula of pathos does not lead them to the authentic folk of the lands (with an origin) but back to earlier theatrical representations: blackface minstrelsy and Irish caricature that predated modernism's use of the primitive and were an insidious circulation of stereotypes that were fashioned into what Elin Diamond refers to as "transatlantic curiosities."[42] Their work simply refers back to something that was already a false copy. Even if this cannot be completely denied, it is the political and perceptual complications that emerge in relation to their person that attends to readings and interpretation of the "intentions" of their ethnographic and artistic work. This echoes earlier critiques explored in this essay where Richard Wright describes Hurston as "not honest" (because he believes she follows a literary form leading back to blackface minstrelsy and not forward to social realism) and George Moore describes Gregory as "not real" (which has the effect of displacing her *un*reality onto her work, which is described as employing artificial language).

Of course, it is not each woman's person that can be denied (they exist), but her *persona*. In large part, these are personae that they themselves created and that are enhanced by their desire to form fictional but powerful kinships with the communities they study. By placing themselves at the center of real stories ("lies") about the folk imagination, they fashion their narratives as ethnographic allegories: they are at once inside the frame and outside, attempting to control its multiple meanings. Gordon Teskey explains the function of persona in allegory in the following excerpt:

> The word *persona* means "mask," literally a thing "to sound through," *per-sonare*, indicating a sonic essence transpiercing a mask that at once represents and conceals the wearer. But in the figure of personification whatever voice that persona has emerges from the logical dissonance of the mask with itself. . . . Personification has been regarded as the sine qua non of allegorical expression. But if this is so, then it is not because personification reveals what is essential to allegory but because it hides what is essential to it so well. One way in which it does this is to give a feminine gender to the figures that confer form, rather than to the female receptacle, so that these "intermediary icons" will already possess Matter's gender. Yet even as they perform this intermediary role feminine agents are both examples of the universals they instantiate and living sources from which those universals cascade into the world.[43]

Thus we are back at the moment of the particular being universal and the universal being particular, the moment where we cannot separate the teller from the tale, or the real woman from the imagined place of "woman." We will see these figures of women in movement again, but the "formula of pathos" might elude our gaze.

Allegories of Salvage

We know by now that Hurston died penniless, buried in an unmarked grave, with all four of her novels, her autobiography, and her two ethnographic studies out of print. The collection of plays now housed at the Library of Congress indicates that she was a prolific playwright who never saw a single play produced in her lifetime. Upon her death in 1960 she was all but forgotten. Hurston was first "rediscovered" by Alice Walker, who writes about her own relationship with Hurston's ethnographic and fictional work in a 1975 article she published in *Ms.* magazine, "In Search of Zora Neale Hurston."[44] By the 1980s Hurston had become—to paraphrase Hazel Carby—an academic industry.[45] In the late 1980s Hurston also joined the heritage industry in the guise of the Zora Neale Hurston Festival of Arts and Humanities held in Eatonville, Florida, since 1988

(Historic Eatonville is now trademarked) and the Zora Neale Hurston National Museum of Fine Art (also in Eatonville since 1990). In addition, Hurston's house in Fort Pierce, Florida, is now a National Historic Landmark.

Hurston also has been the subject of many plays written about her life. Laurence Holder's *Zora Neale Hurston* was first produced off-Broadway in 1989 and has been produced many times in the United States in the last twenty years. Neema Barnette also directed Ruby Dee in the adapted stage play *All About Zora* for the PBS series American Playhouse under the title *Zora Is My Name!* It is now widely available on DVD.[46] Lynda Marion Hill has written about several other incarnations of Hurston's life being adapted for the stage, as well as the landmark production of the never-produced play *Mule Bone*, whose tumultuous history ended the friendship between Hurston and her collaborator, Langston Hughes. Hill writes, "The Broadway production of *Mule Bone* [in 1991] is a landmark in American theater history because for the first time mainstream theater produced a play by a nonliving major black playwright" (in this case, two).[47]

In her biography of Lady Gregory, Elizabeth Coxhead explains that, "within ten years of her death [in 1932], a friend who was almost contemporary could write: 'I perceive no one in Ireland cares in the very least about her. She is almost forgotten already.'"[48] Her plays also fell out of favor after her death, and to this day they are almost never produced. Her ethnographic work has only been the subject of scant critical investigation. Interestingly, however, we find Gregory being revived in the Irish landscape in the 1990s. While she is certainly not an academic industry, her return bears a remarkable resemblance to Hurston's. She, too, has become a fixture in the heritage landscape: "an annual conference, the Lady Gregory Autumn Gathering, has provided a forum for her writing since 1995";[49] the Kiltartan Gregory Museum, opened in 1996, is dedicated primarily to her life and achievements; and her name is now branded on the Lady Gregory Hotel, Conference Centre and Leisure Club in Gort, County Galway, not far from where she lived at Coole Park. There have been numerous biographies of Lady Gregory published in the last thirty years, and her life story has also been the subject of a play by Sam Mc-Cready, *Coole Lady: The Extraordinary Story of Lady Gregory*, which had its premiere in Sligo in 2003.

In her introduction to a special issue of the *Irish University Review*, Anne Fogarty states that, "Despite her ubiquity as a point of orientation in the heritage landscape of modern Ireland and in academic investigations of the Revival period, the iconicity associated with Gregory is a sign less of her continued prestige and influence than of the complex cultural anxieties attaching to her."[50] This understanding of Gregory as being attached to "complex cultural anxieties" and as someone who seems "at once to embody a foundational moment in modern Irish cultural history and remain forever extrinsic to it" could easily be said of Hurston's own return.[51] Indeed, to embody—with one's whole body—a "foundational moment" while remaining extrinsic to the "real" story is what allegorical personae *do*. Their returns are both ubiquitous and singular. Here, Teskey's thoughts come to mind again: "singularity operates in allegory as does the vanishing point in a linear perspective: it is never visible itself, but everything that is visible directs the eye toward it."[52] It is in the contemporary landscape—where Hurston and Gregory are everywhere and nowhere—that we might be able to more firmly grasp the constitutive paradox of authenticity and performance as they animate cultural history, a paradox illuminated by the concept of "allegories of salvage." This ethnographic conceit coined by James Clifford bears startling resemblance to Hurston's and Gregory's spectral return as commodity-icons for heritage tourism in their native landscapes, and their biographical return as "authentic material" for play-texts and staged performances. They continue to trace the formula of pathos where they become "hybrids of archetype and phenomena." That is, their returns mark a curious repetition and revision of their own ethnographic collecting practices and of their use of this material for "authentic" stage performances.

That the primitive (and the "folk") were a means of expressing "authentic" culture, and began circulating in material and performance form as commodity fetish, during modernism's cultural reign in the early twentieth century is well documented. Clifford's statement that ethnography during Boas's time was considered "a last chance rescue operation" underscores the fact that "salvage" was the preoccupation of ethnographers who went to collect geographical "others" and of artists who then interpreted them as historical "others."[53] It was through these "others," it was supposed, that we could glean an authentic and spiritual essence that could save us from "political expansionism and technological and social change."[54]

During the early twentieth century, when the Irish and Harlem Renaissances began to flourish, salvaging the "folk" as a "last chance rescue operation" had a very immediate rationale: the great migration of African Americans from the South to the North and of Irish immigrants to the American North. How do *these* migratory figures in movement "salvaged" by Hurston and Gregory in the early twentieth century help to shed light on Hurston's and Gregory's contemporary return and the "cultural anxieties" attaching to their person? How does their reappearance as "intermediary icons," where their names, images, and biographical lives become landmarks for regional authenticity, tell us something about contemporary Atlantic migration and the continual tracing of the formula of pathos?

We might find that the singular allegorical figures mean other than what they say and say other than what they mean. When migration patterns change—which has happened on a radical scale in the U.S. South and in Ireland in the last fifteen years—formations of national kinship come under scrutiny: How do we incorporate these "new others" into our national story? In many respects, in both Ireland and the U.S. South, this remains at best an open question. Contemporary migrants often occupy the position of being everywhere and nowhere in the landscape, caught in a kind of suspended animation where they too become haptic allegories, "tangible abstractions that one can see and feel and touch."[55]

Cultural anxieties attached to Hurston and Gregory, who were also once "other" to the culture of nationalism, now seem to stand in curious proximity to the cultural *real*. They are names and screens blocking alternative paths into time and space that allegorize the haptic encounters of these new "others." Although Hurston and Gregory are now safely "grounded" in the regional landscape, their restless movements through Atlantic historiography are painful, sensuous reminders of what has not yet passed: the Atlantic voyage to erasure. Recognizing the "singular" returns of gendered specters as "heritage kitsch" doing allegorical work in commodified form might begin to allow us "to make room for the spectres in whose restlessness the rhythms of another mode of living speaks to us."[56]

Notes

1. In his preface to *The Book of American Negro Poetry*, Johnson discusses four African American artistic creations that have "sprung from American soil and been universally acknowledged as distinctive American products." These four "products" are the Uncle Remus stories, "spirituals" or slave songs, the Cakewalk, and ragtime. James Weldon Johnson, Preface, *The Book of American Negro Poetry* ed. Johnson (New York: Harcourt, Brace, 1922), 8.

2. To name but three examples, see Tracey Mishkin's *The Harlem and Irish Renaissances* (Gainesville: University Press of Florida, 1998); Brian Gallagher's "'About Us, For Us, Near Us': The Irish and Harlem Renaissances" and George Bornstein's "Afro-Celtic Connections: From Frederick Douglass to *The Commitments*," both in *Literary Influences and African-American Writers*, ed. Tracy Mishkin (New York: Garland Publishing, 1996), 157–70 and 171–88.

3. Alan Ackerman and Martin Puchner, eds., *Against Theatre: Creative Destructions on the Modernist Stage* (London: Palgrave Macmillan, 2006), 4.

4. Joseph Roach, *Cities of the Dead: Circum-Atlantic Performances* (New York: Columbia University Press, 1996), 5.

5. James Clifford, "On Ethnographic Allegory," in *Writing Culture: The Poetics and Politics of Ethnography*, ed. James Clifford and George Marcus (Berkeley: University of California Press, 1992), 113.

6. Guiliana Bruno, *Atlas of Emotion: Journeys through Art, Architecture, and Film* (New York: Verso, 2002), 6.

7. Susan Buck-Morris, *The Dialectics of Seeing: Walter Benjamin and the Arcades Project* (Cambridge: MIT Press, 1991), 228–29.

8. Giorgio Agamben, *The Signature of All Things: On Method*, trans. Luca D'Isanto (New York: Schocken, 1969), 31.

9. Ibid., 22.

10. Gordon Teskey, *Allegory and Violence* (Ithaca: Cornell University Press, 1996), 5.

11. See Michael Malouf, "Sovereignty at Home and Abroad: Marcus Garvey," in Malouf, *Transatlantic Solidarities: Irish Nationalism and Caribbean Poetics* (Charlottesville: University of Virginia Press, 2009), 44–79; Bruce Nelson, "'Come out of Such Land, You Irishmen': Daniel O'Connell, Slavery and the Making of the Irish 'Race,'" in *Eire/Ireland* 42, nos. 1–2 (Spring/Summer 2007): 58–81.

12. Lady Augusta Gregory, *Our Irish Theatre: A Chapter of Autobiography* (New York: Putnam, 1914), 9.

13. Fred Moten, *In the Break: The Aesthetics of a Black Radical Tradition* (Minneapolis: University of Minnesota Press, 2003), 176.

14. Richard Wright, "Between Laughter and Tears," in *New Masses*, October 5, 1937. Reprinted in *Zora Neale Hurston: Critical Perspectives Past and Present*, ed. Henry Louis Gates Jr. et al. (New York: Amistad Press, 1993), 17.

15. Ibid.

16. George Moore, *Hail and Farewell* (1911), ed. Richard Cave (London: Colin Smythe Ltd., 1985), 547.

17. Ibid., 552.

18. This phrase is taken from Richard Schechner's study *Between Theatre and Anthropology* (Philadelphia: University of Pennsylvania Press, 1985), 35–36, where performance is defined as "the restoration of behavior" or "twice-behaved behavior."

19. Gould quoted in Steve Tillis, *Rethinking Folk Drama* (Westport, Conn.: Greenwood Press, 1999), 171.

20. Elin Diamond, *Unmaking Mimesis: Essays on Feminism and Theatre* (New York and London: Routledge, 1997), iv.

21. Agamben, *The Signature of All Things*, 29.

22. Ibid., 19.

23. Walter Benjamin, "The Work of Art in the Age of Mechanical Reproduction," in *Illuminations: Essays and Reflections*, ed. Hannah Arendt, trans. Harry Zohn (New York: Schocken, 1969), 220.

24. These concerns have been especially prevalent in southern folklore and pop culture studies in the work of James C. Cobb, *Redefining Southern Culture: Mind and Identity in the Modern South* (Athens: University of Georgia Press, 1999); Karl Hagstrom Miller, *Segregating Sound: Inventing Folk and Pop Music in the Age of Jim Crow* (Durham: Duke University Press, 2010); Richard A. Peterson, *Creating Country Music: Fabricating Authenticity* (Chicago: University of Chicago Press, 1997); Jon Smith, "Southern Culture on the Skids: Punk, Retro, Narcissism, and the Burdon of Southern History," in *South to a New Place*, ed. Suzanne Jones and Sharon Monteith (Baton Rouge: Louisiana State University Press, 2002), 76–120; Brian Ward, "That White Man, Burdon: The Animals, Race and the American South," in *Transatlantic Roots Music: Folk, Blues, and National Identities*, ed. Jill Terry and Neil A. Wynn (Jackson: University Press of Mississippi, 2012), 153–78; and David E. Whisnant, *All that is Native and Fine: The Politics of Culture in an American Region* (Chapel Hill: University of North Carolina Press, 1983).

25. Oxford English Dictionary Online, http://www.oed.com.

26. Gregory, *Our Irish Theatre*, 9.

27. Henry Louis Gates, Introduction, in Zora Neale Hurston and Langston Hughes, *Mule Bones: A Comedy of Negro Life* (1931), ed. Henry Louis Gates and George Houston Bass (New York: The Library of America, 1991), 9.

28. Ibid.

29. Hurston in *Zora Neale Hurston: A Life in Letters*, ed. Cara Kaplan (New York: Doubleday, 2001), 116.

30. Hurston, "Characteristics of Negro Expression" in *Hurston: Folklore, Memoirs and Other Writings*, ed. Cheryl A. Wall (New York: The Library of America, 1995), 838.

31. Ibid., 830.

32. Clifford, "On Ethnographic Allegory," 104.

33. See Elin Diamond "Deploying/Destroying the Primitivist Body in Hurston and Brecht," in Ackerman and Puchner, *Against Theatre*, 113.

34. Agamben, *The Signature of All Things*, 29.

35. Lady Augusta Gregory (reprinted with a foreword by Elizabeth Coxhead), *Visions and Beliefs in the West of Ireland* (1920; London: Colin Smythe Ltd., 1970), 15.

36. Hurston, *Mules and Men*, in Wall, *Hurston*, 9.

37. Gregory, *Visions and Beliefs*, 15.

38. Hurston, *Mules and Men*, 13.

39. Ibid., 10.

40. These opinions of Gregory's contemporaries are discussed in Patricia Lysaght, "Perspectives on Narrative Communication and Gender: Lady Augusta Gregory's *Vision and Beliefs in the West of Ireland* (1920)," *Fabula* 3, no. 4 (1998): 256–76; they are espoused by Selina Guinness in her essay "*Visions and Beliefs in the West of Ireland*: Irish Folklore and British Anthropology 1898–1920," *Irish University Review* 6, no. 1 (1998): 37–46.

41. Gregory, *Visions and Beliefs*, 250.

42. Diamond, "Deploying/Destroying the Primitivist Body," 114.

43. Teskey, *Allegory and Violence*, 22.

44. Alice Walker, "In Search of Zora Neale Hurston," *Ms.*, March 3, 1975, 74.

45. Hazel V. Carby, "The Politics of Fiction, Anthropology, and the Folk: Zora Neale Hurston," in *New Essays on "Their Eyes Were Watching God,"* ed. Michael Awkward (New York: Cambridge University Press, 1990), 71–93.

46. *Zora Is My Name!*, directed by Neema Barnette (MCMXC Community Television of Southern California: Monterey Media Inc., 2006), DVD.

47. Lynda Marion Hill, *Social Rituals and the Verbal Art of Zora Neale Hurston* (Washington, D.C.: Howard University Press, 1996), 184.

48. Elizabeth Coxhead, *Lady Gregory: A Literary Portrait* (London: Secker & Warburg, 1966), v.

49. Anne Fogarty, Introduction, *Irish University Review* (special issue on Lady Gregory) 34, no. 1 (2004): viii.

50. Ibid., ix.

51. Ibid.

52. Teskey, *Allegory and Violence*, 5.

53. Clifford writes: "Few anthropologists today would embrace the logic of ethnography in the terms in which it was enunciated in Franz Boas's time, as a last-chance rescue operation. But the allegory of salvage is deeply ingrained." Clifford, "On Ethnographic Allegory," 113.

54. Barkan and Bush quoted in Diamond, "Deploying/Destroying the Primitivist Body," 114.

55. Judy Enders, "Memories and Allegories of the Death Penalty: Back to the Medieval Future," in *Thinking Allegory Otherwise*, ed. Brenda Machosky (Stanford: Stanford University Press, 2010), 39.

56. David Lloyd, "The Indigent Sublime: Spectres of Irish Hunger," *Representations* (special issue on redress), 92 (Fall 2005): 153.

10

·····················

Princess Laura Kofey and
the Reverse Atlantic Experience

NATANYA KEISHA DUNCAN

On March 8, 1928, Princess Laura Adorkor Kofey was assassinated while speaking at a Universal Negro Improvement Association (UNIA) meeting in Miami. A Ghanaian-born royal priestess whose transatlantic journey to the U.S. South took in England, Panama, Detroit, and Canada, Kofey had initially been acclaimed within that organization for her ability to revive struggling UNIA divisions in the Southeast and attract new membership. Between 1926 and 1928 she held camp-style meetings at baseball fields, public parks, church sanctuaries, and Masonic lodge halls such that the overflow forced many listeners to stand outside the edifices and line adjacent streets. As we will see, Kofey's message was imbued with much of the standard black nationalist rhetoric of the 1920s, and she steadily endorsed what she saw as the central tenets of the UNIA program, but it also reflected her unusual background as an African prophetess and emissary to the black population of the United States.

Kofey introduced into the heart of the UNIA a distinctively African and female voice that found particular purchase in Florida, Alabama, and Louisiana. Mobilizing a personal knowledge and understanding of Africa that was quite rare among UNIA leaders and laity, she modified the Association's repatriation agenda by shifting attention from Liberia to Ghana and other less developed areas of the continent and questioned the value of the organization's "missionary" schemes as originally outlined by Marcus Garvey's first wife, Amy Ashwood.[1] More generally, she worked to promote concrete cultural and economic exchange between the United States and Africa that went beyond the sometimes highly romantic dreams of many Garveyites and challenged many of their stereotypes about the continent and its inhabitants. What she called for was simple: African Americans needed to make credible preparations to return to the interior of Africa, not least by developing commercial ties with the continent that were based around the distinctively African or African-derived skills and products that flourished mainly in the U.S. South.

This essay focuses on Kofey's dynamic two-year tenure in the UNIA and her attempts to establish a viable trade agreement between the UNIA and her native Ghana using Jacksonville, Florida, as a hub. These efforts continued even after the Association declared her persona non grata in late 1927, when her burgeoning popularity seemed to threaten the authority of Garvey and the UNIA's largely male, often ministerial leadership in the South, and her militant form of international black nationalism jeopardized the strategic, if tenuous relationships the UNIA formed with local white authorities. Moreover, Kofey couched her work in the United States explicitly in terms of a diplomatic mission sanctioned by the peoples of Africa—more specifically by native Ghanaian authorities based in Accra to whom she had close family ties. Through her demeanor, lineage, and personality as well as through the particulars of her religious and secular teachings, she countered visions of Africans as docile, backward, dysfunctional, and in need of material help and moral uplift from their more sophisticated North American cousins. Whether dealing with matters of repatriation, commerce, religion, education, or politics, she helped to introduce, or more accurately to reintroduce, African American communities of the South and UNIA supporters to alternative, more positive images of Africa and its peoples. Ultimately, however, Kofey's popularity reveals the potency of efforts by her and the UNIA in the South to reach out to and reclaim Africa and themselves, efforts to revalidate the kinds of transatlantic and diasporic connections that Kofey personified.

Diasporic membership is often based on a "culture consciousness" that sets up polar opposites of a "here" and a "there." The "there," according to Paul Tiyambe Zeleza, is "invoked as a rhetoric of self affirmation" and reclamation of a place alleged to be stolen or hidden from the rightful owners.[2] Bridging the gap between "here" and "there," Laura Kofey resembled "Atlantic Creoles" in that she spoke a pidgin English, retained a pride in and utilized many discernibly African cultural, social, and philosophical traits, and attempted to engage in commercial business ties between the continent and the West.[3] Borrowing from the formulation put forward by Tiffany Ruby Patterson and Robin D. G. Kelley, this essay suggests that

Kofey's presence in the UNIA and as a significant—if prematurely silenced—black voice in the South contributed to a "diasporic identity and its social, cultural and political manifestations" while encouraging a "rethinking of the West." A living embodiment of ongoing Atlantic World relationships, Kofey promoted the "continual reinvention of Africa and the Diaspora through cultural work, migrations, transformations in communications, as well as the globalization of capital" within the UNIA and the diaspora at large.[4]

Laura Kofey's Transatlantic Vision

The precise circumstances of Laura Kofey's migration to the United States from Accra, Ghana, are shrouded in mystery. Her early life exemplifies the difficulties that women of African descent often encountered when attempting to enter the United States in the early twentieth century.[5] Kofey's journey from Africa to the U.S. South occurred in phases and introduced her to audiences throughout the diaspora.[6] Along the way she went to England, Canada, and the Panama Canal Zone, where in 1925 she was the featured guest speaker at a UNIA meeting in Colón, Panama. Her presence in Colón brought her a notoriety that followed her to Detroit UNIA circles.[7] Between the summer of 1926 and August 1927, when she visited Marcus Garvey in the Atlanta Penitentiary, Princess Kofey traveled south and established branches of the African Universal Church and Commercial League (sometimes referred to by followers as the Universal African Orthodox Church) in Louisiana, Alabama, and Florida while soliciting members for the UNIA and helping to revitalize struggling branches and divisions.

In this respect, Kofey's work in the UNIA was similar to that of other key female figures in the Garveyite movement, such as Amy Jacques Garvey, Henrietta Vinton Davis, and Maymie Leona Turpeau De Mena, who also visited the South regularly on behalf of the organization. Yet, in places like New Orleans, Mobile, and Jacksonville, Kofey sought to do more than recruit and retain UNIA membership. She asked black southerners to seriously consider repatriation. And those who were not yet ready to physically return to Africa, she encouraged to engage in various business schemes that would extend trade between southerners and the coast of Africa. The exchange with Africa would be based on shared diasporic skills, knowledge, products, and goods common to peoples of

African descent on both sides of the Atlantic. Thus, while Davis and De Mena emphasized UNIA educational and political initiatives in the South, Kofey asked members to see the region as a part of an Atlantic trade network. In her economic program, the African yams, sweet potatoes, and other products that had found such fertile soil in the U.S. South and the peculiar ingenuity and talents of African American farmers and artisans would be the basis for a transatlantic trading relationship between Africa and the United States run for and by Africans and their diasporic cousins in the South. For this emphasis on transatlantic commerce, rooted specifically in transplanted African expertise and crops, Kofey was heralded as a "prophet of Garveyism," while the Miami Division 286 viewed her as the "female John the Baptist."[8]

Kofey believed that the talents and resources African Americans had used to make life livable in the U.S. South were actually no different from those they would need to develop Africa's interior. Thus, beyond their importance in developing new trade links, the skill sets southern blacks had honed as sharecroppers, day laborers, factory workers, educators, journalists, and entrepreneurs were all deemed essential in Kofey's repatriation schemes. According to Mrs. Adel Jennings of Jacksonville, audiences were "taken with her plain folk approach" and responded to her insistence that they could play "an active role in African redemption."[9] In Kofey's program, they could do more than simply buy stock in the fledgling, often ill-fated "back-to-Africa" business enterprises that Garvey privileged or engage in largely symbolic acts of reclamation through dubious African land purchases. Kofey depicted an Africa that was very real, reachable, and, as evidenced by her own diplomatic mission to the United States, eager for their return.

While Garvey and the UNIA staged parades "through the streets of Harlem, boldly claiming those streets as (African-American) political territory," Kofey devoted much of her energy to encouraging her supporters, which included fruit farmers, fishermen, seamen and longshoremen along with their wives in Florida, cotton farmers and their families in Alabama, seamen, schoolteachers, nurses, bricklayers, carpenters and other skilled and unskilled laborers throughout the South, to migrate to Africa. After repatriation, she suggested, that they might choose to revisit the U.S. South temporarily to take full stock of the grim situation that they had left behind. "Make the trip back over here," she urged, and "You will say me smell something stink."[10] The stench in the air of the United

States, particularly in the Jim Crow South, was of racism, discrimination, terror, low self-esteem, gender bias, and ignorance that kept people of the diaspora disconnected from the continent, their pasts, and their potential for economic, social, cultural, and spiritual fulfillment. These ills were enough in Kofey's view to persuade the men and women of the South to return to Africa, where she believed they stood a much better chance to reap the full rewards for their labor.

Kofey's ambition to reconnect Africa and the United States economically on black terms helps to explain her interest in the South. Her Florida converts claimed that she chose Jacksonville as her home due to the city's relative proximity to Africa.[11] More generally, Kofey's focus on the South, particularly the coastal South, reflected the number of ports there that had played a role in the slave trade and that now housed trained black seamen, artisans, and skilled laborers and professionals, and that had in their rural hinterlands a plentiful supply of black agricultural workers—the prerequisites for developing the local African American business interests, the transatlantic trade links, and, ultimately, the repatriation initiatives that she advocated. In Jacksonville, a city plagued by lynching and other acts of racist terror and intimidation, she addressed her audiences in language that fused appeals to "racial uplift," probity, and communal economic progress with a firm focus on Africa: "Negroes, learn to help yourselves, create your own jobs, build your own enterprises. Clean up your lives—love one another, patronize one another. If you don't learn to help yourselves and build industries and commerce with your Motherland Africa you are doomed and done for."[12]

Princess Kofey was hardly the only member of the UNIA or broader Garveyite circles to promote repatriation or advocate closer economic ties with Africa. Yet, for a variety of reasons ranging from bad luck and government harassment to incompetence and fraud, these efforts met with limited success. And they were often hampered from the outset because of their nearly exclusive focus on Liberia. Although the UNIA claimed it was in negotiations with President C. D. B. King of Liberia and sent two delegations over between 1921 and 1924 in hopes of achieving a written agreement to allow, in the UNIA's parlance, the colonization of the country by a new wave of African Americans, King and others in Liberia's government insisted that no such agreement was ever signed. On the contrary, Liberia entered into a land contract with the Firestone Rubber

Company and publicly denounced the UNIA. The Liberian government also banned UNIA members from setting foot in the country by refusing them visas and revoked privileges previously extended to anyone associated with the organization.[13]

Partly because of her awareness of the problems the UNIA had encountered in Liberia, partly because of her belief that African Americans would fare better in areas of Africa where vested political and economic interests were less firmly entrenched, Laura Kofey presented a different strategy for repatriation. Somewhat paradoxically, given the way she repeatedly emphasized her own official mandate from the royal political elite in Ghana into which she had been born, her plans were skeptical of any formal reliance on existing African state or tribal apparatuses to aid repatriating African Americans. Instead, she presented a vision of greater opportunities and wealth for returning African Americans if they were willing to establish new communities in the less developed interior, away from establish centers of jealously guarded economic and political power on the Atlantic coast. Mother Kofey, as she became known, advised that "those of you who go to Africa don't go in the towns that already built up. Go in the interior and build your own towns children. Prepare to build up the old waste places. Children go way out among your people and put up your own stores, because the other fellow is going to have and isn't going to give it away to you."[14]

Despite its prominence in her teachings, Kofey's commitment to and extension of the UNIA's economic agenda, with its emphasis on black capital accumulation and transnational business enterprise, has tended to be downplayed or artificially divorced from her role as a charismatic religious leader in many historical accounts of her career. For example, Barbara Bair and Richard Newman, in their biographical sketches of Kofey's church work, focus primarily on her as a charismatic religious figure.[15] In fact, the roles of spiritual leader and economic visionary intersected. Kofey established branches of the African Universal Church and Commercial League exclusively in major southern ports and transportation hubs such as Jacksonville, New Orleans, and Mobile in the hope that they would serve as centers of black trade and offer easy links to Africa. But in many ways, Kofey's contributions to black nationalist ideals, her conception of repatriation, and her role as a prominent figure in the Black Atlantic, as duly noted by Bair and Newman, were inextricably linked to her ability to reinterpret the UNIA's objectives to southern black audiences through her work as a spiritual leader, with a personal understanding of Ghanaian and broader West African beliefs, political structures, economic resources, and social practices.

That expertise was evident when Kofey challenged UNIA assumptions regarding the spiritual life of Africans, assumptions linked to notions of African backwardness that informed much UNIA rhetoric and policy. According to the UNIA objectives outlined in 1914, the organization sought "To Assist in Civilizing the Backward tribes of Africa, to strengthen the Imperialism of Bas[u]toland, Liberia, etc.," and "To Promote a Conscientious Christian Worship among the Native Tribes of Africa."[16] Kofey proposed that the organization reevaluate the necessity of sending preachers and missionaries to Africa, arguing that Africa was not backward in its religious beliefs or, for that matter, in its governmental systems, and insisting that there was already a strong Christian commitment in Africa.

Here Kofey was helped by the fact that, thanks to the work of its own missionaries, some elements within the UNIA had already begun to reassess their position toward the continent and its spiritual, moral, and political characteristics. Recognition within Association circles that Christianity and civilized values flourished in Africa was first signaled by Henrietta Peters at a New York UNIA meeting in 1919. Mrs. Peters and her husband were missionaries of the African Methodist Episcopalian Zion Church to the Gold Coast of Africa from 1915 to 1925.[17] In Peters's view, the people of the interior of Africa were governed "under the most refined judicial system of law, order and authority," which contrasted sharply with the "time-honored tradition in America that the Negro was a natural and rapid rapine."[18] Her report was followed by that of another AME missionary, Emily Christmas Kinch, who advised in 1920 that Africa was "never in a more receptive mood for the UNIA than today" and that the time was ripe for "going back to Africa and possessing the land."[19] She invoked the "here" and "there" polar opposites central to diasporic identities as she told listeners that

You think it is a wonderful thing to be in Harlem, but you have never enjoyed you[r] manhood until you have walked in Liberia and have come in contact with the black President of that country and received invitations to come to the banquet that is prepared in the State House. You surely cannot go to Washington to one. And so, after all, I would rather be in Liberia to-night, all things being equal, without her trolley cars, without her subways, without her elevated system, and to feel and know that I am a woman for all of that. Black skins or short hair, money or no money, you are a man and have the opportunity of being the greatest person in that republic; for the only requirement of Liberia is that you are black.[20]

It is striking here how explicitly Kinch linked the reclamation of black manhood with setting foot on African soil. Travel to Africa presented the potential for a transformation not only of economic and social status but also of the mind and self-esteem, even if that sometimes took rather traditionally gendered, patriarchal forms. This kind of appeal to black male pride was very much in keeping with the "efficient woman" tradition of the UNIA, in which black women often encouraged men to take a pre-eminent public role in the pursuit of race progress, in part as a pragmatic move to help restore a sense of black manhood, self-respect, and purposefulness that had been compromised by multiple forms of racial, economic, political, and social oppression.[21] Still, as she closed her remarks, Kinch carefully noted that "the only requirement in Liberia is that you are black," indicating that African American women and children would also enjoy new possibilities.

Within the UNIA, women were often especially eager to see particular programs and agendas actualized. One such area was education, where the UNIA's objective "To Establish Universities, Colleges and Secondary Schools for the Further Education and Culture of our Boys and Girls" led to the formation of Liberty University in Virginia.[22] The pursuit of education as an instrument of liberation was viewed throughout the diaspora as a means to overcome imperialism and racism. Laura Kofey also saw educational initiatives in the United States as vital to dispelling stereotypes about Africa and preparing African Americans for eventual repatriation. Just as Kofey advocated a literal approach to repatriation that included building new towns in Africa and establishing trade with existing native-run enterprises, so she supported a race-based education that would "enlighten" her audiences to the realities of an Africa well "managed by native people."[23]

In addition to setting up a small training school in her Jacksonville home, Kofey encouraged all peoples of the diaspora to acquire the skills and knowledge that would help them to build stronger, more prosperous nations in Africa in cooperation with, rather than simply as visiting tutors of, those Africans already living in less developed regions of the continent. Here Kofey deviated slightly from the UNIA's official approach to education, which primarily sought to train boys and girls for temporary service in Africa. This agenda was exemplified by the work of Liberty University in Claremont, Virginia. Generally speaking, the UNIA's success in Virginia was due to its ability to co-opt or participate in preexisting programs that mitigated the worst evils of Jim Crow and empowered local blacks.[24] The founding of Liberty University, which really amounted to the purchasing of Smallwood-Corey Industrial Institute in 1926, was heralded as one of Garvey's foremost early achievements. His original intention had been to create a Tuskegee-like institution in Jamaica that would "in time furnish competent men and women as technical missionaries to be sent to the mother country—Africa."[25] With the demise of the UNIA's short-lived Booker T. Washington University in New York, Liberty was as close as Garvey came to realizing that goal in America. The university was used to promote both figurative and literal links with Africa, as the school's site was alleged to be "the spot where Negro slaves landed in 1622" and near the disembarking point of "the first cargo of (American) slaves in 1619."[26] By buying this property, the UNIA thus attempted to reconnect itself, via the history of the slave South, with an African past that was transformed, but never severed, by the Middle Passage. The president and vice-president of Smallwood-Corey and members of the UNIA, Caleb Robinson and Dr. St. Clair Drake, contended, "because of the history of the place and its sacredness to (our) group we are deciding to make it the Southern Headquarters of the Garvey 'Back to Africa' movement, and have there a great school to teach and train boys and girls, men and women of African descent."[27]

The training offered at Liberty was designed to enable students "to live in Africa" and "be an asset and not a liability."[28] *Negro World* described the university as a

> distinct school for Negro people, in which they may learn some-thing about themselves and their race, and about Africa, their

Motherland, which they could not learn in other race schools, nor in the white schools open to them. . . .

To be taught that the Negro has as many rights as any other racial group and that he needs a country and a flag of his own in order to make effective his rights, is something new in Negro education.[29]

While UNIA officials stressed the importance of education in fostering a generation of African Americans ready to serve and work in a backward Africa, the Africa Kofey portrayed did not usually suffer from a lack of educated and able people. Although she noted that many areas remained economically underdeveloped, she spent much more time stressing that Africa was a continent of intelligent, knowledgeable landed peoples with an impressive and highly effective social and economic infrastructure that ought to inspire African Americans. She proclaimed, "it is the natives, who, in many countries of Africa, own and control their homelands. And since they owned and controlled their homelands it is the Africans themselves who carried on industries and commerce of their own countries, selling their raw materials to the markets of the world and in turn buying all kinds of manufactured goods."[30]

To counter prevailing narratives of African primitivism, Kofey frequently depicted a modern Africa of "cities operated and managed by African people."[31] Many of these cities, she insisted, sometimes with considerable creative license, had "every modern convenience—of black mayors, city authorities, houses of legislature of Natural Rulers, kings and leaders."[32] Her recourse to such relentlessly positive imagery was motivated by a desire to galvanize her audiences, instill racial pride, and undermine the negative, condescending images of the continent that dominated American consciousnesses, black as well as white, and assumed the superiority of European social, economic, and cultural practices. According to historian Tunde Adekele, even the UNIA approached Africa with "Europeans as the bearers of civilization of universal and normative values that Africans should emulate." In so doing they "came to [view] Africa with cultural arrogance and a sense of superiority, just like the Europeans, and they objectified Africans as primitives who lacked the capacity for self-enhancement."[33] Kofey, much like Henrietta Peters, Emily Kinch, and other African Americans who had actually returned across the Atlantic to visit Africa, vehemently denied that the continent was bereft of Christian virtue, economic enterprise, efficient social structures, and governmental competence.

Laura Kofey's Rise and Demise

Laura Kofey attempted to reformulate the basis for UNIA repatriation efforts in a number of ways: by questioning the wisdom of working with established African states like Liberia, with its vested political and economic interests; by emphasizing the special role that the African American workers and professionals of the South might play in a new mode of transatlantic trade and re-migration; and by calling for educational initiatives that would promote both a better understanding of Africa and develop the kinds of knowledge and skills that would be most valuable in the South and for those returning to the homeland.

In accounting for Kofey's success in attracting support for this program, her African credentials were undoubtedly an important factor. Her personal lineage gave her a unique air of authority and prestige. Indeed, she was one of the few Africans who openly invited African Americans to return to their ancestral homeland. While African Americans and various colonization societies in America and England had raised funds and devised plans for the return of slaves and their descendants to Africa, few documented formal invitations to former slaves and free people of color emanated from within the continent itself.

As a charismatic spiritual leader, Kofey took care to present herself to pious UNIA crowds as doing the work of "her Ol' Man God." However, she began most of her speeches by invoking the authority she derived from her father, King Kenispi, and from the community elders of the Gold Coast who had decided to "endorse a mission to America and supply her with documents, credentials, and power of attorney to represent them." Kofey explained how she had been furnished with "samples of their products and raw materials and above all she was given a MESSAGE by them to their people in America."[34] Thus she presented herself as a native-born African on a formal diplomatic mission from Accra, sent to ask African Americans to "let us know" if they wanted to "come home"; "and if you don't want to come, let us know."[35]

Kofey also presented herself and her message in terms readily understood and appreciated by people of the diaspora. Her vernacular rhetorical style was easily accessible to the black agricultural workers and laborers of the South, while her central focus on greater trade links with and eventual return to an Africa that she refused to stereotype or reduce to a monolith struck a chord with UNIA members and non-members alike, both working class and elite. The historic and future greatness of Africa that she proclaimed was often spoken of by UNIA officials, many of whom—including self-styled provisional president general of Africa, Marcus Garvey—held fictional leadership positions, often modeled on European dynastic aristocratic titles that were supposed to symbolically link them to the continent.[36] But Garvey's Africa was not represented to the UNIA lay membership as a series of discrete countries or tribal districts; instead it was depicted as one large occupied state, crushed and largely disabled by imperial power and in desperate need of saving by African Americans. In this context, Kofey's claims to genuine African royal blood (rather than to an ersatz title) and her descriptions of complex systems of African political organization both seemed particularly attractive. If she sometimes exaggerated the degree of African autonomy and agency, she actually presented a more nuanced and credible view of indigenous attempts to exercise power in the face of European domination.

Her credibility was also bolstered by her appearance. Unlike Garvey, Kofey never promoted a vision of Africa that required dressing in European-style uniforms and plumed hats. Instead, she was described by her followers as a "beautiful brown-skinned woman of medium height in her early 30s with a head full of lovely hair, but not straightened." She wore at all times "only plain Western-style dresses and except for harboring an African-made gold broach, there was no jewelry seen on her."[37] Her choice of dress and natural hairstyle, deftly yoking Western and African influences in a sartorial expression of her own transatlantic provenance, also served to endear her to southern audiences: she looked and sounded much like them.

As a consequence of all of these factors, Kofey's influence in the black South soared. In April 1927 alone she single-handedly registered one thousand new members for the UNIA. Word of her impact in Florida, especially, attracted national attention within the UNIA.[38] At first her work on behalf of the Association was reported positively, despite the independent spin she sometimes put on some of its core programs. In the summer of 1927 the pages of the *Negro World* were filled with glowing assessments from the lay membership describing Kofey as "marvelous" and arguing that she was responsible for the fact that "Garveyism (was) spreading like wild fire" in the South, where she had "done untold good and [was] still doing it."[39]

Yet this official endorsement of popular good feelings toward Kofey from within the UNIA hierarchy was short lived; she quickly became a victim of her own success and of the paranoia and jealousy of various Association leaders. Kofey's popularity in the South, and the prospect that it might spread still further, posed several problems for the UNIA and for African American ministers. While Kofey aggressively signed up members for the UNIA and recruited to her branches of the African Universal Church and Commercial League, her efforts upset the delicate balance between local preachers and UNIA officials: her Sunday-afternoon meetings and weeklong, revival-style rallies left churches and collection plates empty. As her popularity burgeoned she held meetings in baseball fields, where "without the benefit of public notices, people (would) line the streets long before opening hour." Many of her speaking engagements became "standing room only" events.[40] Moreover, some of her speeches directly criticized both local ministers and UNIA officials, causing resentments. Her admonitions against "do nothing preachers" and men who used the UNIA for their "personal self-interest" did not go unnoticed.[41]

In September 1927, Miami division president Claude Green made an appearance before Marcus Garvey, then imprisoned in the Atlanta Penitentiary, to answer Kofey's charges of widespread indolence and corruption among preachers and UNIA leaders. It appears that Green not only succeeded in refuting Kofey's accusations but also managed to discredit her work and convince Garvey that she was a poisonous influence within the UNIA. As Garvey sat in prison, the idea that someone outside his inner sanctum was drawing crowds that rivaled participation at officially sanctioned UNIA events seemed to pose a tangible threat to his own prestige and leadership.

Shortly after Garvey met with Green, Kofey was declared persona non grata by the UNIA. Garvey and other UNIA officials, particularly his lawyer and confidant J. A. Craigen, sent "directives" to branches throughout the South, banning Kofey from UNIA meetings and expelling her supporters.[42] Although the *Negro World* denounced her as a "fake," Kofey continued to receive invitations to speak; contributions to her church flowed in uninterrupted, and people throughout Florida and Alabama demonstrated their support by buying passage on some Japanese ships she was attempting to purchase for a voyage to the Gold Coast.[43]

As official UNIA denunciations of Kofey escalated, so did more overt acts of intimidation. In Florida it had become routine for members of the paramilitary African Legion affiliated with the Miami UNIA branch to heckle her at public appearances. On March 7, 1928, Kofey's supporters and legion members had clashed at the Miami UNIA's Liberty Hall in Coconut Grove. In response the police had padlocked the facility and prohibited its use by either group. Rather than cancel a meeting scheduled for the following night, Kofey's followers decided to move to the nearby Fox Thompson's Hall. As they were not in an official UNIA building, Kofey and her audience believed the African Legion would leave them alone.[44] At the meeting, a single shot rang out, piercing Kofey in the head and silencing her instantly. The shot was apparently fired from the back of the hall, a distance of fifty feet, indicating that a person of some skill would have been the assassin. That person, to date, has yet to be identified.

Laura Kofey's murder presented many ironies. One of the most glaring is that she did not heed her own advice regarding the ways in which those in power tend to protect their own interests from perceived external threats. She had warned UNIA members that those in power in Liberia would be reluctant to share that power with or cede it to returning Africans from the United States. Yet, she seemed to underestimate the determination of entrenched UNIA leaders, national and local, to crush any incipient challenges to their authority and power. Kofey had focused her attentions in the South, far from the UNIA's metropolitan headquarters in New York, but she could not escape its grasp.

A further irony is that, despite her formal estrangement from Garvey and his organization, she never abandoned what she believed were the core ideals of the UNIA. On the night of her murder she was actually speaking, not on behalf of the church she was attempting to establish in Miami, but on behalf of the UNIA. She never lost faith in a mode of black nationalism that privileged diasporic racial pride alongside return to an Africa she knew through personal experience, not from imagination and fancy. At the nadir of Jim Crow with its rigid racist structures of segregation, disenfranchisement, and terror, she recognized the particular appeal of this message to southern blacks, just as she assigned them a special place in her plans for a return transatlantic journey to redeem Africa.

Laura Kofey's Life and Lessons

There are various contexts in which Laura Kofey's life can be used to interrogate the long African American freedom struggle, black gender politics, and international black nationalism. According to Barbara Bair, "the violent martyrdom of Laura Kofey can serve as a metaphor in examining gender politics and ideas of power and authority that imbued the Garvey movement."[45] This is undoubtedly true. Although a gendered reading of Kofey's career is not the main preoccupation of this essay, it is clear that she was frequently at odds with the UNIA's male leadership and that she also shared some important programmatic priorities with other women in and around the UNIA. This included a marked interest in education and a pragmatic willingness to help encourage black male pride, self-respect, and leadership potential in order to promote black economic progress, communal and family stability, and racial uplift. This was the essence of the "efficient womanhood" that typified the work of so many female black activists.[46]

Contemplating Kofey's life also offers a way to respond to the appeal by Amy Jacques Garvey's biographer Ula Taylor that historians should present accounts of the UNIA that "challenge our understanding of Marcus Garvey and Garveyism and unveil the complicated reality of a black radical."[47] Rodney Carlisle has defined black nationalism during the interwar years as a belief that black powerlessness could be overcome by "setting up mechanisms of self-determination."[48] It has also been defined by Wilson Jeremiah Moses as more than a mere "a dissatisfaction with conditions in the United States"; it was a dissatisfaction that was translated into an "impulse toward self determination among Africans transplanted to the New World by the slave trade."[49] Moreover, Moses argues, their goals were defined as "racial goals," as race was central to the environment in which they lived.[50] This typology certainly rings true for Laura Kofey, who placed diasporic racial progress and racial pride at the core of her program. At one of her camp-style meetings she encouraged her audience to "Enroll your names with your Mother, children. If you don't have but one drop of black blood in you, and know you cannot pass for white, enroll your name with Mother."[51]

In this essay, however, the emphasis has been primarily on how Laura Adorkor Kofey's life can be used to illuminate aspects of the Black Atlantic and, more specifically, the transatlantic connections between Africa and the U.S. South. At a basic level, Kofey's story, with its series of journeys around the Atlantic from Africa to the U.S. South, reminds us that Atlantic World exchanges—human, cultural, economic, and ideological—continued long after the period from roughly the sixteenth century to the early nineteenth century, which is usually the focus for Atlantic World histories. Perhaps most significantly for this volume, it is evident that as Kofey worked to enact her vision to "see Africa redeemed and my children in Africa," she envisioned a special role for southern blacks in that enterprise and targeted the region as especially fertile soil for her message of diasporic racial pride, repatriation, and transatlantic economic exchange and cooperation.[52] She worked hard to emphasize the inclusiveness of her vision, stressing the roles that could be played by ordinary black laborers, as well as skilled workers, artisans, and professionals, in developing black economic strength in the South and in Africa. Indeed, she frequently stressed the similarities between black southern and African workers to promote a sense of shared identities, expertise, and ambitions. In Florida, Alabama, and Louisiana, Kofey admonished her audiences to "serve God, love your Motherland Africa" and encouraged black workers to aspire to become "dedicated men and women who are skilled workers such as engineers, carpenters, bricklayers, mechanics, ice men, and men and women trained and qualified in the professions" in order to help those already working in those capacities to build the Motherland.[53] In Kofey's mind a redeemed and economically strong Africa needed workers of every kind, and her rhetoric tended to downplay class differences and hierarchies within the black community, giving every person—male and female, lawyer and bricklayer—equal significance.

After Kofey's death, her adherents continued her work. In keeping with her desire that African Americans should stick together and pool their money in support of collective community enterprises, monies raised from the viewing of her body were used to build a church and establish homes for congregants residing in Jacksonville. Two years later, the training school she had originally established in her front parlor was relocated to a building of its own, purchased in part with funds from her funeral and donations from church members.[54]

In Mobile, members of the African Universal Church established there by Kofey learned to pray in Banta and were taught Xhosa group songs in preparation for eventual repatriation.[55] In 1931 the church sent six men to Africa in a bid to start schools and negotiate trade agreements, although the enterprise was short lived because church finances could not maintain the effort.[56] Despite Kofey's ambivalence toward missionary work in Africa, following her death her churches sponsored a total of four missions to Ghana, Nigeria, and Kenya, hoping to further her plans for black-run transatlantic trade links and to establish schools on the continent.[57] By the 1940s, however, although the three southern churches Kofey founded were still adorned with her image, they had all begun to take on a life and ideology of their own that, while influenced by her teachings, did not strictly adhere to them.

The founding of these churches and their attempts to fulfill Kofey's twin goals of fostering closer educational and economic links with Africa while preparing African Americans for eventual repatriation suggest something of her impact in the interwar South, along with that of the UNIA, whose core program she always claimed to be honoring. Consequently, her life and legacy speak to the need for sensitivity to the peculiarities of the region within broader studies of the UNIA, the Black Atlantic, pan-Africanism, and domestic black nationalism that do not resort to simplistic notions of southern exceptionalism. Laura Kofey is a useful vehicle for such a project precisely because she appreciated the complex mix of connectedness and distinctiveness, of parallelism and convergence, of departure and arrival that has always characterized the Black Atlantic experience and the U.S. South's relationships with various Atlantic worlds.

Notes

1. The aims of the UNIA, including its missionary projects, were first published in a series of pamphlets coauthored by Marcus Garvey and Amy Ashwood in Kingston, Jamaica, dated July–August 1914. Another series of pamphlets authored by Garvey carry the same date. Robert Hill, ed., *Marcus Garvey and the Universal Negro Improvement Association Papers*, vol. 1 (Berkley: University of California Press, 1983), 55–70.

2. Paul Tiyambe Zeleza, "Re-Writing the African Diaspora: Beyond the Black Atlantic," *African Affairs* 104, no. 414 (2005): 41. Zeleza notes that in the diaspora "The emotional and experiential investment in 'here' and 'there' and the points in between obviously changes in response to the shifting material, mental, and moral orders of social existence. Diaspora is simultaneously a state of being and a process of becoming, a kind of voyage that encompasses the possibility of never arriving or returning, a navigation of multiple belongings. It is a mode of naming, remembering, living and feeling group identity molded out of experiences, positionings, struggles and imaginings of the past and the present, and at times the unpredictable future, which are shared across the

boundaries of time and space that frame 'indigenous' identities in the contested and constructed locations of 'there' and 'here' and the passages and points in between."

3. Ira Berlin uses the term "Atlantic Creoles" in reference to West Africans living in Africa who were active in the slave trade and "connected by long-standing business and personal ties to other slave traders in African and England." Berlin, "From Creole to African: Atlantic Creoles and the Origin of African-American Society in Mainland North America," *William and Mary Quarterly* 53 (1996): 251–88. For more on the significance of the Atlantic in linking African Americans and Africans, see Robin Law and Paul E. Lovejoy, "The Changing Dimensions of African History: Reappropriating the Diaspora," in *Rethinking African History*, ed. Simon A. McGrath and Christopher Fyfe (Edinburgh: Centre of African Studies, University of Edinburgh, 1997), 181–200.

4. Tiffany Ruby Patterson and Robin D. G. Kelley, "Unfinished Migrations: Reflections on the African Diaspora and the Making of the Modern World," *African Studies Review* 43, no. 1 (2000): 13.

5. For governmental policy and its effects on immigrations patterns and quotas among women of the diaspora, see Nancy Foner, *Islands in the City: West Indian Migration to New York City* (Berkeley: University of California Press, 2001); Irma Watkins Owens, *Blood Relations: Caribbean Immigrants and the Harlem Community, 1900–1930* (Bloomington: Indiana University Press, 1996).

6. Aimee M. Glocke, "Two Steps Forward and One and a Half Steps Back: Maria Stewart and Mary Ann Shadd Cary's Fight for Inclusion into Early Black Nationalism, 1803–1893" (master's thesis, University of California, Los Angeles, 2001).

7. Convention Division Reports reprinted in the *Negro World*, August 1926.

8. *Negro World*, June 11, July 23, 1927; Richard Newman, "'Warrior Mother of Africa's Warriors of the Most High God': Laura Adorkor Kofey and the African Universal Church," in *Black Power and Black Religion: Essays and Reviews*, ed. Newman (West Cornwall, Conn.: Locust Hill Press, 1987), 131; Barbara Bair, "'Ethiopia Shall Stretch Forth Her Hands Unto God': Laura Kofey and the Gendered Vision of Redemption in the Garvey Movement," in *A Mighty Baptism: Race, Gender, and the Creation of American Protestantism*, ed. Susan Juster and Lisa MacFarlane (Ithaca and London: Cornell University Press, 1996), 56.

9. Laura Kofey, *Mother's Sacred Teachings* (Jacksonville: African Universal Church, n.d.), 8, Box 2, Folder 1, Precious Duncan Papers (Private Collection: Atlanta, Georgia, 2004), 62–64.

10. Ibid., 67.

11. Ibid., 69, 35.

12. Ibid., 60.

13. *New York World*, June 29, 1924; Martin Summers, *Manliness and Its Discontents: The Black Middle Class and the Transformation of Masculinity, 1900–1930* (Chapel Hill: University of North Carolina Press, 2003), 81–83; Ibrahim Sundiata, *Brothers and Strangers: Black Zion, Black Slavery, 1914–1940* (Durham: Duke University Press, 2003), 30–41.

14. Kofey, *Mother's Sacred Teachings*, 52. For the official correspondence between Liberia, the U.S. government, and the UNIA see Robert Hill, ed., *Marcus Garvey and*

the Universal Negro Improvement Association Papers, vol. 10 (Berkley: University of California Press, 2006), 200–250.

15. Bair, "'Ethiopia,'" 38–61; Barbara Bair, "Renegotiating Liberty: Garveyism, Women, and Grassroots Organizing in Virginia," in *Women of the American South*, ed. Christine Anne Farham (New York: New York University Press, 1996), 221–40; Newman, "'Warrior Mother,'" 131–43.

16. Hill, *Garvey Papers*, 1:67.

17. David H. Bradley, *A History of the A.M.E. Zion Church, 1796–1968: Part I, 1796–1872* (Nashville: Parthenon Press, 1956); Mt. Zion A.M.E. Church Records, 1884–1949 (Charleston, South Carolina: Mt. Zion AME Church).

18. *Negro World*, June 14, 1919.

19. Emily Christmas Kinch traveled in West Africa from 1908 to 1910. She also worked as a missionary in Sierra Leone and Liberia, where she established the Eliza Turner Primary School, and authored a pamphlet based on her time in Africa titled *West Africa: An Open Door*. For more on Kinch see Randall Burkett, *Black Redemption: Churchmen Speak for the Garvey Movement* (Philadelphia: Temple University Press, 1978), 43–46; Robert Hill, ed., *Marcus Garvey and the Universal Negro Improvement Papers*, vol. 2 (Berkley: University of California Press, 1983), 3; *Negro World*, June 26, 1920.

20. *Negro World*, June 26, 1920.

21. See Natanya Duncan, "The 'Efficient Womanhood' of the Universal Negro Improvement Association: 1919–1930" (Ph.D. diss., University of Florida, 2009).

22. The pursuit of an independent school was first expressed in the series of 1914 pamphlets believed to be authored by Amy Ashwood Garvey. See Hill, *Garvey Papers*, 1:55–70.

23. Kofey, *Mother's Sacred Teachings*, 18.

24. Claudrena N. Harold, *The Rise and Fall of the Garvey Movement in the Urban South, 1918–1942* (New York: Routledge, 2007), 91; Bair, "Renegotiating Liberty," 223.

25. Amy Jacques Garvey, *Garvey and Garveyism* (1963; reprint, New York: Octagon, 1978), 13, 173; Robert Hill, ed., *Marcus Garvey and the Universal Negro Improvement Association Papers*, vol. 6 (Berkley: University of California Press, 1989), 338–39.

26. Caleb Robinson to John Powell, March 26, 1926, John Powell Collection, Special Collections, Alderman Library, University of Virginia, Charlottesville.

27. Ibid.

28. Ibid.

29. *Negro World*, January 8, 1927.

30. Kofey, *Mother's Sacred Teachings*, 18.

31. Ibid., 27.

32. Ibid., 18.

33. Tunde Adekele, *UnAfrican Americans: Nineteenth-Century Black Nationalists and the Civilizing Mission* (Lexington: University Press of Kentucky, 1998), 25.

34. Kofey, *Mother's Sacred Teachings*, 8. Members of Kofey's family, who held political office in Ghana until the mid-1980s, continued to defend the legitimacy of her claims to royal ancestry and affirmed the authority given to her by the people and govern-

ment of Accra to simply ask if and when African Americans intended to return to their homeland.

35. Ibid., 17.

36. Within the UNIA hierarchy, Garvey bestowed titles that reflected the government in exile status the UNIA claimed. He was "Provisional President" and had appointed a "Leader of the Negro People in America" and a "Leader of the People of the West Indies" as well as a host of other fictive officers in anticipation of a winning a battle for control of the continent. For the UNIA's government in exile see Jahi Issa, "The Universal Negro Improvement Association in Louisiana: Creating a Provisional Government in Exile" (Ph.D. diss., Howard University, 2005).

37. Kofey, *Mother's Sacred Teachings*, 15–16.

38. *Negro World*, May 14, 1927.

39. *Negro World*, June 11, July 23, 1927.

40. Kofey, *Mother's Sacred Teachings*, 23; Bair, "'Ethiopia,'" 55; *Negro World*, May 7, May 14, 1927; *Mobile Register*, August 18, 1926.

41. Kofey, *Mother's Sacred Teachings*, 9.

42. *Negro World*, October 22, 1927.

43. Ibid.; Kofey, *Mother's Sacred Teachings*, 41.

44. *Miami Daily News*, March 9, 1928; *Miami Herald*, March 12, 1928; *Daily Gleaner*, April 3, 1928.

45. Bair, "'Ethiopia,'" 38.

46. For more on the gender politics of the UNIA, see Karen Adler, "'Always Leading Our Men in Service and Sacrifice': Amy Jacques Garvey, Feminist Black Nationalist,'" *Gender and Society* 6, no. 3 (1992): 346–75; Barbara Bair, "Pan-Africanism as Process: Adelaide Casely Hayford, Garveyism, and the Cultural Roots of Nationalism," in *Imagining Home: Class, Culture, and Nationalism in the African Diaspora*, ed. Sidney J. Lemelle and Robin D. G. Kelley (London: Verso, 1994), 121–44; Bair, "Renegotiating Liberty"; Bair, "'Ethiopia'"; Barbara Bair, "True Women, Real Men: Gender, Ideology and Social Roles in the Garvey Movement," in *Gendered Domains: Rethinking Public and Private in Women's History*, ed. Dorothy O. Helly and Susan M. Reverby, (Ithaca: Cornell University Press, 1992), 154–66; Duncan "'Efficient Womanhood'"; Anne S. Macpherson, "Colonial Matriarchs, Garveyism, Maternalism, and Belize's Black Cross Nurses, 1920–1952," *Gender and History* 15 (2003): 507–27; Tony Martin, "Women in the Garvey Movement," in *Garvey: His Work and Impact*, ed. Rupert Lewis and Patrick Bryan (Trenton, N.J.: Africa World Press, 1991), 67–72; Beryl Satter, "Marcus Garvey, Father Divine and the Gender Politics of Race Difference and Race Neutrality," *American Quarterly* 48, no. 1 (2003): 43–76; Ula Y. Taylor, "Intellectual Pan-African Feminists: Amy Ashwood-Garvey and Amy Jacques Garvey," *ABAFAZI: The Simmons College Journal of Women of African Descent* 9, no. 1 (1998): 10–18; Ula Y. Taylor, "'Negro Women Are Great Thinkers as Well as Doers': Amy Jacques Garvey and Community Feminism in the United States, 1924–1927," *Journal of Women's History* 12, no. 2 (2000): 1014–126.

47. Ula Yvette Taylor, *The Veiled Garvey: The Life and Times of Amy Jacques Garvey* (Chapel Hill: University of North Carolina Press, 2002), 1.

48. Rodney P. Carlisle, *The Roots of Black Nationalism* (New York: Kennikat, 1975), 6.

49. Wilson J. Moses, *Classical Black Nationalism: From American Revolution to Marcus Garvey* (New York: New York University Press, 1996), 2–3.

50. Ibid., 6.

51. *Miami Herald*, March 12, 1928; Kofey, *Mother's Sacred Teachings*, 44; *The Church: Why Mother Established the Church and What It Stands For* (Jacksonville, Fla.: n.p., n.d.).

52. Kofey, *Mother's Sacred Teachings*, 46.

53. Ibid., 49.

54. *Jacksonville Times Union*, April 12, 1930.

55. *African Universal Hymnal* (Jacksonville: Missionary African Universal Church, 1961), 6.

56. Peter F. Anson, *Bishops at Large* (London: Faber and Faber, 1964), 278–79.

57. Richard Newman, "Laura Adorkor Kofey and the African Universal Church," Box 1, Folder 7, The New York Public Library Manuscripts, Archives and Rare Books Division, Schomburg Center for Research in Black Culture, New York.

11

....

Dish-Washing in the Sea of Ndayaan

What We Make of Our Souths in Atlantic World Initiation

KEITH CARTWRIGHT

"Gimme the tea, Guitar. Just the tea. No geography."
"No geography? Okay, no geography. What about some history in your
    tea? Or some sociopolitico—No. That's still geography. Goddam, Milk,
    I do believe my whole life's geography."
"Don't you wash pots out for people before you cook water in them?"

Milkman Dead and Guitar Baines in Toni Morrison, Song of Solomon

For those of us studying the American South in the aftermath of the election of President Barack Obama (and the backlash from the right's Tea
Party), there is much to ponder in this scene from Toni Morrison's *Song of
Solomon*. I particularly like the geography lesson that Florida-born Michigan resident Guitar Baines gives to his friend Milkman Dead with his
cup of tea: "I live in the North now. So the first question come to mind is
North of what? Why, north of the South. So North exists because South
does. But does that mean North is different from South? No way! South
is just south of North."[1] Guitar goes on to school Milkman most playfully
on global politics and economy, putting North and South (the American
nation) into relation with India (and tea), France, and the Congo. We see
that North exists (in global tea-partying economy) because South does.
And we come to see that North has existed as a destination for black Flo-
ridians because something called the South has existed on the plantation
frontiers of hell.

Mostly, however, I think it is the other way around. The South has been
determined and defined by relations with a magnetically fixed northern
compass point. This has been as true of global, colonized souths as much
as it is true of the U.S. South. In the United States, New England and the

North are so central to the national narrative as city on a hill—with the whole accompanying march of originating chronology (1620, 1776)—that the North is no region. It is nation. East and west coasts become North too in relation to a South, according to Leigh Anne Duck, that is every bit as abject, scene and stage of national crimes, disasters, and supposedly peculiar institutions.[2] As "the nation's region" and internal other, the South has come to be seen as an unprogressive, backward space, but—as often happens with such spaces—the South also gets tapped as storehouse of what has been kept most real, what is most "country" or "folk," most authentically or conservatively nationalist, most Christian(ist), and even most feudally English.[3] The South is a chronotope (time-space) that makes North and Nation possible as positive or progressive time-space. But the plantation economy of this relation leaves much to be desired.

As much as I like Guitar Baines's teatime geography lessons, his friend Milkman's question of pot-washing may be even more compelling. Putting the South into relation with a larger Atlantic World offers us a cleansing expansion of regional scale, an alternative to national and sectional pots so crusty we can hardly cook with them. This is not to say that the Atlantic provides an escape from the racialized traumas of the "Dirty" South. Legacies of conquest, enslavement, and genocidal and environmental devastation are, of course, writ large across this originary ocean of modernity. Nevertheless, circum-Atlantic chartings of the South may foster fresh approaches to agency in the long cross-cultural encounter. In "Consuming Subjects: Theorizing New Models of Agency for Literary Criticism in African Studies," Wendy Belcher recently argued that a "reciprocal enculturation model of agency" can help us understand how Western texts may be infused and shaped by the discursive agency of African genius.[4] Belcher attends to modes of "transcultural intertextuality" by which the words, speech, tales, music, and performances of a colonized culture's repertoire may "penetrate, we might even say animate or possess, European identities and literatures."[5] The entire Atlantic World—and perhaps the U.S. South and the circum-Caribbean in particular—may be recognized as a locus of transcultural possessions: a space shaped by asymmetrical relations of power but also by reciprocal routes of enculturation. This is an initial and initiating gulf-space in which we can wash our pots.

The Atlantic World's rhizomatic interpenetrations, according to Édouard Glissant, wrought "not merely an encounter," not merely a synthesis or "a *métissage*, but a new and original dimension" best "summed up in the word *creolization*."[6] We find recognition of this "original dimension" in the first monograph written by the first *great* writer of the Americas, Inca Garcilaso de la Vega's *History of Florida* (1605). Garcilaso's *La Florida* presented and defined "creole" (*criollo*) as a word coined by Africans and adopted by enculturated Spaniards to mark a new nativity: children born of African (or Old World) parents in the New World.[7] "Creole" signifies new ethnic assemblage, new language, new pots for seasoned cooking . . . native to an abyssal trauma-space recognized by African parental authority.

For literary scholars, the study of a regional southern literature has tended to be housed in English departments. But much as the South never quite worked as a new England, the English department may not be the best container for cooking a Louisiana gumbo, a Florida perlou or *ajiaco*, or even a low-country okra soup. American studies programs have gone hemispheric, and comparative literature has its history of support for transnational and inter-arts approaches to literary studies. Atlantic studies, however, may offer southernists their best pot-scrubbing and re-seasoning thus far, an interdisciplinary expansion of regional scale that fosters awareness of a *longue durée*, a glimpse into deep time, taking us beyond 1776, 1620, 1607, and beyond English too—in cross-cultural dialogue very much oriented to present needs and conditions.[8]

Historians of southern spaces have been well ahead of literary scholars on this front because of their discipline's wider geopolitical range. English departments tend to adhere to two filiations: British and Anglo-American canons (informed by French theory), beyond which everything else gets attached paradoxically as "minority" and "world." This kind of structure, even in its most radical kinds of praxis, has the disturbing tendency to reinforce a British and Anglo-American "fortress homogeneity" (as Wilson Harris put it) that isolates English departments from what is happening (and has long been happening) to shape the mosaic expressive traditions of the world.[9] This state of "fortress homogeneity" is healthy for none of us, and it is perhaps doubly damning for southern institutions that accept and foster their secondary provincial status in the making and circulation of knowledge.

My own entry into circum-Atlantic readings of southern texts emerged as a necessary response to my Peace Corps experience in Senegal and as an ongoing movement toward a *hippikat* (Wolof, "open-eyed") attentiveness to the unaccredited basilect (the low-prestige, generally most deeply

Africanized end of the Creole sociolinguistic continuum) as well as the prestige acrolect (closest to standard Euro-metropolitan usage) of a Creole cultural grammar unaddressed in my schooling.[10] I am not really a southernist but a southerner and comparativist who works with local texts and backward notions (like community, identity, sense of place) in transnational context against the grain of various American nationalisms and against the grain of English departments' reduction of literary study to histories of nationalism. It is easy to understand how Atlantic studies benefits a cosmopolitan trend (and real need) in southern studies. What we should also be asking, however, is how Gullah/Geechee, Floridian, or Gulf Souths may answer folks' needs across the waters. What use is the South elsewhere? And how might what gets done with the South—across the Atlantic, the Gulf, and the Caribbean—foster reciprocally enculturating work with and in our home spaces?

Circum-Atlantic models of travel and transcultural performance offer indispensable positioning for study of a dynamic Black Atlantic counterculture of modernity.[11] This Black Atlantic "cosmopolitanism from below," as Ifeoma Nwankwo refers to it, continues to be marginalized within the humanities even when the work is based in archivally and culturally accredited sources such as the autobiography or the novel.[12] Historians of the Atlantic World, despite their pioneering work in establishing the field, often prove reluctant to rely upon Atlantic models for the historiography of periods and events after 1830, the decade of British abolition of slavery. To seal off Atlantic studies from the remarkable agency of post-abolition black travel, music, religion, art, politics, and literature has the inoculatory effect—not necessarily the intention—of safeguarding the field, the discipline, and the academy from the reciprocal enculturations and potentiality of Black Atlantic and creolist scholarship. The magisterial path-opening work of innovators like Bernard Bailyn or Jack Greene may be left open to the familiar charge that Atlantic history is simply a repackaging of imperial European history. We get a new "subject" defined primarily by the old players (the British, French, Spanish, Portuguese, Dutch, and early U.S. Republic). But the temporal boundaries placed on this subject safeguard it from those of us (consuming subjects) who would put its full creolizing force into play. Limiting Atlantic history to 1830—or even to 1860—has the effect of relegating the post-plantation Atlantic World to the status of geopolitical (and disciplinary) ghetto. This may indeed be an apt description of much of the Atlantic after abolition: the post-plantation world as ghetto. Still, however, for southern comparativists and scholars of a transcultural cosmopolitanism from below, our post-abolition, post-plantation, postcolonial, and postmodern Atlantic worlds remain utterly compelling crucibles of an increasingly creolizing planet.

Washing the Calabash: Bush Travels of Initiation

This washing of our calabashes in the Atlantic follows trends that gained momentum with Paul Gilroy's publication of *The Black Atlantic* (1993). Largely because Gilroy privileges an acrolectal literature and archival record (even as he gestures innovatively to the basilect of black music's "politics of transfiguration" and "slave sublime")—and because he works within a nexus of North Atlantic relations (the black United States and Britain)—*Black Atlantic* has circulated fairly well within English departments.[13] I would argue, however, that Gilroy's generally archival and An-glo–North Atlantic orientation should be supplemented by the further-reaching, anthropologically oriented scholarship of folk such as Melville Herskovits, Sidney Mintz and Richard Price, Robert Farris Thompson, and J. Lorand Matory.[14] We have all but forgotten that it was Thompson's stunning work on ritual arts of Nigeria, Mali, Congo, Togo, Cuba, Haiti, the U.S. South, Suriname, and Mexico that introduced us (back in 1983) to the "art and philosophy connecting black Atlantic worlds."[15] Thompson's Atlantic is a bigger and often deeper ocean than is Gilroy's equally path-clearing work. One thing they do share is an utter contemporaneity routed through the travels and musics of a deep Atlantic time-space.

On a recent CD titled *Give and Take*, the Senegalese music star Youssou Ndour invokes a tradition of travel as initiatory agency, singing, "Who doesn't travel can't know where sweetness is."[16] Youssou Ndour has been singing of the virtues and challenges of travel for a long time, at least since *Immigrés*—the 1985 breakthrough of his band Super Etoile (and their mix of Cuban *rhumba* and *son*, southern soul and rock, with indigenous West African sounds) onto an emergent "world music" scene. Super Etoile's notion of travel remains initiatory, guarding dialogue with the deep bush and with deep time, but it is also circum-Atlantic and transfigurational, pointing "to the formation of a community of needs and solidarity which is magically made audible in the music itself."[17] This is a cosmopolitanism by which we may wash our containers, fill them with a musical *supakanje* (an okra-based Senegalese dish akin to gumbo), take three cups of hot green tea, and come to be reinitiated into the South's own Atlantic and Gulf coasts.

A fundament of West African and Black Atlantic societies, the "travel" of initiatory sequestering removes the initiatory seeker from domestic space, presenting a series of tests—a learning to give and take in the wilderness, an undoing and redoing of the fostered self in bush schools of rebirth and reaffiliation. In one very widespread Afro-Atlantic tale of an orphan's initiation, her bush travel is enabled by what Bahamians would call "broughtupsy," or the guiding presence of the dead mother. Let's look at a Wolof example paraphrased from a tale often told in accompaniment to three rounds of evening tea.

The Wolof orphan tale features two girls named Kumba, "Orphan Kumba" and "Kumba-with-a-mother." The father remains alive, but a surviving co-wife parents both girls. She uses orphan Kumba as a virtual slave until she sends the orphan (when the girl comes of age) on an infanticidal task: to cross the wilderness to wash a dirty calabash in the Sea of Ndayaan (the Atlantic). The orphan meets a jujube tree that is chopping itself down and a skillet doing its own cooking. In each case she greets the wonder with openness, pays her respects, and is hospitably rewarded with food. She finally encounters a crone in her path, a woman with only one leg, arm, eye, ear, and finger. Keeping her composure, and following the crone's instructions to cook a single bone and to pound and boil a single grain of millet, orphan Kumba enjoys a plentiful meal of meat and couscous. Come morning the bush crone gives Kumba three eggs with instructions for breaking them in the forest on her way home. Following instructions, the orphan bursts the eggs to arrive home with the wealth that crowns her new status. Of course, the stepmother responds to the orphan's transformation by sending her own blood-daughter Kumba into the bush. This Kumba's bush encounter turns deadly as she can't "give and take" in the spirit realm, can't abandon preconceptions of normalcy, ridicules everything, does not follow directions, and is finally killed by the beasts that emerge from the eggs she receives. Of the failed traveler, the tale says simply that vultures fed on her entrails and cried out, high over both Kumbas' home village: "Here is the heart of the little girl who set out for the wilderness by the Sea of Ndayaan."[18]

So what do we gain by washing our calabashes in this Sea of Ndayaan? In facing waters considered nigh-absolute boundaries, we may see that the Africans whose social personalities were swallowed up by plantation systems did not enter the belly of that beast unprepared to reorganize and consume New World materials. Kumba's undoing and redoing in initiatory wilderness steeled her against trauma and encouraged her to foster others' reincorporation. The story of Kumba washing her (menses-stained?) calabash in the Atlantic serves as generic tale of all initiation. Kumba is both girls: the one devoured and the one "crowned" in sublime travel. She totes a fear-overcoming composure that helps her navigate encounters with a crone disfigured by frequentation of the sublime (a one-eyed, one-armed, one-legged spirit known across the Atlantic as herbalist of initiatory transformation, Osain).[19]

Both the name and the enculturating initiate agency of Kumba are omnipresent in the Gullah/Geechee low country of South Carolina from the colonial period to the War of 1812. In Georgia we find a number of "Cumbas" traveling to the Bahamas after the Revolutionary War, leaving for British refuge and the island of Trinidad during the War of 1812, and spreading an Afro-Baptist faith throughout the Atlantic World.[20] We can follow Cumba to Louisiana and Florida, into Seminole country, and all over the Caribbean. Her orphan's tale shows up across the Atlantic too, from Senegal, Gambia, and Nigeria to Louisiana, Grenada, St. Lucia, Dominica, Guadeloupe, Haiti, the Bahamas, St. Kitts, South Carolina, Florida, and the Dominican Republic.[21] Lodged within these repeating tales are some of the mechanisms whereby black subjects evaded reduction to consumable chattel within the symbolic order of plantation slavery and remained consuming subjects within a world of their own making. Attentiveness to these tales of plantation and wilderness reveals a multilingual, transnational literature that is unquestionably circum-Atlantic. A body of polyglot creole narrative links the basilect of southern literature to African, Creole, and American Indian literatures beyond U.S. boundary waters. Such initiatory travel repertoires, however, remain orphaned, bastard even—having not received their due as essential grounding of literatures and modes of knowledge emergent from our early contact zones.

Kumba's orphan initiation, Brer Rabbit's and Turtle's tales of tricksterism, divination tales of hunters and animal shape-shifters: this body of narrative constitutes a mythopoetic literary base of Atlantic contact zones, our Ovid, our Old Testament. It is a body of work shared by Joel Chandler Harris, Zora Neale Hurston, the Creek writer Earnest Gouge, the Cuban Lydia Cabrera, the Senegalese Birago Diop, and the Nigerians Amos Tutuola and Chinua Achebe, among many others. We must open our eyes and foster such texts beyond the national categorizations that consign them to minoritarian orphan status.[22] That is one of the first things a good calabash-washing in the Atlantic may do for the way we receive and transmit narratives of our deepest souths.

"I Have a Dream": Cross-Cultural Poetics and Imagination

Caribbean writers like Antonio Benítez-Rojo, Wilson Harris, and Éd-ouard Glissant essay a post-plantation terrain of cross-cultural imagination. They are well aware that the region's traditions of narrative performance have shaped the matrix of a literature that cuts across national and linguistic boundaries, across the Caribbean and Atlantic in their own fiction and in the work of William Faulkner or Morrison, Wole Soyinka or Gabriel García Márquez. These three Caribbean practitioner-theorists' interest in the U.S. South is simultaneously intrinsic and strategic. The North American South, as bridge between so-called first and third worlds, provides a recognizable global currency of common touchstones (Martin Luther King, Faulkner, Elvis, Muddy Waters) useful to writers and theorists from more southerly souths in their exploration of circum-Atlantic literatures and histories.

Benítez-Rojo's repeated references in *Sea of Lintels* and *The Repeating Island* to St. Augustine, Florida, as Spanish Caribbean space remind us of North America's ties to the Spanish formations of an Atlantic World system. Although Florida remains at the frontier margins, Benítez-Rojo represents it as the crucial piece in the construction of "the Grandest Machine on Earth" completed when "in 1565 Pedro Menéndez de Avilés, after slaughtering, with indifferent calm, nearly five hundred Huguenots who had settled in Florida, finished his network of fortified cities with the founding of St. Augustine, today the oldest city in the United States."[23] A fortified Florida frontier secured the Gulf Stream return route for Spain's fleet system of capital intake and supply distribution, guarding Spanish control of transatlantic capital flows. Benítez-Rojo's Florida remains part of the Latin Caribbean, and we should recall that Florida was governed by Spain through Cuba for a longer period of time than it has been under British and U.S. jurisdiction lumped together. Among historians, Jane Landers has worked steadily to help us understand Florida's long circum-Caribbean positioning. She insists that "immigration has once again made Florida a part of the Afro-Hispanic Caribbean, changing the way it looks and sounds."[24] The Caribbean keeps intervening in Florida's deep time-space: from the slaughter of Jean Ribault's men at Matanzas Inlet to the 1993 Supreme Court ruling on Santeria practitioners' rights to animal sacrifice.

Most southerners, however, seem willing to relinquish local agency and cosmopolitanism in exchange for the national narrative's fortress protection of Anglo-supremacy. For example, against Benítez-Rojo's placement of Florida as a key cog in the early machinery of circum-Atlantic capital flow, we get the Florida legislature's post-9/11 reinstitutionalization of nationalist narrative signed into law by Jeb Bush in 2006: "American history shall be viewed as factual, not as constructed, shall be viewed as knowable, teachable, and testable, and shall be defined as the creation of a new nation based largely on the universal principles stated in the Declaration of Independence."[25] This removal of Floridian perspective (in deference to nationalist *patria*) keeps the patrimony of Anglo-American founding fathers at the center of our every relation. Folk content with such non-constructed factuality deny their/our capacity for transfiguring calabash-washings along our own beaches. Interestingly, when Benítez-Rojo offers an example of a consummate Caribbean performer in *The Repeating Island*, he turns again to "idiosyncratic" margins, looking northward (from his Cuba-centered narrative) to a southerner, Martin Luther King, and to King's articulations of initiatory discontent: "his improvisatory vocation, his ability to seduce and be seduced, and, above all, his vehement condition as a dreamer (I have a dream . . .) and as an authentic performer make up the Caribbean side of a man unquestionably idiosyncratic in North America. Martin Luther King occupies and fills the space in which the Caribbean connects to the North American, a space of which jazz is also a sign."[26]

St. Augustine's Castillo de San Marcos, the civil rights movement, and jazz all occupy Benítez-Rojo's cusp of Caribbean and North American connection. Ultimately, Benítez-Rojo's Caribbean is a "confluence of marine flowings that connects the Niger with the Mississippi, the China Sea with the Orinoco, the Parthenon with a fried food stand in an alley in Paramaribo."[27] These are the waters in which we must wash our frypots. The Caribbean is their confluence or gulf-matrix.

While Martin Luther King provided Benítez-Rojo with an exemplary circum-Caribbean performer to match fortressed St. Augustine as the cusp of Caribbean space, Wilson Harris found a gateway to the cross-cultural imagination in the work of another idiosyncratic North American: William Faulkner. Guyana's Harris launched the introduction and opening chapter of *The Womb of Space: The Cross-Cultural Imagination* (1983) with a complex response to Faulkner's *Intruder in the Dust* (1948), the novel that has been dismissed more than any other in the Yoknapatawpha oeuvre as Faulkner's "most provincial novel."[28] Harris argues, however, that the novel's imagery and language work to undercut the South's "fortress homogeneity" as the text pushes its white protagonist (the young Charles Mallison) into an icy Yoknapatawpha creek and forces him to rely upon the hospitality of a black elder (Lucas Beauchamp)—bringing "a transformed mosaic of community . . . into play."[29] Although *The Womb of Space* discusses writers from across the world, the book's three opening chapters address southern writers: Faulkner, Edgar Allan Poe, and Ralph Ellison. Faulkner's South provides the Guyana-born and -raised Harris with the authorial currency and post-plantation creole spaces for a foray into new kinships and contexts of reading.

Harris sees Faulkner's novel as enacting a double engulfment or intrusion: first, within a debt of hospitality to the other, and second, within an "intuitive constellation . . . the nightsky of a culture that invokes the spectre of dead Gowrie [a dead white man] as nightmare protuberance, pregnant hate, 'sent dead' against the living to draw blood."[30] Here Harris makes the startling move (in 1983) of applying concepts from Alfred Métraux's *Voodoo in Haiti* to his reading of *Intruder in the Dust* as he takes up the vodou notion of the "*l'envoi mort*" ("sent dead") intervening in the lives of the lynchable Lucas and his young white erstwhile guest to force the opening of Vinson Gowrie's grave. Métraux reports that when a spirit or spirits of the dead get "sent against someone," the targeted person will waste away and die if not diagnosed and treated by a ritual specialist.[31] The Gulf and Caribbean dead remain in rapport with the living. And for Harris it is "that hidden *rapport* between Faulkner's intuitive imagination and Lucas Beauchamp's anonymous black kith and kin in the Caribbean [that] gives an original twist to the drama of psychical awakening from . . . the ceaseless nightmare of history."[32] In other words, in the face of a fortress white South's sent dead, Faulkner's text provides diagnostic potential for treating an apartheid regime that conceals its indebtedness to Afro-creole genealogies of enculturation.

That Faulkner (or Lawyer Gavin Stevens's rhetoric in the end) may not consciously authorize what the text raises as possibility in no way negates our "perception of cross-cultural capacity" within *Intruder*.[33] Harris points to how the novel exposes the "dead-end of a cultural homogeneous model" as "the shadow of conscience drapes itself everywhere to become . . . a potential bridge" to "twinship" or "cross-cultural mind" that finally "freezes and aborts itself" in the daylight world and icy creeks of white supremacist Mississippi.[34] *Intruder in the Dust* turns out to be more than a thematic initiation novel; it helped launch a circum-Atlantic/deep southern *Womb of Space* into "automatic carnival" and uncanny cross-culturality, opening "potential heterogeneity," "hidden antecedents."[35]

Yoknapatawpha ports from Frenchman's Bend to New Orleans have also served the Martinican Édouard Glissant as a space of cross-cultural transport for his *Poetics of Relation* (1997) redistilled in Glissant's *Faulkner, Mississippi* (1999). In *Poetics of Relation* (published in French in 1990) Glissant points to how the entire plantation system (in the Caribbean, Brazil, the U.S. South, and Indian Ocean islands) constitutes a "territory of *créolité*" bearing "the modern vectors of civilization."[36] Here "the Plantation is one of the focal points for the development of present-day modes of Relation."[37] Glissant insists that the oral literature of the plantation shares such a "web of filiations" that the vernaculars, musics, and novels of post-plantation spaces have "made it no longer possible to consider these literatures as exotic appendages of a French, Spanish, or English literary corpus; rather, they entered suddenly, with the force of a tradition that they built themselves, into the relation of cultures."[38] He mentions Saint-John Perse, Franketienne, Alejo Carpentier, Kamau Brathwaite, and Gabriel García Márquez as writers of the exploded "ruins of the Plantation," a "cultural *métissage*" inflected with Afro-creole musication become multilingual "speech of the world."[39] Glissant sees these "extensions of the Plantation," their "*Baroque speech, inspired* [like Louis Armstrong's scat] *by all possible speech*," as having moved opaquely from a closed place to a creolizing open word.[40] The challenges that accompany such a post-plantation rereading of literary texts and history are considerable. We must find new containers, or scrub our old calabashes in saltwater.

In *Faulkner, Mississippi*, Glissant turns even more explicitly to the South and Faulkner to articulate his notion of a cross-cultural poetics. For Glissant, Faulkner's work is valuable for its grounding within a frontier from which it points to "a secret" obsessively underscored and hidden in deferral: "the unstoppable conjunction" of "Creolization" "and the damnation of those who fight it."[41] Here, Glissant argues, "the entire South is not only the catastrophic victim of the breakup of legitimacy but also the symbolic place—the very dynasty—where this legitimacy is broken."[42] Faulkner's texts defer and repeat, Glissant notes, in ways akin to jazz and blues, like the "Dream Deferred" of King's "I Have a Dream" speech, utilizing a "method whereby an element isolated from the real . . . insistently reenters the discourse."[43] A cumulative, repeating, circular writing (affected by techniques of orature) works "to undo the vision of reality and truth as singular, introducing the multiple, the uncertain, the relative instead."[44] For Glissant, Yoknapatawpha endlessly discloses such frontiers. Whether in its plantation space or its wilderness, "we find ourselves to be an open frontier."[45] As Glissant sees it, Faulkner initiated a relational poetics, "a way of respecting the opacity of the Other" while also disclosing a foundational, dependent relation with the Other and discovering a composite "new type of 'origin.'"[46] In Yoknapatawpha Glissant met his maimed one-eyed initiatrice. He came to his relational poetics via another's frontier space: "the marginal (which you enter only through initiation into the wilderness of the unnamed)."[47] Glissant found in Yoknapatawpha's "Hunting season . . . the wilderness's carnival," texts "forever on a hunt, tracking game through a bush impossible to possess" as "Thought rides from one person to another, the way the [vodou]loas . . . ride those they have chosen to possess."[48]

Glissant addresses Faulkner as an initiating author of a new kind of creolizing origin. Both Glissant and Harris find a carnivalesque cross-culturality in Faulkner's prose, and both turn to vodou-inflected readings in response. For Glissant, Yoknapatawpha is a space in which thought and perception ride folk the way spirits of vodou ride their "mounts." Harris reads Yoknapatawpha as a contact zone wherein the dead may be sent against the living and from which fortress Western territoriality gets breached. With Faulkner, as with much of the South's deeply creolized cultural agency, we get a horse for forces of reciprocal enculturation (or discursive possession) that the ridden mount (or author) intuits but cannot in full consciousness see.

"A nod is as good as a wink . . . to a blind horse": Homeboy Cosmopolitans

In Oxford, Mississippi, the West African novelist Tierno Monénembo recently spoke of his chance discovery of Faulkner back in the 1970s in a university dormitory in the Ivory Coast: "To read Faulkner is to be initiated, to detach ourselves from the world in which we had lived in order to enter into another world more obscure, more vertiginous." Separating his "transformational" experience of Yoknapatawpha from the neocolonial "formation" of his Ivory Coast university, Monénembo sees Faulkner's Big Woods and flow of words as offering two seemingly contradictory things at once: first, a standing in for old initiation rites receding in the face of Islam, Christianity, and modern secular consumerism; and second, an ushering into a new poetics of relation—the give and take of entry into world markets.[49] Monénembo uncannily equates his reading of *The Sound and the Fury* with his response to the music of rock and soul, self-fashionings generated out of the South: "I tell myself, you don't understand what the Beatles are saying either, but you still spend your time humming 'Yesterday,'" so "I put Mr. Faulkner away next to the Beatles and the Rolling Stones, Otis Redding and James Brown . . . who spoke to me about the demons and the marvels of my era in a language that was foreign to me."[50] This music (Faulkner's, Otis's) carried a countercultural, opaque, foreign-language modernity from one southern periphery to another. For Monénembo, the initiatory Faulkner shares with the Stones a performance in which "Black characters abound. . . . They are secondary characters, it's true, but they are deciding factors in the configuration of white characters and in the unfolding of the story."[51] Seeking to tap into *hippikat* knowledge, stories everywhere came to depend on black Mississippians as deciding factors in our local and global unfolding. And it may be Caribbean and West African writers who best open our eyes to this reciprocally enculturating agency . . . even when it is carried or mediated by British or white southern performers such as the Stones or Elvis.

One of the most eloquent testimonies to the role of rock music in the lives of West African youth of the late 1960s and early 1970s is Manthia Diawara's 2003 memoir *We Won't Budge* (titled after the Salif Keita anthem "Nou Pas Bouger" and inspired in response to anti-immigrant policies in France as well as by the police shooting of Amadou Diallo in New York). Diawara's memoir alerts us to how musical frontiers schooled his generation of African bush travelers: "Rock and roll strengthened our sense of inner spirituality against organized religions and pushed us to rebel against tradition."[52] "The Rockers" in Bamako "had discovered Led Zeppelin in 1969, not in 1975," wailing "When the Levee Breaks" with Robert Plant.[53] Listening to the guitarist of the Faces, Ron Wood, sing "Memphis, Tennessee," some of the Rockers argued "that Wood was even better than Chuck Berry, who had originally sung that song."[54] A teenage Diawara, however, insisted that Rod Stewart was the true superstar of the Faces "because his voice had soul like a blues musician from the Mississippi Delta." The author, embarrassed now by his youthful passion for Stewart, reflects, however, "that Stewart had succeeded where many rock and roll singers had failed, because he had accumulated the habitus of black soul singers in his body and his voice, while at the same time preserving unchanged the kitsch of rock and roll." For West African youth, popular British singers like Stewart, Plant, and Mick Jagger offered a gateway: "we imitated Stewart imitating black soul musicians" and thereby "acquired the resources of the black soul music habitus."[55] We see that British youth or white southerners (like Elvis or Faulkner) could serve as "crossover" carriers of black cultural (or "soul") possessions back to African source cultures in a complex and ongoing Atlantic counterculture of modernity.

It was the British musicians' imperfect mimicry of black soul musicians (or white rockers' mimicry with a kitsch difference) that led the teenage Diawara to his interpretation of the hermetic words on the Faces' album cover: "A nod is as good as a wink . . . to a blind horse."[56] Authorized by his high school English and his one trip to Liberia, Diawara read the Faces' hip "nod" as signifying an awareness of their always imperfect Mississippi mimesis—soul signs taken for wonders, productive of their hybrid powerplay. From minstrelsy to the Stones, black southern music has long stirred mimetic desire. But the politics of the music industry's production of stars (preferential promotion of white crossover performers) did not travel so well to the Malian teenagers styling themselves after Rod Stewart over three cups of tea. Diawara writes that "Even before globalization as we know it today, the success of the market depended on the invisibility of the real conditions of production in the objects we consume," so that "By the time it hit us in Bamako, rock and roll was . . . cut off from the history of the conditions of its production in the United States and United Kingdom."[57]

Diawara hardly invokes the South directly, but in implicit relation, assessing issues of civil rights, national identity, and citizenship in an America and France that have faced their different southern subjects. Diawara depicts a France increasingly hospitable to the ideas of Jean-Marie Le Pen's National Front, a France "afraid of including Africans in the redefinition of the new France."[58] The French, Diawara writes, "believe in a philosophy of assimilation into their culture, which they call universal, and they do not think of Africans as capable of such an integration."[59] Since "France and Africa have contaminated each other" in ways more familiar to the Americas but common to the Old World now, he insists on the give and take of travel: "People have to be willing to lose something, in every cultural encounter with the other, to have a real . . . coexistence."[60] The New York–based Diawara, who took early cues from not only British imitations of Mississippi musicians but also Richard Wright's *Native Son*, pens his memoir not in French but English, as native son of *hippikat* Atlantic codes he terms "homeboy cosmopolitan."[61] Diawara guides us into networks of relation—to guilt, memory, (in)justice—that made the son of an East African immigrant, Obama, electable as U.S. president precisely because of his lack of discernible ties to the black South, slavery, or the civil rights movement (save through marriage), revealing how France likewise would favor the son of a black American over anyone from its own colonial souths. Malians and Senegalese summon too immediately France's historic guilt and the Republic's unmet responsibilities.

The homeboy cosmopolitanism of *We Won't Budge* is attuned to how white rock and roll seemed to carry an initiatory message of revolutionary change even as it glossed over structural injustice (in relation to domestic or colonial souths) to become a market brand promoted over anything emerging more directly from the music's Afro-southern cultural sources. Diawara nods slyly to Joseph Conrad's gothic voice in speaking of the music industry in terms of plantation product: "if only the housewives in England knew that the coffee and tea they were drinking every morning were produced through human suffering and exploitation elsewhere."[62] We find an Aquarian hippie and Black Atlantic *hippikat* double consciousness in Diawara's gothic nod, fortified by a West African cosmopolitanism born of trans-Saharan orientations older than the Black Atlantic. Diawara reminds us that tea economies traveled not only across oceans with imperial England but also via an imperializing Islam in the three-cup ritual crucial to the reproduction of Islamic domestic space. Rocked, however, from identification with traditionalisms of both the mosque and neocolonial education, Diawara came to know—through songs like "Johnny B Goode" and "Memphis, Tennessee"—that "Sitting around and drinking tea all day was not for you."[63] The music issued its call to initiatory travel. And if the music industry hid its political economy (its masking as "savage other" in seeking certain kinds of white liberty) in a nod or wink, we may find similar structures at work in our academic disciplines. We should recall that even those traditions that seem most local or domestic—such as southern addiction to ultra-sugary iced tea—may bear witness to long exchanges linking Asia on the one hand to circum-Caribbean sugar plantations on the other. No south exists in isolation, only in relation.

Conclusion: *Goodbye Solo*

We may argue for a planetary approach to shift or extend the circum-Atlantic turn in southern studies. However, we still need to understand the history and reach of Atlantic contact zones. Study of the U.S. South stands to gain much by the regional expansion of scale that Atlantic studies provides. Although there is a growing consensus (discernible in this volume) that we should move beyond Atlantic regionalisms to embrace global histories of movement and exchange, I want to offer two cautionary concerns supporting a circum-Atlantic framework for study of the South: first, a reminder that literary scholars lag behind historians in their application of Atlantic models to southern studies and thus have much work to do—structurally and departmentally—in a terrain that many historians seem ready to abandon for the next vanguardist approach; and second, a suggestion that once literary and cultural studies scholars have looked seriously at the basilectal narratives and countercultural epistemologies of African, American Indian, and creole post-plantation souths, then the historians will realize they have far more work to do than they may have realized. We need to give our containers and heads a thorough initiatory washing in Atlantic waters before we move on to seemingly bigger worlds.

We can no longer content ourselves with pointing out the obvious: the notion that the American South (or the United States in general) has been shaped by cultural and historical forces from beyond its borders and from beyond Euro-colonial ports of origin. We have all long been shaped by transatlantic and global matrices of relation. The greater challenge to our articulation and to our (inter)disciplinary curricula is the study of new modes of cross-cultural initiatory agency rising out of the American South and out of global souths' creole countercultures of modernity: an almost counterintuitive backwater cosmopolitanism.

I want to conclude in this vein by returning to the flying Africans of *Song of Solomon* via Ramin Bahrani's 2008 film *Goodbye Solo*, starring Souléymane Sy Savané and the remarkably cast Red West—a former Elvis friend and bodyguard. Bahrani, a North Carolina native son of Iranian immigrant parents, scripts the Senegalese cabbie Solo giving a ride to the gruffest elderly redneck, William (ex-Memphis mafia member, West). William, facing the alienation of a nursing home, offers Solo a thousand dollars to drive him one way from Winston-Salem to Blowing Rock for what Solo intuits as an impending suicidal leap. Although he appears to be cast in the too-familiar role of goodhearted black sidekick and initiatory savior, Solo, studying to become a flight attendant, dominates the film's airtime and exceeds the nurse role. Despite Solo's West African respect for elders and his shock in facing American elder care, it remains hard to fathom why he invests himself so deeply in William's plight. Still, Solo succeeds in drawing the emotionally maimed William into a zone of renewed psychic openness. The film has us read their encounter allegorically (within or against the South's old Atlantic contact cultures), with the Senegalese immigrant serving as final flight attendant for an aging, changing, inarticulate South perfectly summoned by the mannerisms of Red West. Solo's Mexican American wife, Quiera, has little patience for her husband's investment in William's life, but her daughter responds with fully empathetic innocence in accompanying Solo on this suicide-fare to the mountains. Blowing Rock—an Appalachian cliff site where updrafts are said to give flight to thrown objects—provides the film's final magnificent images in the peak of autumn leaf season. We see a panorama of autumn mountains and sublime wind blasts, with Solo on the rock-edge, arms outraised, his stepdaughter by his side, both strangely transported by William's otherwise undepicted flight. The film signifies on Morrison's *Song of Solomon* (itself deeply indebted to Afro-Atlantic folk narrative and initiation tales): "If you surrendered to the air, you could ride it."[64] William helps Solo become flight attendant. Solo fosters new ancestors while William opens himself to new community. Bahrani's film gives a deterritorializing launching beyond our nativist enshrinements of ancestry and identity. The film's featuring of a redneck, a West African, and Solo's Mexican American wife and stepdaughter reshuffles presences from our core Atlantic formations. But Bahrani's film also presents us with a North Carolina no longer defined by Atlantic space. This is a composite world of flight and satellite. Under the piloting of Ramin Bahrani, Blowing Rock is an apt launching pad that puts everything into flight while offering wondrous planetary grounding. Here, we feel the air of changing-world relations and unguessed cross-cultural hospitality, a goodbye to our flying solo.

Notes

1. Toni Morrison, *Song of Solomon* (New York: Knopf, Everyman's Library, 1995), 127.

2. Leigh Anne Duck, *The Nation's Region: Southern Modernism, Segregation, and U.S. Nationalism* (Athens: University of Georgia Press, 2006).

3. On the South's use as national container of the abject, see ibid. For the South as sign of the "real" see Scott Romine, *The Real South: Southern Narrative in the Age of Cultural Reproduction* (Baton Rouge: Louisiana State University Press, 2008); and on the South's use in the creation of an American national literature, see Jennifer Rae Greeson, *Our South: Region, World, and the Rise of a National Literature* (Cambridge: Harvard University Press, 2010).

4. Wendy Laura Belcher, "Consuming Subjects: Theorizing New Models of Agency for Literary Criticism in African Studies," *Comparative Literature Studies* 46, no. 2 (2009): 213.

5. Ibid., 228.

6. Édouard Glissant, *Poetics of Relation*, trans. Betsy Wing (Ann Arbor: University of Michigan Press, 1997), 34.

7. Inca Garcilaso de la Vega, *The Florida of the Inca*, trans. John Grier Varner and Jeanette Johnson Varner (Austin: University of Texas Press, 1981), 106.

8. Valérie Loichot's *Orphan Narratives: The Postplantation Literature of Faulkner, Glissant, Morrison, and Saint-John Perse* (Charlotteville: University of Virginia Press, 2007) argues for interdisciplinary and comparative approaches to a hemispheric postplantation literature. By "deep time" I borrow from Wai Chee Dimock, *Through Other Continents: American Literature across Deep Time* (Princeton: Princeton University Press, 2006). In 1958 Fernand Braudel proposed a history "of the *longue durée*" in "History and the Social Sciences: The Longue Durée," in *On History*, trans. Sarah Matthews (Chicago: University of Chicago Press, 1980), 25–54.

9. Wilson Harris, *The Womb of Space: The Cross-Cultural Imagination* (Westport, Conn.: Greenwood Press, 1983), xviii.

10. Acrolect and basilect are rather basic (though in many ways contested) terms within studies of Creole linguistics and culture. They are important to any effort to address the complex parameters and perspectives of cultural agency in the Atlantic World. Still, these terms tend to be just as foreign to English professors (even among the New Southern Studies crowd) as they are to most historians. But how do we do Atlantic

studies or talk about an Atlantic World without grounding in antiphonal frameworks of basilect and acrolect . . . a kind of Atlantic Creole double consciousness? See Keith Cartwright, *Reading Africa into American Literature: Epics, Fables, Gothic Tales* (Lexington: University of Kentucky Press, 2002).

11. See Paul Gilroy, *The Black Atlantic: Modernity and Double Consciousness* (Cambridge: Harvard University Press, 1993), and the title of the book's opening chapter: "The Black Atlantic as a Counterculture of Modernity."

12. Ifeoma Nwankwo, *Black Cosmopolitanism: Racial Consciousness and Transnational Identity in the Nineteenth-Century Americas* (Philadelphia: University of Pennsylvania Press, 2005), 14.

13. Gilroy, *The Black Atlantic*, 37–38, 131.

14. The key works here are Melville Herskovits, *The Myth of the Negro Past* (New York: Harper, 1941); Sidney W. Mintz and Richard Price, *The Birth of African-American Culture: An Anthropological Perspective* (Boston: Beacon Press, 1976, 1992); Robert Farris Thompson, *Flash of the Spirit: African and Afro-American Art and Philosophy* (New York: Random House, 1983); and J. Lorand Matory, *Black Atlantic Religion: Tradition, Transnationalism, and Matriarchy in the Afro-Brazilian Candomblé* (Princeton: Princeton University Press, 2005).

15. Thompson, *Flash of the Spirit*, xvii. From the introduction, "The Rise of the Black Atlantic Visual Tradition," to the end of the book, Thompson introduced us to the better part of what we recognize as the Black Atlantic.

16. Youssou Ndour, *Rokku Mi Rokka (Give and Take)* (Nonesuch Records 266044-2, 2007).

17. Gilroy, *The Black Atlantic*, 37.

18. Lilyan Kestelot and Cherif Mbodj, *Contes et mythes Wolof* (Dakar: Les nouvelles éditions africaines, 1983), 24–31.

19. See Thompson, *Flash of the Spirit*, 42–51.

20. "Cumba" appears in the low country in Joel Chandler Harris, *Nights with Uncle Remus* (New York: Penguin, 2003), 232; Whittington B. Johnson, *Black Savannah* (Fayetteville: University of Arkansas Press, 1996), 93; Lorenzo Dow Turner, *Africanisms in the Gullah Dialect*, (Ann Arbor: University of Michigan Press, 1973), 117; Philip D. Morgan, *Slave Counterpoint*, (Chapel Hill: University of North Carolina Press, 1998), 448; Larry Koger, *Black Slaveowners: Free Black Slave Masters in South Carolina, 1790–1860* (Columbia: University of South Carolina Press, 1995), 113–15; and Daniel L. Schafer, *Anna Madgigine Jai Kingsley* (Gainesville: University Press of Florida, 2003), 28. On Cumba in the Bahamas see Michael Craton and Gail Saunders, *Islanders in the Stream* (Athens: University of Georgia Press, 1992), 338, as well as her different listings on Bahamian slave registries. On Cumba's leaving Georgia for Trinidad, look to John McNish Weiss, *The Merikens: Free Black American Settlers in Trinidad 1815–16* (London: McNish and Weis, 2002), 41, 42, 45. See Sylvia R. Frey and Betty Wood, *Come Shouting to Zion: African American Protestantism in the American South and British Caribbean to 1830* (Chapel Hill: University of North Carolina Press, 1998), 116–17, 131, on Georgians and the spread of the Baptist faith in the Atlantic World.

21. On Cumba's presence in the British Caribbean, see the online database "Slave Registries of Former British Colonial Dependencies," ancestry.co.uk. On Cumba among the Seminole, see Rebecca Bateman, "Naming Patterns in Black Seminole Ethnogenesis," *Ethnohistory* 49, no. 2 (2002): 227. One of several sources for Cumba in Louisiana may be found in Gwendolyn Midlo Hall, *Africans in Colonial Louisiana* (Baton Rouge: Louisiana University Press, 1993), 409. For Franco-creole versions of Kumba's tale from Grenada, St. Lucia, and Dominica, see Elsie Clews Parsons, *Folk-lore of the Antilles, French and English*, part 1 (New York: American Folk-lore Society, 1933), 87–88, 142–44, 422–25. For versions from Guadeloupe, Marie-Galante, St. Kitts, and Haiti, see Elsie Clews Parsons, *Folk-lore of the Antilles, French and English*, part 2 (New York: American Folk-lore Society, 1943), 159–60, 277–78, 367–69, 569–70. For a version from Haiti via Miami, see Liliane Nerette Louis, *When Night Falls, Kric! Krac!: Haitian Folktales* (Englewood, Colo.: Libraries Unlimited, 1999), 71–74. And for the Louisiana tale, see Alcée Fortier, *Louisiana Folk-Tales in French Dialect and English Translation* (New York: American Folklore Society, 1895), 117–19. For the tale in the Bahamas, look to Elsie Clews Parsons, *Folk-Tales of Andros Island Bahamas* (New York: American Folk-lore Society, 1918), 5–6; and Patricia Glinton, *An Evening in Guanima* (Nassau: Guanima Press, 1994), 39–49. A truncated variant appears in Elsie Clews Parsons, *Folk-Lore of the Sea Islands, South Carolina* (New York: American Folklore Society, 1923), 137–38. See also Manuel J. Andrade, *Folk-lore from the Dominican Republic* (New York: American Folk-lore Society, 1930), 216–18. A partial sampling of other African sources may be found in Francois-Victoire Equilibecq, *Contes populaires d'Afrique occidentale* (Paris: G.-P. Maisoneuve et Larose, 1972), 276–82, 384–86; and Emil Magel, *Folktales from the Gambia: Wolof Fictional Narratives* (Washington, D.C.: Three Continents Press, 1984), 90–95. In the New World tales, the orphan has no African name and is sometimes called "Cinderella" even as she undertakes Kumba's initiatory tasks—as in a compelling version from St. Kitts.

22. Loichot's *Orphan Naratives* insists on this need to foster an intertextual postplantation body of literature across linguistic boundaries.

23. Antonio Benítez-Rojo, *The Repeating Island: The Caribbean and the Postmodern Perspective*, trans. James E. Maraniss (Durham: Duke University Press, 2001), 6, 8.

24. Jane Landers, *Black Society in Colonial Florida* (Urbana: University of Illinois Press, 1999), 253.

25. Quoted in Leigh A. Neithardt, "Florida Legislation Mandates How to Teach History," http://www.teachablemoment.org/high/justthefacts.html (accessed September 29, 2010).

26. Benítez-Rojo, *The Repeating Island*, 24.

27. Ibid., 16.

28. Edmond L. Volpe quoted in W. Harris, *Womb of Space*, 4. Harris quotes from Volpe's *William Faulkner* (London: Thames & Hudson, 1964).

29. W. Harris, *Womb of Space*, 4, 5.

30. Ibid., 9.

31. Métraux quoted and summarized in ibid., xviii–xix. See Alfred Métraux, *Voodoo in Haiti*, trans. Hugo Charteris (New York: Schocken, 1972), 274–85.

32. W. Harris, *Womb of Space*, xviii.

33. Ibid., xvii.

34. Ibid., 11–13.

35. Ibid., 12, 6. For an earlier examination of Caribbean responses to Faulkner, see Randy Boyagoda, "Just Where and What Is 'the (comparatively speaking) South'? Caribbean Writers on Melville and Faulkner," *Mississippi Quarterly* 57, no. 1 (2003–4): 65–73.

36. Glissant, *Poetics of Relation*, 63, 64.

37. Ibid., 65.

38. Ibid., 71.

39. Ibid., 72, 74, 73.

40. Ibid., 75.

41. Édouard Glissant, *Faulkner, Mississippi*, trans. Barbara Lewis and Thomas C. Spear (New York: Farrar, Straus and Giroux, 1999), 3, 30.

42. Ibid., 131.

43. Ibid., 200.

44. Ibid., 197.

45. Ibid., 218.

46. Ibid., 65, 195.

47. Ibid., 138.

48. Ibid., 137, 176.

49. Tierno Monénembo, "Faulkner and Me," in *Global Faulkner: Faulkner and Yoknapatawpha*, ed. Annette Trefzer and Ann J. Abadie (Jackson: University Press of Mississippi, 2009), 177.

50. Ibid., 176.

51. Ibid., 181.

52. Manthia Diawara, *We Won't Budge: An African Exile in the World* (New York: Basic *Civitas*, 2003), 117.

53. Ibid., 103.

54. Ibid., 119.

55. Ibid., 119–20.

56. Ibid., 118.

57. Ibid., 116.

58. Ibid., 144.

59. Ibid., 155.

60. Ibid., 149, 146.

61. Ibid., 228, viii.

62. Ibid., 117.

63. Ibid., 79.

64. Morrison, *Song of Solomon*, 337.

Contributors

Martyn Bone is associate professor of American literature at the University of Copenhagen. He is the author of *The Postsouthern Sense of Place in Contemporary Fiction* (2005) and the editor of *Perspectives on Barry Hannah* (2007). His articles have appeared in *American Literature, Journal of American Studies, Comparative American Studies, New Centennial Review, Mississippi Quarterly,* and other journals.

Trevor Burnard is the author of several books on Atlantic history and on white slave owners in the Chesapeake and Jamaica, including *Mastery, Tyranny and Desire: Thomas Thistlewood and His Slaves in the Anglo-Jamaican World* (2004). He has also written a large number of articles on such things as the history of early Jamaica; gender, whiteness, and slavery in plantation societies; and the character of the planter class in the British Atlantic World. He is head of the School of Historical and Philosophical Studies at the University of Melbourne.

Keith Cartwright is associate professor of English at the University of North Florida. He has published *Reading Africa into American Literature* (2002) and a number of articles in journals such as *American Literature, Callaloo, Yearbook of Comparative and General Literature, Yinna, Southern Quarterly Review,* and *Mississippi Quarterly.*

Leigh Anne Duck is associate professor of English at the University of Mississippi. Her research focuses on modern and contemporary literature, film, and documentary concerning the southern United States. She also studies the modern and contemporary literature of South Africa and the United States, constructions of race and nation, and theories concerning space, narrative, and neoliberalism. She is the author of *The Nation's Region: Southern Modernism, Segregation, and U.S. Nationalism* (2006) and has published essays in venues such as *Journal of American Folklore, CR: New Centennial Review,* and *American Literary History.*

Natanya Keisha Duncan is assistant professor of history at Morgan State University. Her research on black nationalist practices among female members of the Universal Negro Improvement Association and associated groups will appear as *Crossing Waters, Fighting Tides: The "Efficient Womanhood" of the Universal Negro Improvement Association, 1919–1930*.

Kathleen M. Gough is a lecturer in theatre studies in the School of Culture and Creative Arts at the University of Glasgow. She has published articles and reviews in *Journal of American Studies, Modern Drama, Performance Research, TDR,* and *New Theatre Quarterly* as well as in several edited collections. She is currently completing a monograph, *Haptic Allegories: Kinship and Performance in the Black and Green Atlantic,* which examines the unlikely kinship between African American and Irish social actors, using gender and performance to revise historiographical practices in Atlantic studies, while also revising, reimagining, and redeploying concepts central to performance studies.

Martha S. Jones is associate professor of history and Afro-American and African studies and a member of the affiliated Faculty of Law at the University of Michigan. Her work examines the history of race, law, and African American politics and culture in the United States and extends into the history of the Atlantic World through an emphasis on the Haitian diaspora in the United States. She is the author of *All Bound Up Together: The Woman Question in African-American Public Culture, 1830–1900* (2007) and is currently working on a book project, *Riding the Atlantic World Circuit: One Household's Journey through Slavery and Law in the Era of the Haitian Revolution*.

Jeffrey R. Kerr-Ritchie is associate professor of history at Howard University. He has published scholarly articles in *The Journal of African American History; Nature, Society, and Thought; Slavery and Abolition; Radical History Review;* and *Souls: A Critical Journal of Black Politics, Culture, and Society* and has contributed chapters to several book anthologies. He is the author of *Freedpeople in the Tobacco South: Virginia, 1860–1900* (1999) and *Rites of August First: Emancipation Day in the Black Atlantic World* (2007) and has edited an electronic anthology, *African-American Social Movements* (2005). His current projects include *Freedom's Seekers: Essays in Comparative Emancipation; August Address: An Anthology of West Indies Emancipation Day Speeches;* and a popular history of emancipation.

William A. Link is the Richard J. Milbauer Professor of History at the University of Florida, a position he has held since 2004. His publications include *Roots of*

Secession: Slavery and Politics in Antebellum Virginia, Righteous Warrior: Jesse Helms and the Rise of Modern Conservatism, and *Links: My Family in American History.* His current book project, a study of race and memory in Atlanta titled *Cradle of the New South: Race and the Struggle for Meaning in the Civil War's Aftermath,* will appear in 2013.

Jon Sensbach teaches early American history at the University of Florida. He is the author of *Rebecca's Revival: Creating Black Christianity in the Atlantic World* (2005) and *A Separate Canaan: The Making of an Afro-Moravian World in North Carolina, 1763–1840* (1998), as well as many articles and book chapters.

Jennifer K. Snyder is currently finishing her dissertation, titled "Black Flight: Tracing the Loyalist Slave Diaspora throughout the Revolutionary Atlantic World," at the University of Florida, from where she also holds an M.A. in early American history. Her research interests include diasporas and kinship networks in the Revolutionary Atlantic.

Brian Ward is professor in American Studies at Northumbria University. In addition to many journal articles and book chapters, his major publications include *The Making of Martin Luther King and the Civil Rights Movement* (coedited with Tony Badger, 1996), *Just My Soul Responding: Rhythm and Blues, Black Consciousness and Race Relations* (1998), *Media, Culture and the Modern African American Freedom Struggle* (2001), *Radio and the Struggle for Civil Rights in the South* (2004), and *The 1960s: A Documentary Reader* (2009).

Natalie Zacek is a lecturer in American history at the University of Manchester. She is the author of *Settler Society in the English Leeward Islands, 1670–1776* (2010), winner of the Gladstone Prize of the Royal Historical Society, as well as of articles in *Slavery and Abolition, History Compass,* and the *Journal of Peasant Studies,* and of chapters in a number of edited collections. She is currently at work on a monograph on the cultural history of thoroughbred horse racing in nineteenth-century America.

Index